The
Lineal Ascent
of
Edgar Osden
FULLMER:
A
Travis Wayne GOODSELL
Genealogical
Ancestry

Compiled by: Travis Wayne Goodsell

Dedication

This is dedicated to my three children, Malissa, Clayton, and Emma.

Introduction

This book is volume 3 of A Travis Wayne Goodsell Genealogical Ancestry. It contains the genealogical ancestry of Edgar Osden FULLMER, the Great-Grandfather of Travis Wayne Goodsell. The information collected is from unknown family members, so the further back the line goes the more uncertain is the accuracy of the information. But it is clear that a lot of time and hard work in research was made to discover the family tree.

The collection is composed of three parts. The first part is the pedigree of Edgar Osden Fullmer. The second part is the ancestral listing in book form. And the third part is an ancestry chart. No attempt was made to provide the family group sheets. This book is entirely dedicated to the lineal ancestors of Edgar Osden Fullmer. This work was made possible with the assistance of Ancestral Quest Basics. The pages are scanned from the originals.

This work is published in a book form primarily for the benefit of Travis Wayne Goodsell. Having a printed copy of the genealogical information is more easily accessible and researchable. Travis spends much of his time searching for lines to extend and Temple ordinances to perform. In The Church of Jesus Christ of Latter-Day Saints, Temple rituals are performed by proxy for deceased ancestors. It is necessary for a welding link from the living member of The Church to family members as far back as possible. It all stems from a belief concerning one's afterlife status.

The volumes in the series are:

1. Joseph Franklin GOODSELL
2. Olive Emeline HOOPES
3. Edgar Osden FULLMER
4. Rhoda Maie CAMERON
5. Hamlin Hannibal SMITH
6. Rhoda Elizabeth PERRY
7. Nathan Melvin YEARSLEY
8. Josephine JONES

Pedigree Chart

8 Peter FULLMER-83   2
B: 25 Feb 1774
P: Reading,Berks,P,British America
M: 2 Mar 1802 - 42
P: Schuylkill Township,S,P,United States
D: 6 Jan 1857
P: Salt Lake City,Salt Lake,UT,United States

4 John Solomon FULLMER-40
B: 21 Jul 1807
P: Huntington Mills,L,P,United States
M: 24 May 1837 - 20
P: Nashville,Davidson,T,United States
D: 8 Oct 1883
P: Springville,Utah,UT,United States

9 Susannah ZERFASS-84   3
B: 17 Sep 1783
P: Whitehall,Allegheny,P,United States
D: 11 Nov 1856
P: Salt Lake City,Salt Lake,UT,United States

2 Samuel David FULLMER-20
B: 4 Nov 1856
P: Salt Lake City,SL,UT,United States
M: 24 Oct 1878 - 10
P: of Springville,Utah,Utah,USA
D: 29 Jul 1921
P: Blackfoot,Bingham,I,United States

10 John PRICE-85   4
B: 23 Dec 1790
P: Nashville,Davidson,T,United States
M: 29 Dec 1814 - 43
P: Rutherford,Tennessee,United States
D: 27 Dec 1848
P: Vicksburg,Warren,M,United States

5 Mary Ann PRICE-41
B: 16 Sep 1815
P: Nashville,Davidson,T,United States
D: 28 Mar 1897
P: Marysvale,Piute,Utah,United States

11 Johanna RUCKER-86   5
B: 19 Apr 1786
P: Shockoe,Richmond City,V,United States
D: 6 Feb 1822
P: Nashville,Davidson,T,United States

1 Edgar Osden FULLMER-10
B: 3 May 1884
P: Mapleton,Utah,Utah,United States
M: 5 Jun 1913 - 5
P: Cache,Utah,United States
D: 11 Apr 1959
P: Blackfoot,Bingham,Idaho,United States

12 Levi KENDALL-87   6
B: 13 Jun 1798
P: Royalston,Worcester,M,United States
M: 10 Apr 1820 - 44
P: Lockport,Niagara,New York,United States
D: 19 Apr 1822
P: Lockport,Niagara,New York,United Staes

6 Levi Newell KENDALL-42
B: 19 Apr 1822
P: Lockport,Niagara,NY,United States
M: 29 Nov 1852 - 21
P: Salt Lake City,SL,Utah,United States
D: 10 Mar 1903
P: Mapleton,Utah,Utah,United States

Rhoda Maie CAMERON-11
(Spouse of no. 1)

13 Lorena (Laura) LYMAN-88   7
B: 27 Jul 1804
P: Canada
D: 27 Dec 1860
P:

3 Roxey Jane KENDALL-21
B: 21 Dec 1859
P: Springville,Utah,Utah,United States
D: 18 Jun 1934
P: Rexburg,Madison,Idaho,United States

14 Albert N CLEMENTS-89   8
B: 19 Mar 1801
P: Fort Ann,Washington,NY,United States
M: 21 Jan 1821 - 45
P: Fort Ann,Washington,NY,United States
D: 2 Apr 1883
P: Springville,Utah,Utah,United States

7 Elizabeth CLEMENTS-43
B: 17 May 1836
P: Liberty,Clay,Missouri,United States
D: 1 Feb 1924
P: Oxford,Franklin,Idaho,United States

15 Ada WINCHELL-90   9
B: 24 Dec 1801
P: Hebron,Washington,NY,United States
D: 4 Mar 1890
P: Oxford,Franklin,Idaho,United States

Pedigree Chart

No. 1 on this chart is the same as No. **8** on chart no. **1**.

8 Hans Jacob VOLLMAR-663   10
B: 6 Mar 1697
P: K,E,R,Baden-Württemberg, Germany
M: 16 Aug 1718 - 358
P: Rosswag,Neckar,Württemberg
D: 25 Jan 1762
P: Tulpehocken,Berks,Pennsylvania

4 Johann Jacob VOLLMAR-346
B: 2 Apr 1721
P: Roßwag,Vaihingen,W,Germany
M: 25 Jan 1742 - 181
P: Tulpehocken,Berks,Pennsylvania
D: 20 Sep 1758
P: Tulpehocken,Berks,Pennsylvania

9 Marie Agnes RAU-664   11
B: 16 Nov 1695
P: Eberdingen,V,N,Württemberg, Germany
D: 6 Apr 1735
P: Roßwag,V,N,Württemberg, Germany

2 Johann Michael FOLLMER-170
B: 29 Sep 1744
P: TT,Berks,Pennsylvania,United States
M: -- 86
P:
D: 14 Mar 1817
P:

10 John Michael KARCHER-666   12
B: Bef 22 Aug 1685
P: Konstanz,Baden,Germany
M: -- 360
P:
D: 1787
P:

5 Justina Catharina KAERCHER-347
B: Abt 1720
P: Dobel,Neuenbürg,W,Germany
D: 17 Jan 1820
P: TT,Berks,Pennsylvania,United States

11 Maria Catharina KNOELLER-667   13
B: 23 Mar 1697
P: Neuenburg,Schwarzwaldkreis,W,Germany
D: 11 Feb 1802
P: Hamburg,Berks,P,United States

1 Peter FULLMER-83
B: 25 Feb 1774
P: Reading,Berks,P,British America
M: 2 Mar 1802 - 42
P: Schuylkill Township,S,P,United States
D: 6 Jan 1857
P: Salt Lake City,Salt Lake,U,United States

12 Hanss Otto KESSLER-668   14
B: 17 Feb 1673
P: Idar-Oberstein,Rhineland,Prussia,Germany
M: 19 Feb 1697 - 361
P: Birkenfeld,Oldenburg,Rheinland,Germany
D: 19 Sep 1749
P: Idar-Oberstein,Rhineland,Prussia,Germany

6 Johann Georg KESSLER-348
B: 11 Oct 1711
P: Georg,W,B,Rheinland, Germany
M: 17 Apr 1735 - 182
P: Evangelisch,Mettlach,R,Prussia
D: 1 Jul 1760
P: Georg,W,B,Rheinland, Germany

Susannah ZERFASS-84
(Spouse of no. 1)

13 Elisabeth Maria PURPUR-669   15
B: Abt 1676
P: Germany
D: Deceased
P:

14 Johann Frantz KLEIN-670   16
B: 1681
P: Windesheim,Bad Kreuznach,R,Germany
M: 17 Jan 1707 - 362
P: Weiderscheim,Rhineland,Germany
D: 26 Jan 1733
P: Windesheim,Bad Kreuznach,R,Germany

3 Anna Juliana KESSLER-171
B: 16 May 1745
P: W,I,B,Rheinland-Pfalz, Germany
D: 17 Jan 1820
P: Reading,Berks,P,United States

7 UNKNOWN-349
B: 1715
P: Of Georg-Weierbach,B,R,Germany
D: 21 Oct 1762
P: Georg,W,B,Rheinland, Germany

15 Anna Maria SECKLER-671   17
B: 1680
P: Gensingen,Bingen,R,Hessen, Germany
D: 1 Sep 1735
P: Rhineland,Prussia,Germany

07 Nov 2015

Pedigree Chart

No. 1 on this chart is the same as No. **9** on chart no. **1** .

Chart no. **3**

8 Ulysses (Zerfass) SURFACE-672   **18**
B: Abt 1685
P: Germany
M: Abt 1708 - 363
P: Palatine Area, Germany
D: 1740
P: Germany

4 Johan Nicholas ZERFASS-350
B: 1709
P: Rheinland-Pfalz, Germany
M: -- 183
P:
D: 1 Oct 1784
P: Cocalico, Lancaster, P, United States

9 Mrs. Ulysses Zerfass -673
B: Abt 1689
P: Germany
D: Deceased
P:

2 Captain Johann Adam ZERFASS-173
B: 25 Jan 1742
P: Whitehall Township, N, P, United States
M: 6 Mar 1768 - 88
P: Whitehall Township, L, P, United States
D: 18 Aug 1806
P: Whitehall Township, L, P, United States

10 Herman HELWIG-674
B: Abt 1676
P: Kirschroth, M, Rhineland, Prussia, Germany
M: Abt 1702 - 364
P: Rheinland, Germany
D: Deceased
P:

5 Maria Elisabeth HELWIG-351
B: 1705
P: Germany
D: Abt 1742
P: Salisbury Township, L, P, United States

11 Sabina E VON KIRSCHROTH-675
B: Abt 1680
P: Kirschroth, M, Rhineland, Prussia, Germany
D: Bef 1779
P:

1 Susannah ZERFASS-84
B: 17 Sep 1783
P: Whitehall, Allegheny, P, United States
M: 2 Mar 1802 - 42
P: Schuylkill Township, S, P, United States
D: 11 Nov 1856
P: Salt Lake City, Salt Lake, U, United States

12 Hanss Adam SCHNEIDER-678   **22**
B: Abt 1694
P: Germany
M: 19 Jul 1722 - 366
P: Heselwangen, Heselwangen, W, Germany
D: 3 Nov 1769
P: Haiterbach, Calw, B, Germany

6 Peter SHAFER-353
B: 1720
P: Schuylkill, Pennsylvania, United States
M: Abt 1745 - 185
P: Of, Schuylkill, Pennsylvania
D: 1825
P: White Hill, Cumberland, P, United States

Peter FULLMER-83
(Spouse of no. 1)

13 Anna HUNTZINGER-679   **23**
B: 11 Feb 1698
P: Heselwangen, B, S, Württemberg, Germany
D: 26 Nov 1721
P:

3 Mary Elizabeth SHAFER-174
B: 11 Feb 1746
P: Whitehall Township, N, P, United States
D: 16 Mar 1800
P: Whitehall Township, N, P, United States

14
B:
P:
M:
P:
D:
P:

7 Catherine LORICH-354
B: 1724
P: Panama
D: 16 Aug 1818
P:

15
B:
P:
D:
P:

07 Nov 2015

Pedigree Chart

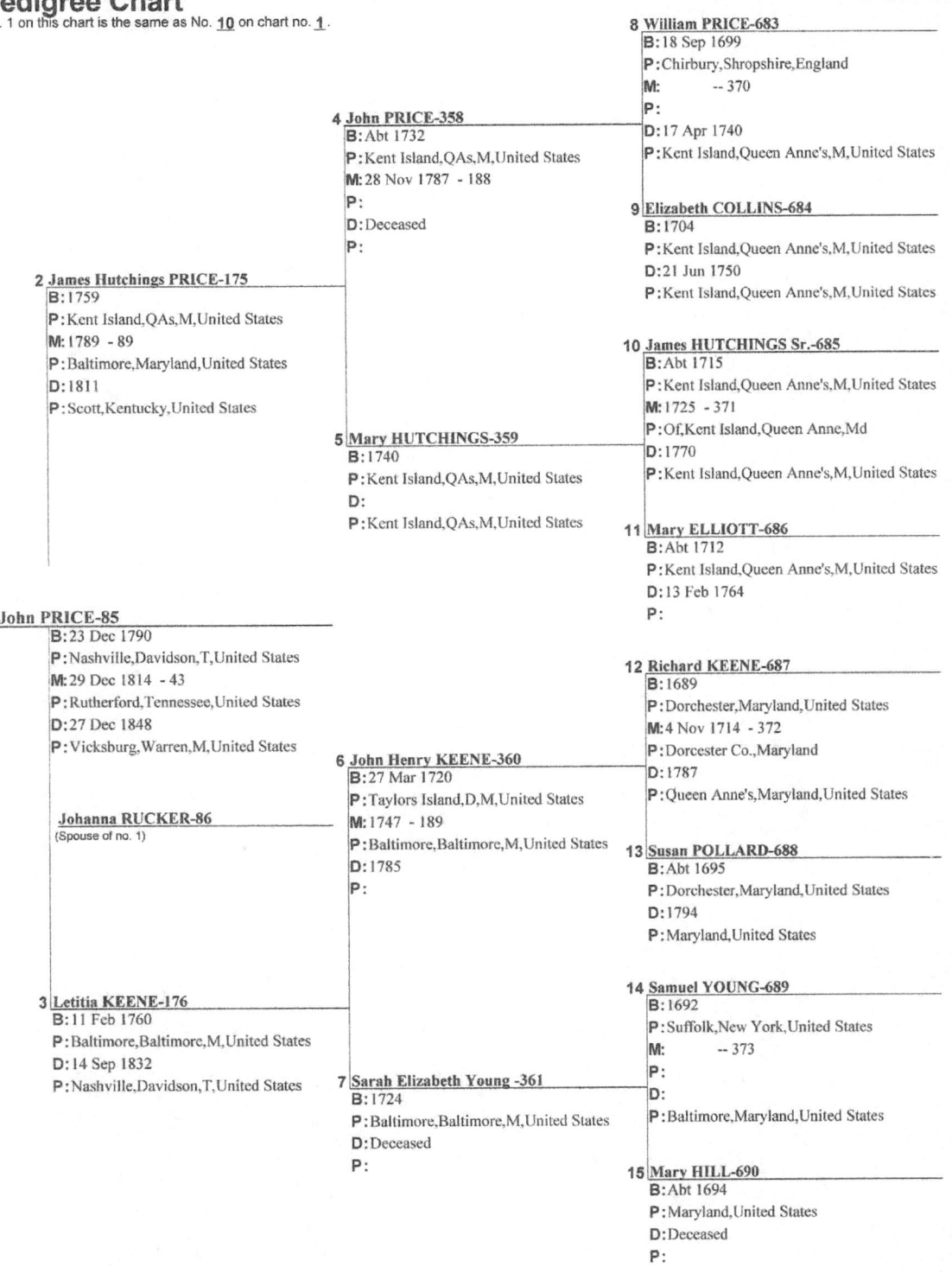

8 William PRICE-683
B: 18 Sep 1699
P: Chirbury, Shropshire, England
M: -- 370
P:
D: 17 Apr 1740
P: Kent Island, Queen Anne's, M, United States

4 John PRICE-358
B: Abt 1732
P: Kent Island, QAs, M, United States
M: 28 Nov 1787 - 188
P:
D: Deceased
P:

9 Elizabeth COLLINS-684
B: 1704
P: Kent Island, Queen Anne's, M, United States
D: 21 Jun 1750
P: Kent Island, Queen Anne's, M, United States

2 James Hutchings PRICE-175
B: 1759
P: Kent Island, QAs, M, United States
M: 1789 - 89
P: Baltimore, Maryland, United States
D: 1811
P: Scott, Kentucky, United States

10 James HUTCHINGS Sr.-685
B: Abt 1715
P: Kent Island, Queen Anne's, M, United States
M: 1725 - 371
P: Of, Kent Island, Queen Anne, Md
D: 1770
P: Kent Island, Queen Anne's, M, United States

5 Mary HUTCHINGS-359
B: 1740
P: Kent Island, QAs, M, United States
D:
P: Kent Island, QAs, M, United States

11 Mary ELLIOTT-686
B: Abt 1712
P: Kent Island, Queen Anne's, M, United States
D: 13 Feb 1764
P:

1 John PRICE-85
B: 23 Dec 1790
P: Nashville, Davidson, T, United States
M: 29 Dec 1814 - 43
P: Rutherford, Tennessee, United States
D: 27 Dec 1848
P: Vicksburg, Warren, M, United States

12 Richard KEENE-687
B: 1689
P: Dorchester, Maryland, United States
M: 4 Nov 1714 - 372
P: Dorcester Co., Maryland
D: 1787
P: Queen Anne's, Maryland, United States

6 John Henry KEENE-360
B: 27 Mar 1720
P: Taylors Island, D, M, United States
M: 1747 - 189
P: Baltimore, Baltimore, M, United States
D: 1785
P:

Johanna RUCKER-86
(Spouse of no. 1)

13 Susan POLLARD-688
B: Abt 1695
P: Dorchester, Maryland, United States
D: 1794
P: Maryland, United States

14 Samuel YOUNG-689
B: 1692
P: Suffolk, New York, United States
M: -- 373
P:
D:
P: Baltimore, Maryland, United States

3 Letitia KEENE-176
B: 11 Feb 1760
P: Baltimore, Baltimore, M, United States
D: 14 Sep 1832
P: Nashville, Davidson, T, United States

7 Sarah Elizabeth Young -361
B: 1724
P: Baltimore, Baltimore, M, United States
D: Deceased
P:

15 Mary HILL-690
B: Abt 1694
P: Maryland, United States
D: Deceased
P:

Pedigree Chart

No. 1 on this chart is the same as No. 11 on chart no. 1.

8 John RUCKER-691
B: 1699
P: Essex,CoV,British Colonial America
M: 1729 - 374
P: Essex,CoV,British Colonial America
D: Jan 1743
P: Orange,Virginia,United States

4 Benjamin RUCKER-362
B: Abt 1730
P: Orange,Orange,Virginia,United States
M: <1755> - 190
P: ,,Virginia
D: 1 Feb 1810
P: Amherst,Amherst,V,United States

9 Susannah Lloyd PHILLIPS-692
B: 1684
P: Orange,Virginia,United States
D: 28 Aug 1742
P: Orange,Orange,Virginia,United States

2 Rev. James RUCKER-177
B: 4 Sep 1758
P: Amherst,Amherst,V,United States
M: 31 Jan 1788 - 90
P: Lynchberg,Amherst,Virginia
D: 10 Sep 1819
P: ,Rutherford,Tennessee,United States

10 James BENNETT-693
B: 1706
P: Amherst,Virginia,United States
M: 1730 - 375
P: Orange,Virginia
D: Deceased
P:

5 Elizabeth UNKNOWN-363
B: Abt 1725
P: Amherst,Virginia,United States
D: Deceased
P:

11 Mrs. James BENNETT-694
B: Abt 1710
P: Virginia,United States
D: Deceased
P:

1 Johanna RUCKER-86
B: 19 Apr 1786
P: Shockoe,Richmond City,V,United States
M: 29 Dec 1814 - 43
P: Rutherford,Tennessee,United States
D: 6 Feb 1822
P: Nashville,Davidson,T,United States

John PRICE-85
(Spouse of no. 1)

12 John READE-697
B: Abt 1708
P: Elizabeth City,Virginia,United States
M: -- 378
P:
D: 1739
P: Henrico,Virginia,United States

6 William READE-366
B: Aft 1729
P: Chesterfield,Virginia,United States
M: Abt 1751 - 192
P: ,,Virginia,British Colony
D: 24 Sep 1798
P: Bedford,Virginia,United States

13
B:
P:
D:
P:

3 Nancy Ann READE -178
B: 12 May 1765
P: Bedford,Virginia,United States
D: 3 Nov 1843
P: Murfreesboro,R,T,United States

14 Thomas JONES-701
B: 8 Jul 1715
P: Chesterfield,Chesterfield,V,United States
M: 1735/1736 - 382
P:
D: 1782
P: Shepherdstown,Jefferson,V,United States

7 Johanna JONES-367
B: 1736
P: Henrico,Virginia,United States
D: 23 Mar 1797
P: Bedford,Virginia,United States

15 Sarah HANCOCK-702
B: 1719
P: Henrico,Mecklenburg,V,United States
D: 1769
P: Granville,North Carolina,United States

07 Nov 2015

Pedigree Chart

No. 1 on this chart is the same as No. 12 on chart no. 1.

8 Samuel KENDALL-703
B: 1529
P: Norfolk,England
M: -- 383
P:
D:
P: Norfolk,England

4 Jesse KENDALL-368
B: 15 May 1727
P: Woburn,Middlesex,M,United States
M: Mar 1749 - 193
P: Woburn,Middlesex,M,United States
D: 14 Apr 1797
P: Athol,Worcester,M,United States

9 Elizabeth PEIRCE-704
B: 1687
P:
D: 10 Jan 1742
P: Woburn,Middlesex,M,United States

2 Andrew KENDALL-179
B: 17 Apr 1766
P: Athol,Worcester,M,United States
M: 23 Feb 1796 - 91
P: Royalston,Worcester,M,United States
D: 3 May 1829
P: Royalston,Worcester,M,United States

10 Andrew EVANS-706
B: 26 Jan 1708
P: Malden,Middlesex,M,United States
M: 4 Dec 1730 - 385
P: Woburn,Middlesex,M,United States
D: 18 Dec 1778
P: Woburn,Middlesex,M,United States

5 Elizabeth EVANS-369
B: 6 Jan 1732
P: Woburn,Middlesex,M,United States
D: 22 Jun 1813
P: Athol,Worcester,M,United States

11 Mary RICHARDSON-707
B: 13 Mar 1710
P: Woburn,Middlesex,M,United States
D: 31 Aug 1781
P: Woburn,Middlesex,M,United States

1 Levi KENDALL-87
B: 13 Jun 1798
P: Royalston,Worcester,M,United States
M: 10 Apr 1820 - 44
P: Lockport,Niagara,NY,United States
D: 19 Apr 1822
P: Lockport,Niagara,NY,United Staes

12
B:
P:
M: -- 386
P:
D:
P:

Lorena (Laura) LYMAN-88
(Spouse of no. 1)

6 Benjamin JENNINGS-370
B: 16 Jul 1730
P: Springfield,Hampden,M,United States
M: 1 Nov 1750 - 194
P: Brookfield,Worcester,MA
D: 18 Dec 1796
P: Brookfield,Worcester,M,United States

13 Zerviah COOLEY-708
B: 29 Feb 1708
P: Springfield,Hampshire,M,United States
D: 23 Feb 1781
P: Springfield,Hampden,M,United States

14 Thomas GILBERT 1V-709
B: 1 Aug 1695
P: Brookfield,Worcester,Massachusetts
M: 1 Dec 1718 - 387
P: Brookfield,MA.
D: 13 Feb 1781
P: Brookfield,Worcester,M,United States

3 Hannah JENNINGS-180
B: 1 Apr 1768
P: Brookfield,Worcester,M,United States
D: 14 Jul 1811
P: Brookfield,Worcester,M,United States

7 Elizabeth GILBERT-371
B: 16 Jun 1732
P: Brookfield,Worcester,M,United States
D: 16 Sep 1785
P: Brookfield,Worcester,Ma

15 Judith GOSS-710
B: 10 Apr 1699
P: Lancaster,Worcester,M,United States
D: Deceased
P:

07 Nov 2015

Pedigree Chart

No. 1 on this chart is the same as No. 13 on chart no. 1.

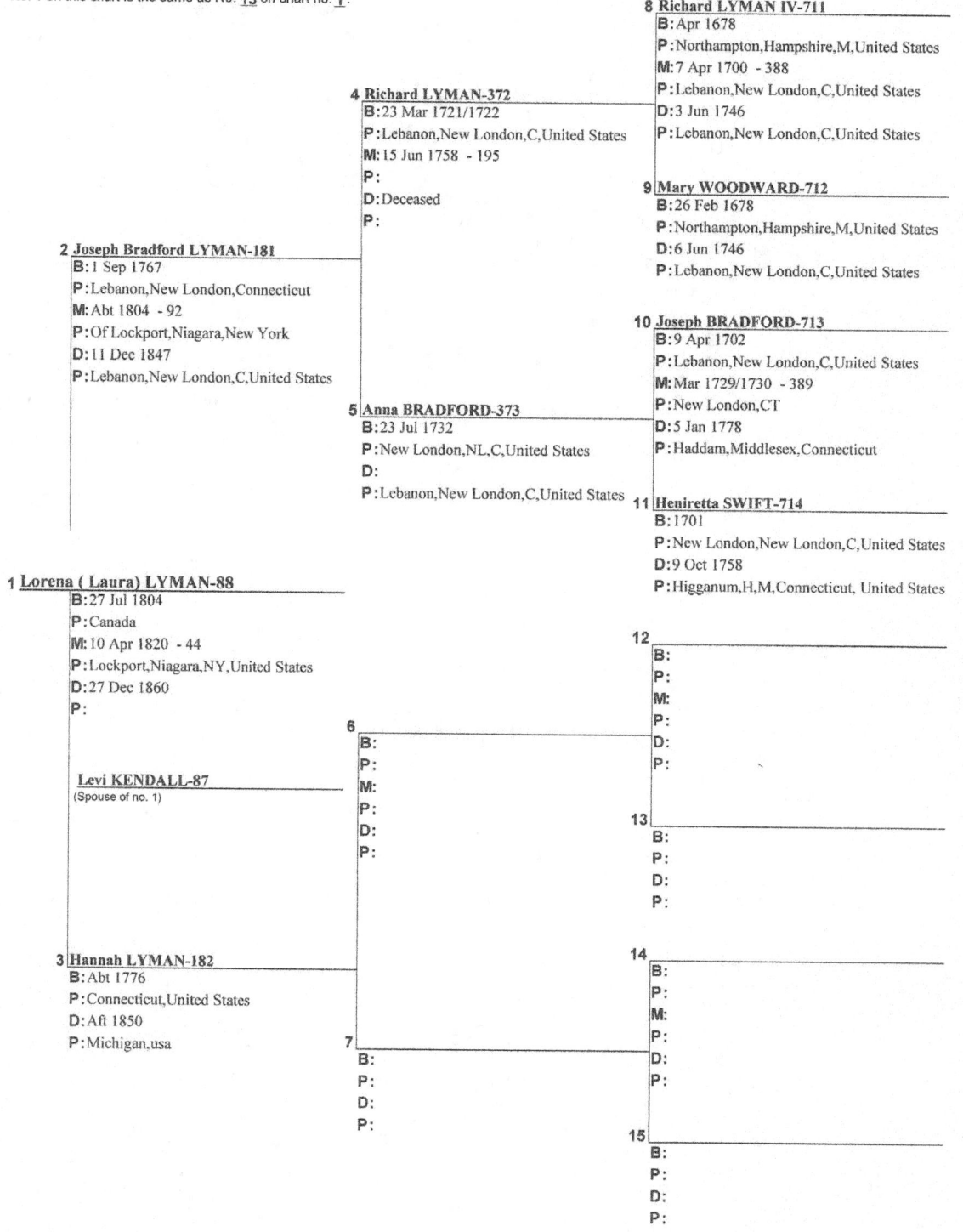

8 Richard LYMAN IV-711
B: Apr 1678
P: Northampton,Hampshire,M,United States
M: 7 Apr 1700 - 388
P: Lebanon,New London,C,United States
D: 3 Jun 1746
P: Lebanon,New London,C,United States

4 Richard LYMAN-372
B: 23 Mar 1721/1722
P: Lebanon,New London,C,United States
M: 15 Jun 1758 - 195
P:
D: Deceased
P:

9 Mary WOODWARD-712
B: 26 Feb 1678
P: Northampton,Hampshire,M,United States
D: 6 Jun 1746
P: Lebanon,New London,C,United States

2 Joseph Bradford LYMAN-181
B: 1 Sep 1767
P: Lebanon,New London,Connecticut
M: Abt 1804 - 92
P: Of Lockport,Niagara,New York
D: 11 Dec 1847
P: Lebanon,New London,C,United States

10 Joseph BRADFORD-713
B: 9 Apr 1702
P: Lebanon,New London,C,United States
M: Mar 1729/1730 - 389
P: New London,CT
D: 5 Jan 1778
P: Haddam,Middlesex,Connecticut

5 Anna BRADFORD-373
B: 23 Jul 1732
P: New London,NL,C,United States
D:
P: Lebanon,New London,C,United States

11 Heniretta SWIFT-714
B: 1701
P: New London,New London,C,United States
D: 9 Oct 1758
P: Higganum,H,M,Connecticut, United States

1 Lorena (Laura) LYMAN-88
B: 27 Jul 1804
P: Canada
M: 10 Apr 1820 - 44
P: Lockport,Niagara,NY,United States
D: 27 Dec 1860
P:

12
B:
P:
M:
P:
D:
P:

6
B:
P:
M:
P:
D:
P:

Levi KENDALL-87
(Spouse of no. 1)

13
B:
P:
D:
P:

3 Hannah LYMAN-182
B: Abt 1776
P: Connecticut,United States
D: Aft 1850
P: Michigan,usa

14
B:
P:
M:
P:
D:
P:

7
B:
P:
D:
P:

15
B:
P:
D:
P:

07 Nov 2015

Pedigree Chart

No. 1 on this chart is the same as No. **14** on chart no. **1** .

8 Johannes Peter CLEMENTS-715
B: 8 Nov 1702
P: Flammersfeld,A,R,Prussia, Germany
M: 25 Jun 1727 - 390
P: Tarrytown,Westchester,New York
D: 31 Oct 1780
P: Beekman,Dutchess,NY,United States

4 Peter CLEMENTS-374
B: 12 Feb 1747
P: Sleepy Hollow,W,NY,United States
M: Abt 1775/1776 - 196
P: Fort Ann,Washington,New York,X
D: 21 Dec 1834
P: Fort Ann,Washington,N,United States

9 Maritie Mary MEY-716
B: 1706
P: ,,Netherlands
D: Nov 1780
P: Flushing,Queens,New York,United States

2 James H CLEMENTS-183
B: 1780
P: Saratoga,Saratoga,NY,United States
M: 1796 - 93
P: Fort Ann,Washington,N,United States
D: 27 Aug 1866
P: Glens Falls,Warren,NY,United States

10 James SEELEY-717
B: Abt 1735
P: Bedford,Westchester,New York,Usa
M: Abt 1750 - 391
P: Stillwater,Saratoga,NY
D: 10 Feb 1819
P: Stillwater,Saratoga,NY,United States

5 Anna SEELEY-375
B: Abt 1755
P: Stillwater,Saratoga,New York
D: 10 Mar 1813
P: Stillwater,Saratoga,NY,United States

11 Elizabeth BROWN-718
B: 1736
P: Bedford,Westchester,NY,United States
D: 25 Jan 1828
P: Stillwater,Saratoga,NY,United States

1 Albert N CLEMENTS-89
B: 19 Mar 1801
P: Fort Ann,Washington,NY,United States
M: 21 Jan 1821 - 45
P: Fort Ann,Washington,NY,United States
D: 2 Apr 1883
P: Springville,Utah,Utah,United States

12
B:
P:
M:
P:
D:
P:

6 Ananias OWEN-376
B: 1756
P: Fort Ann,Washington,N,United States
M: 1775 - 197
P: ,,Tennessee
D: Deceased
P:

Ada WINCHELL-90
(Spouse of no. 1)

13
B:
P:
D:
P:

3 Lucy OWEN-184
B: 26 Jan 1781
P: Fort Ann,Warren,NY,United States
D: 26 Jan 1851
P: Harrisburg,Warren,NY,United States

14
B:
P:
M:
P:
D:
P:

7 Lucy SALES-377
B: 1758
P: Fort Ann,Washington,N,United States
D: Deceased
P:

15
B:
P:
D:
P:

07 Nov 2015

Pedigree Chart

No. 1 on this chart is the same as No. **15** on chart no. **1** .

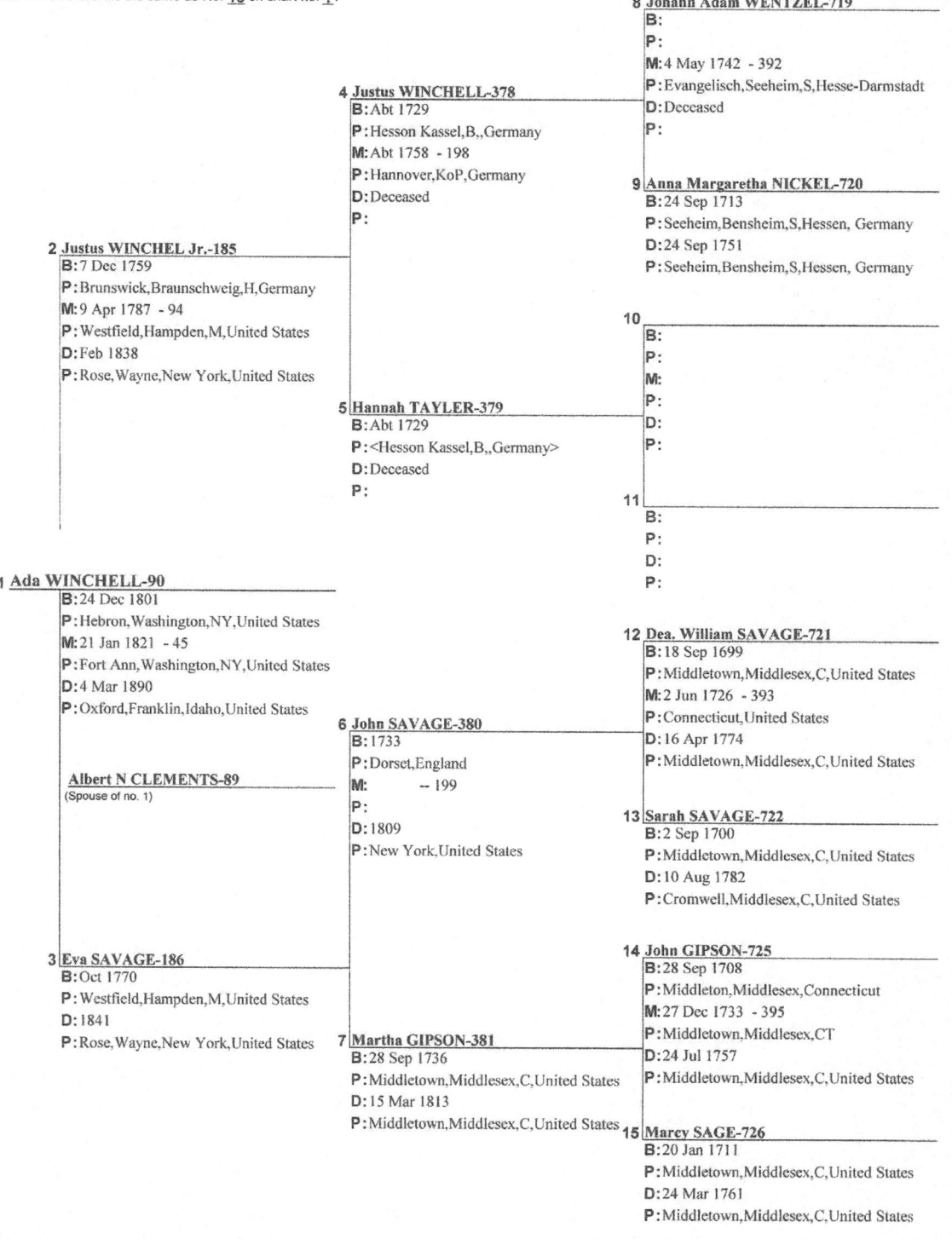

8 Johann Adam WENTZEL-719
B:
P:
M: 4 May 1742 - 392
P: Evangelisch,Seeheim,S,Hesse-Darmstadt
D: Deceased
P:

4 Justus WINCHELL-378
B: Abt 1729
P: Hesson Kassel,B,,Germany
M: Abt 1758 - 198
P: Hannover,KoP,Germany
D: Deceased
P:

9 Anna Margaretha NICKEL-720
B: 24 Sep 1713
P: Seeheim,Bensheim,S,Hessen, Germany
D: 24 Sep 1751
P: Seeheim,Bensheim,S,Hessen, Germany

2 Justus WINCHEL Jr.-185
B: 7 Dec 1759
P: Brunswick,Braunschweig,H,Germany
M: 9 Apr 1787 - 94
P: Westfield,Hampden,M,United States
D: Feb 1838
P: Rose,Wayne,New York,United States

10
B:
P:
M:
P:
D:
P:

5 Hannah TAYLER-379
B: Abt 1729
P: <Hesson Kassel,B,,Germany>
D: Deceased
P:

11
B:
P:
D:
P:

1 Ada WINCHELL-90
B: 24 Dec 1801
P: Hebron,Washington,NY,United States
M: 21 Jan 1821 - 45
P: Fort Ann,Washington,NY,United States
D: 4 Mar 1890
P: Oxford,Franklin,Idaho,United States

Albert N CLEMENTS-89
(Spouse of no. 1)

12 Dea. William SAVAGE-721
B: 18 Sep 1699
P: Middletown,Middlesex,C,United States
M: 2 Jun 1726 - 393
P: Connecticut,United States
D: 16 Apr 1774
P: Middletown,Middlesex,C,United States

6 John SAVAGE-380
B: 1733
P: Dorset,England
M: -- 199
P:
D: 1809
P: New York,United States

13 Sarah SAVAGE-722
B: 2 Sep 1700
P: Middletown,Middlesex,C,United States
D: 10 Aug 1782
P: Cromwell,Middlesex,C,United States

14 John GIPSON-725
B: 28 Sep 1708
P: Middleton,Middlesex,Connecticut
M: 27 Dec 1733 - 395
P: Middletown,Middlesex,CT
D: 24 Jul 1757
P: Middletown,Middlesex,C,United States

3 Eva SAVAGE-186
B: Oct 1770
P: Westfield,Hampden,M,United States
D: 1841
P: Rose,Wayne,New York,United States

7 Martha GIPSON-381
B: 28 Sep 1736
P: Middletown,Middlesex,C,United States
D: 15 Mar 1813
P: Middletown,Middlesex,C,United States

15 Marcy SAGE-726
B: 20 Jan 1711
P: Middletown,Middlesex,C,United States
D: 24 Mar 1761
P: Middletown,Middlesex,C,United States

07 Nov 2015

Pedigree Chart

No. 1 on this chart is the same as No. 8 on chart no. 2 .

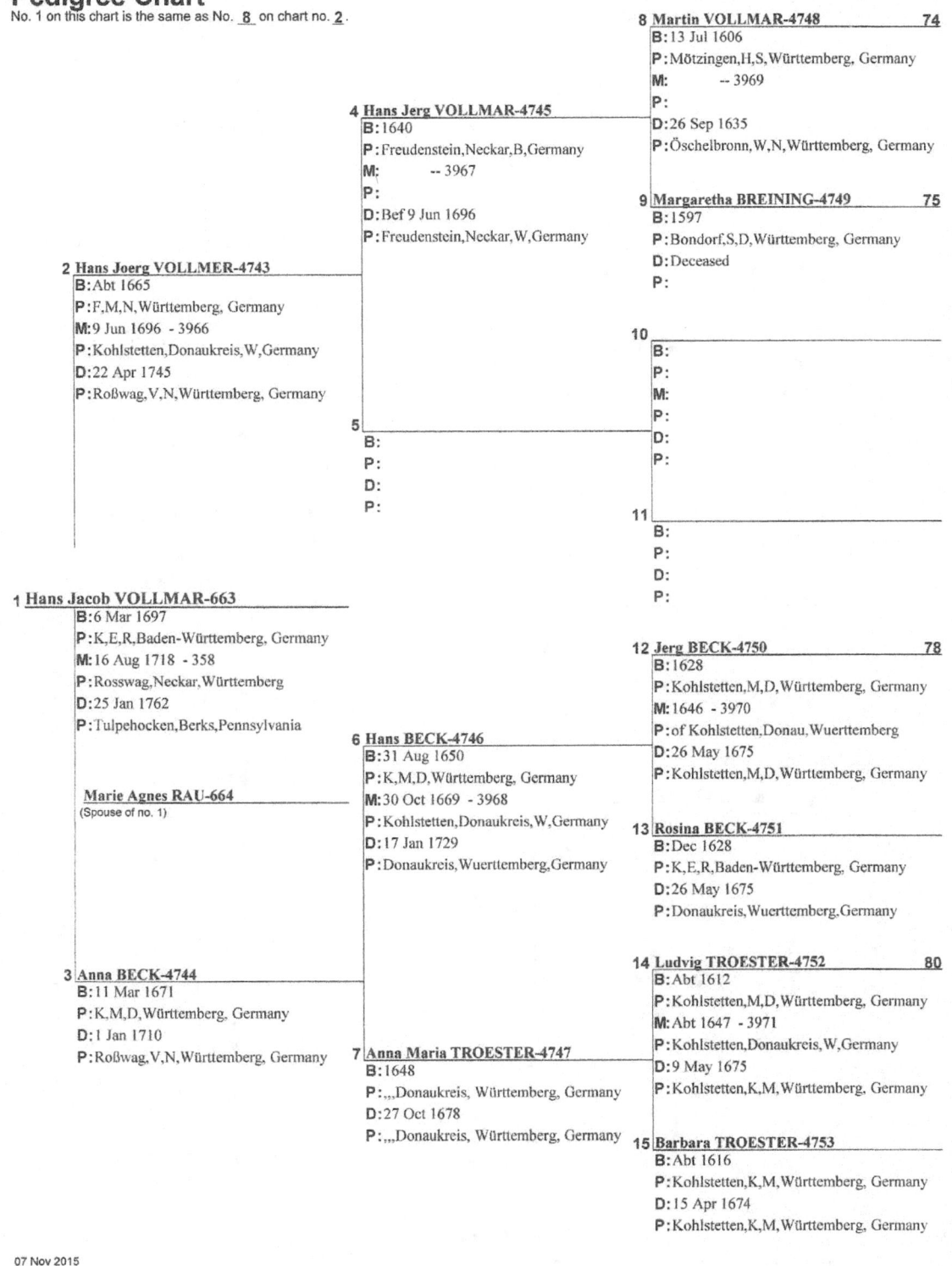

8 Martin VOLLMAR-4748   74
B: 13 Jul 1606
P: Mötzingen,H,S,Württemberg, Germany
M: -- 3969
P:
D: 26 Sep 1635
P: Öschelbronn,W,N,Württemberg, Germany

4 Hans Jerg VOLLMAR-4745
B: 1640
P: Freudenstein,Neckar,B,Germany
M: -- 3967
P:
D: Bef 9 Jun 1696
P: Freudenstein,Neckar,W,Germany

9 Margaretha BREINING-4749   75
B: 1597
P: Bondorf,S,D,Württemberg, Germany
D: Deceased
P:

2 Hans Joerg VOLLMER-4743
B: Abt 1665
P: F,M,N,Württemberg, Germany
M: 9 Jun 1696 - 3966
P: Kohlstetten,Donaukreis,W,Germany
D: 22 Apr 1745
P: Roßwag,V,N,Württemberg, Germany

10
B:
P:
M:
P:
D:
P:

5
B:
P:
D:
P:

11
B:
P:
D:
P:

1 Hans Jacob VOLLMAR-663
B: 6 Mar 1697
P: K,E,R,Baden-Württemberg, Germany
M: 16 Aug 1718 - 358
P: Rosswag,Neckar,Württemberg
D: 25 Jan 1762
P: Tulpehocken,Berks,Pennsylvania

12 Jerg BECK-4750   78
B: 1628
P: Kohlstetten,M,D,Württemberg, Germany
M: 1646 - 3970
P: of Kohlstetten,Donau,Wuerttemberg
D: 26 May 1675
P: Kohlstetten,M,D,Württemberg, Germany

Marie Agnes RAU-664
(Spouse of no. 1)

6 Hans BECK-4746
B: 31 Aug 1650
P: K,M,D,Württemberg, Germany
M: 30 Oct 1669 - 3968
P: Kohlstetten,Donaukreis,W,Germany
D: 17 Jan 1729
P: Donaukreis,Wuerttemberg,Germany

13 Rosina BECK-4751
B: Dec 1628
P: K,E,R,Baden-Württemberg, Germany
D: 26 May 1675
P: Donaukreis,Wuerttemberg,Germany

14 Ludvig TROESTER-4752   80
B: Abt 1612
P: Kohlstetten,M,D,Württemberg, Germany
M: Abt 1647 - 3971
P: Kohlstetten,Donaukreis,W,Germany
D: 9 May 1675
P: Kohlstetten,K,M,Württemberg, Germany

3 Anna BECK-4744
B: 11 Mar 1671
P: K,M,D,Württemberg, Germany
D: 1 Jan 1710
P: Roßwag,V,N,Württemberg, Germany

7 Anna Maria TROESTER-4747
B: 1648
P: ,,,Donaukreis, Württemberg, Germany
D: 27 Oct 1678
P: ,,,Donaukreis, Württemberg, Germany

15 Barbara TROESTER-4753
B: Abt 1616
P: Kohlstetten,K,M,Württemberg, Germany
D: 15 Apr 1674
P: Kohlstetten,K,M,Württemberg, Germany

07 Nov 2015

Pedigree Chart

No. 1 on this chart is the same as No. _9_ on chart no. _2_.

Chart no. 11

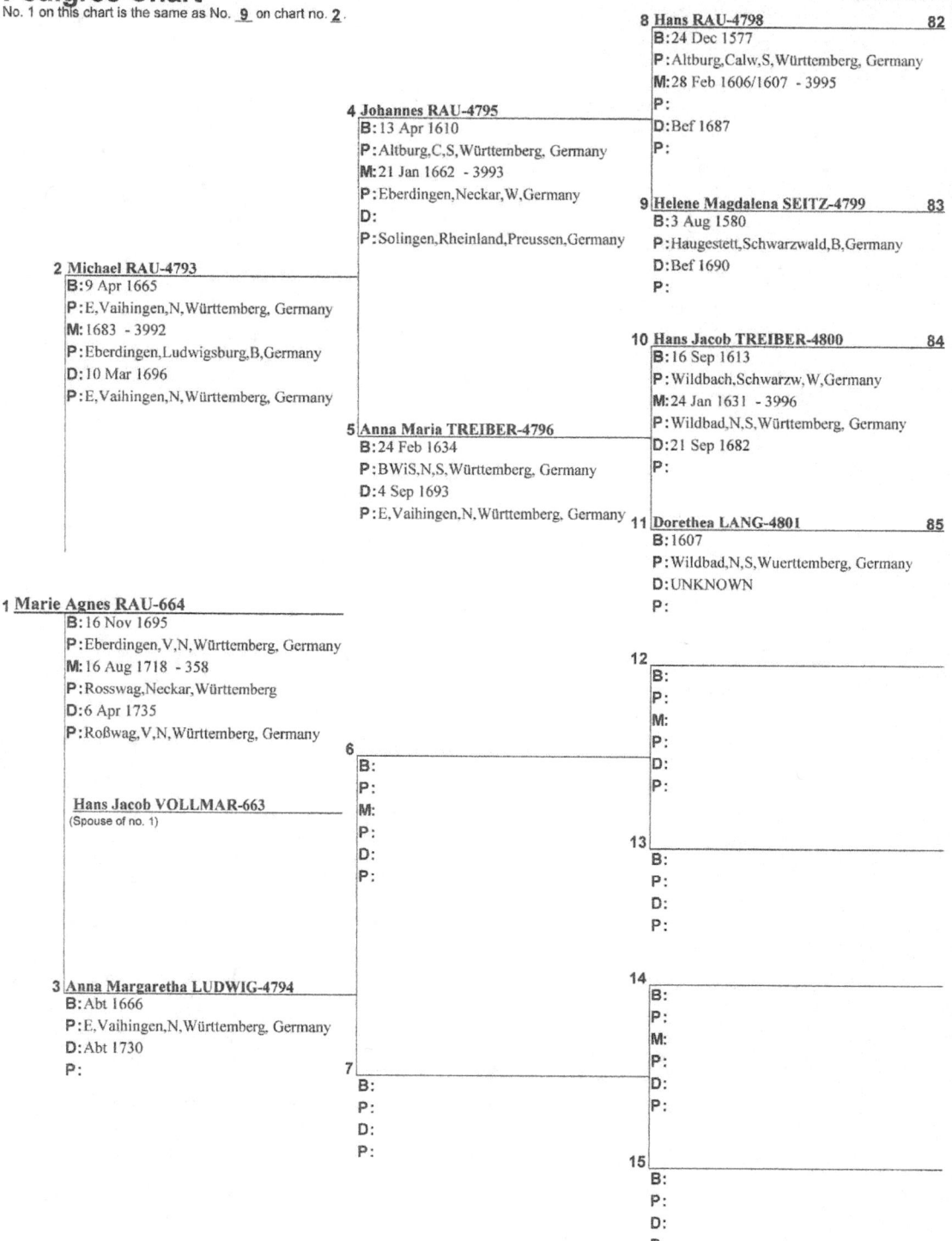

8 Hans RAU-4798   82
B: 24 Dec 1577
P: Altburg,Calw,S,Württemberg, Germany
M: 28 Feb 1606/1607 - 3995
P:
D: Bef 1687
P:

4 Johannes RAU-4795
B: 13 Apr 1610
P: Altburg,C,S,Württemberg, Germany
M: 21 Jan 1662 - 3993
P: Eberdingen,Neckar,W,Germany
D:
P: Solingen,Rheinland,Preussen,Germany

9 Helene Magdalena SEITZ-4799   83
B: 3 Aug 1580
P: Haugestett,Schwarzwald,B,Germany
D: Bef 1690
P:

2 Michael RAU-4793
B: 9 Apr 1665
P: E,Vaihingen,N,Württemberg, Germany
M: 1683 - 3992
P: Eberdingen,Ludwigsburg,B,Germany
D: 10 Mar 1696
P: E,Vaihingen,N,Württemberg, Germany

10 Hans Jacob TREIBER-4800   84
B: 16 Sep 1613
P: Wildbach,Schwarzw,W,Germany
M: 24 Jan 1631 - 3996
P: Wildbad,N,S,Württemberg, Germany
D: 21 Sep 1682
P:

5 Anna Maria TREIBER-4796
B: 24 Feb 1634
P: BWiS,N,S,Württemberg, Germany
D: 4 Sep 1693
P: E,Vaihingen,N,Württemberg, Germany

11 Dorethea LANG-4801   85
B: 1607
P: Wildbad,N,S,Wuerttemberg, Germany
D: UNKNOWN
P:

1 Marie Agnes RAU-664
B: 16 Nov 1695
P: Eberdingen,V,N,Württemberg, Germany
M: 16 Aug 1718 - 358
P: Rosswag,Neckar,Württemberg
D: 6 Apr 1735
P: Roßwag,V,N,Württemberg, Germany

12
B:
P:
M:
P:
D:
P:

6
B:
P:
M:
P:
D:
P:

13
B:
P:
D:
P:

Hans Jacob VOLLMAR-663
(Spouse of no. 1)

3 Anna Margaretha LUDWIG-4794
B: Abt 1666
P: E,Vaihingen,N,Württemberg, Germany
D: Abt 1730
P:

14
B:
P:
M:
P:
D:
P:

7
B:
P:
D:
P:

15
B:
P:
D:
P:

Pedigree Chart

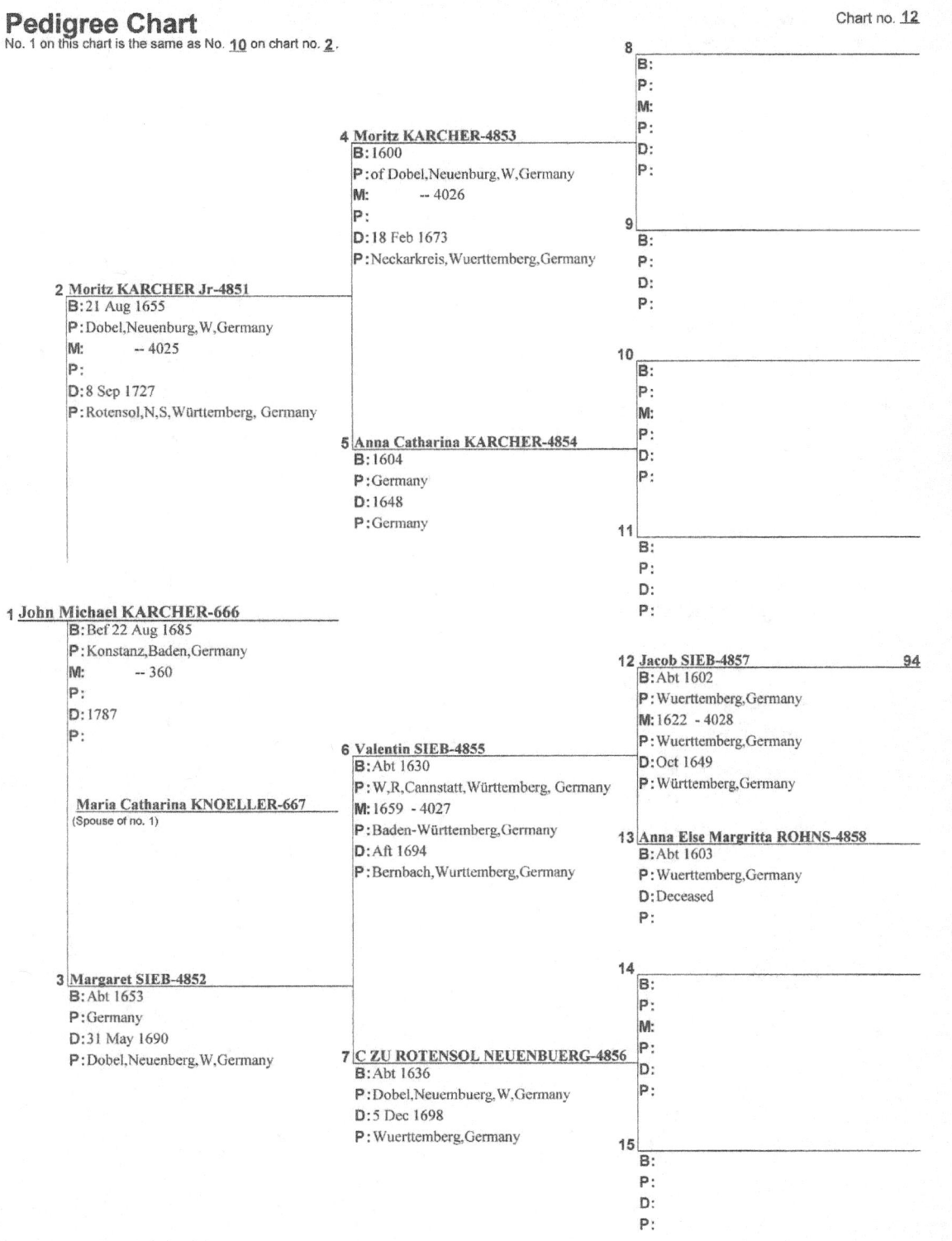

4 <u>Moritz KARCHER-4853</u>
B: 1600
P: of Dobel, Neuenburg, W, Germany
M: -- 4026
P:
D: 18 Feb 1673
P: Neckarkreis, Wuerttemberg, Germany

2 <u>Moritz KARCHER Jr-4851</u>
B: 21 Aug 1655
P: Dobel, Neuenburg, W, Germany
M: -- 4025
P:
D: 8 Sep 1727
P: Rotensol, N, S, Württemberg, Germany

5 <u>Anna Catharina KARCHER-4854</u>
B: 1604
P: Germany
D: 1648
P: Germany

1 <u>John Michael KARCHER-666</u>
B: Bef 22 Aug 1685
P: Konstanz, Baden, Germany
M: -- 360
P:
D: 1787
P:

<u>Maria Catharina KNOELLER-667</u>
(Spouse of no. 1)

6 <u>Valentin SIEB-4855</u>
B: Abt 1630
P: W, R, Cannstatt, Württemberg, Germany
M: 1659 - 4027
P: Baden-Württemberg, Germany
D: Aft 1694
P: Bernbach, Wurttemberg, Germany

3 <u>Margaret SIEB-4852</u>
B: Abt 1653
P: Germany
D: 31 May 1690
P: Dobel, Neuenberg, W, Germany

7 <u>C ZU ROTENSOL NEUENBUERG-4856</u>
B: Abt 1636
P: Dobel, Neuernbuerg, W, Germany
D: 5 Dec 1698
P: Wuerttemberg, Germany

8 _____
B:
P:
M:
P:
D:
P:

9 _____
B:
P:
D:
P:

10 _____
B:
P:
M:
P:
D:
P:

11 _____
B:
P:
D:
P:

12 <u>Jacob SIEB-4857</u>   94
B: Abt 1602
P: Wuerttemberg, Germany
M: 1622 - 4028
P: Wuerttemberg, Germany
D: Oct 1649
P: Württemberg, Germany

13 <u>Anna Else Margritta ROHNS-4858</u>
B: Abt 1603
P: Wuerttemberg, Germany
D: Deceased
P:

14 _____
B:
P:
M:
P:
D:
P:

15 _____
B:
P:
D:
P:

Pedigree Chart

No. 1 on this chart is the same as No. **11** on chart no. **2**.

8
B:
P:
M: -- 4033
P:
D:
P:

4 Mathias KNOELLER-4864
B: Jan 1622
P: Dobel,Calw,B,Germany
M: 14 May 1650 - 4032
P: Dobel Neuenbuerg,S,Wuerttemberg
D: 31 May 1687
P:

9 M -4866
B: 1594
P: Dobel Neuenbuerg,S,W,Germany
D: Deceased
P:

2 Hanns Ludwig KNOELLER-4861
B: 2 Jan 1657
P: Neusatz,N,S,Württemberg, Germany
M: Abt 1687 - 4030
P: of Neusatz,Neuenburg,Wuerttemberg
D: 2 May 1719
P: Neusatz,N,S,Württemberg, Germany

10 Elias RAU-4869   **100**
B: 23 Apr 1592
P: Dobel,N,S,Württemberg, Germany
M: 2 Mar 1614/1615 - 4036
P: Dobel,Germany
D: 21 Feb 1668
P: Dobel,N,S,Württemberg, Germany

5 Martha RAU-4865
B: 20 Nov 1620
P: Dobel,Calw,B,Germany
D: 24 Nov 1687
P:

11 Rosina STAHL-4870   **101**
B: Abt 1598
P: Dobel,Neuenbuerg,W,Germany
D: Bef 1660
P:

1 Maria Catharina KNOELLER-667
B: 23 Mar 1697
P: Neuenburg,S,Wuerttemberg,Germany
M: -- 360
P:
D: 11 Feb 1802
P: Hamburg,Berks,P,United States

12
B:
P:
M:
P:
D:
P:

John Michael KARCHER-666
(Spouse of no. 1)

6
B:
P:
M:
P:
D:
P:

13
B:
P:
D:
P:

3 Anna Maria -4862
B: Abt 1661
P: Dobel,Neuenbuerg,W,Germany
D: 1741
P:

14
B:
P:
M:
P:
D:
P:

7
B:
P:
D:
P:

15
B:
P:
D:
P:

07 Nov 2015

Pedigree Chart
No. 1 on this chart is the same as No. **12** on chart no. **2** .

Chart no. **14**

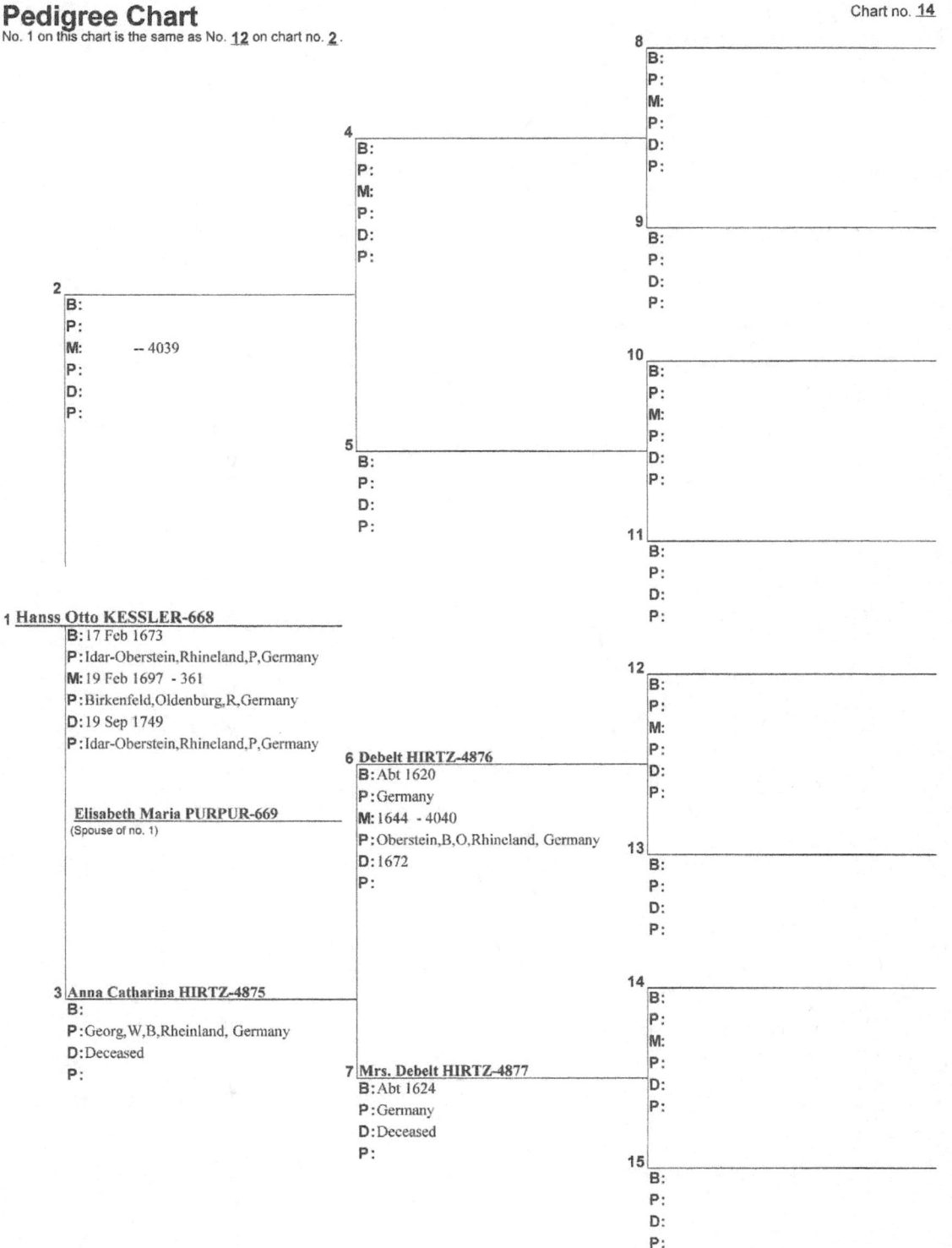

8
B:
P:
M:
P:
D:
P:

4
B:
P:
M:
P:
D:
P:

9
B:
P:
D:
P:

2
B:
P:
M: -- 4039
P:
D:
P:

10
B:
P:
M:
P:
D:
P:

5
B:
P:
D:
P:

11
B:
P:
D:
P:

1 Hanss Otto KESSLER-668
B: 17 Feb 1673
P: Idar-Oberstein,Rhineland,P,Germany
M: 19 Feb 1697 - 361
P: Birkenfeld,Oldenburg,R,Germany
D: 19 Sep 1749
P: Idar-Oberstein,Rhineland,P,Germany

12
B:
P:
M:
P:
D:
P:

6 Debelt HIRTZ-4876
B: Abt 1620
P: Germany
M: 1644 - 4040
P: Oberstein,B,O,Rhineland, Germany
D: 1672
P:

Elisabeth Maria PURPUR-669
(Spouse of no. 1)

13
B:
P:
D:
P:

3 Anna Catharina HIRTZ-4875
B:
P: Georg,W,B,Rheinland, Germany
D: Deceased
P:

14
B:
P:
M:
P:
D:
P:

7 Mrs. Debelt HIRTZ-4877
B: Abt 1624
P: Germany
D: Deceased
P:

15
B:
P:
D:
P:

07 Nov 2015

Pedigree Chart

No. 1 on this chart is the same as No. **13** on chart no. **2** .

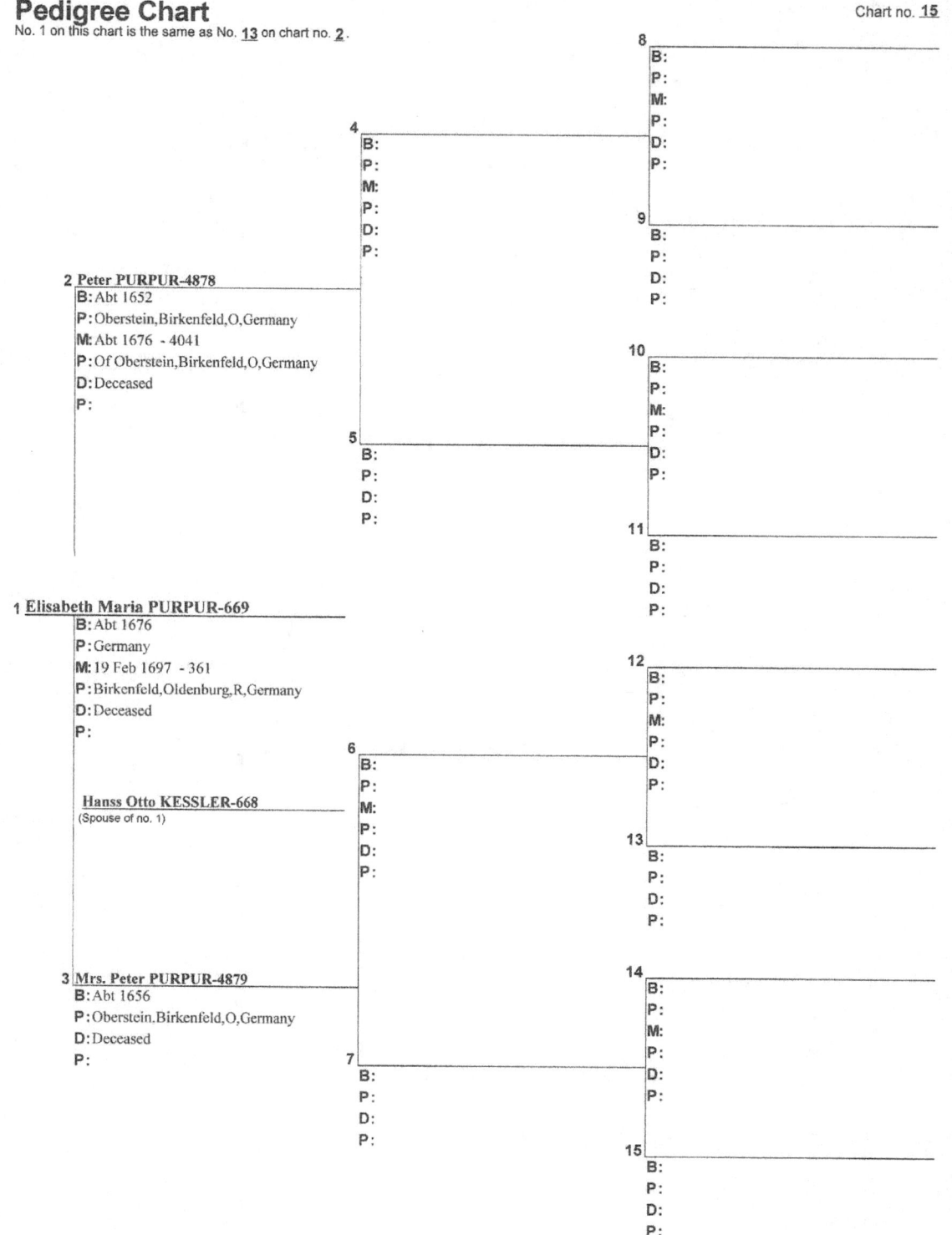

2 Peter PURPUR-4878
B: Abt 1652
P: Oberstein,Birkenfeld,O,Germany
M: Abt 1676 - 4041
P: Of Oberstein,Birkenfeld,O,Germany
D: Deceased
P:

1 Elisabeth Maria PURPUR-669
B: Abt 1676
P: Germany
M: 19 Feb 1697 - 361
P: Birkenfeld,Oldenburg,R,Germany
D: Deceased
P:

Hanss Otto KESSLER-668
(Spouse of no. 1)

3 Mrs. Peter PURPUR-4879
B: Abt 1656
P: Oberstein.Birkenfeld,O,Germany
D: Deceased
P:

4
B:
P:
M:
P:
D:
P:

5
B:
P:
D:
P:

6
B:
P:
M:
P:
D:
P:

7
B:
P:
D:
P:

8
B:
P:
M:
P:
D:
P:

9
B:
P:
D:
P:

10
B:
P:
M:
P:
D:
P:

11
B:
P:
D:
P:

12
B:
P:
M:
P:
D:
P:

13
B:
P:
D:
P:

14
B:
P:
M:
P:
D:
P:

15
B:
P:
D:
P:

07 Nov 2015

Pedigree Chart

No. 1 on this chart is the same as No. 14 on chart no. 2.

8 Nickel KLEIN-4886   122
- B: 1575
- P: Bischmisheim,S,R,Prussia, Germany
- M: 1593 - 4045
- P: Bischmisheim,Saarbruchen,Germany
- D: 1621
- P: Bischmisheim,S,R,Prussia, Germany

4 Hans KLEIN-4882
- B: 1595
- P: Bischmisheim,S,R,Prussia, Germany
- M: 1620 - 4043
- P: ,,Prussia,(Germany)
- D: Bef 9 Nov 1655
- P: Bischmisheim,S,R,Prussia, Germany

9 Gertraud BECKER-4887   123
- B: 1576
- P: Germany
- D: 1621
- P: Bischmisheim,S,R,Prussia, Germany

2 Joseph KLEIN-4880
- B: 1621
- P: Rhineland,Prussia,Germany
- M: Abt 1672 - 4042
- P: Weiderscheim,Rhineland,Germany
- D: 24 May 1708
- P: Windesheim,BK,R,Prussia, Germany

10 Engeland SCHERER-4888   124
- B: Abt 1570
- P: Bischmisheim,S,R,Prussia, Germany
- M: Abt 1605 - 4046
- P: of,Bischmisheim,Saar,Germany
- D: Bef 1622
- P:

5 Catharina SCHERER-4883
- B: 1595
- P: Bischmisheim,S,R,Prussia, Germany
- D: 24 Apr 1686
- P: Bischmisheim,S,R,Prussia, Germany

11 Engel KLEIN-4889   125
- B: Abt 1570
- P: Bischmisheim,S,R,Prussia, Germany
- D: Bef 11 Jun 1624
- P:

1 Johann Frantz KLEIN-670
- B: 1681
- P: Windesheim,Bad Kreuznach,R,Germany
- M: 17 Jan 1707 - 362
- P: Weiderscheim,Rhineland,Germany
- D: 26 Jan 1733
- P: Windesheim,Bad Kreuznach,R,Germany

12 Eberhard FRANTZ-4890   126
- B: Abt 1590
- P: Irmenach,Bernkastel-Wittlich,R,Germany
- M: Abt 1609 - 4047
- P: Kleinich,,Rhineland-Pfalz,Germany
- D: 30 Jan 1614
- P: Kleinich,Bernkastel-Wittlich,R,Germany

6 Eberhard FRANTZ-4884
- B: Abt 1610
- P: Kleinich,B,R,Prussia, Germany
- M: 12 Aug 1632 - 4044
- P: Evangelisch,Kleinich,R,Prussia
- D: 8 Mar 1690
- P: Kleinich,B,Rheinland-Pfalz,Germany

Anna Maria SECKLER-671
(Spouse of no. 1)

13 Elisabetha HERBERTS-4891   127
- B: Abt 1590
- P: Irmenach,Bernkastel-Wittlich,R,Germany
- D: 6 Nov 1632
- P: Kleinich,Bernkastel-Wittlich,R,Germany

14 Hans BAUR-4892
- B:
- P:
- M: -- 4048
- P:
- D: Deceased
- P:

3 Johanna FRANTZ-4881
- B: 1633
- P: Windesheim,BK,R,Germany
- D: Deceased
- P:

7 Marie BAUR-4885
- B: 7 Oct 1603
- P: Hochscheid,B,R,Prussia, Germany
- D: 10 May 1635
- P: Hochscheid,B,R,Germany

15 Geze -4893
- B:
- P:
- D: Deceased
- P:

Pedigree Chart

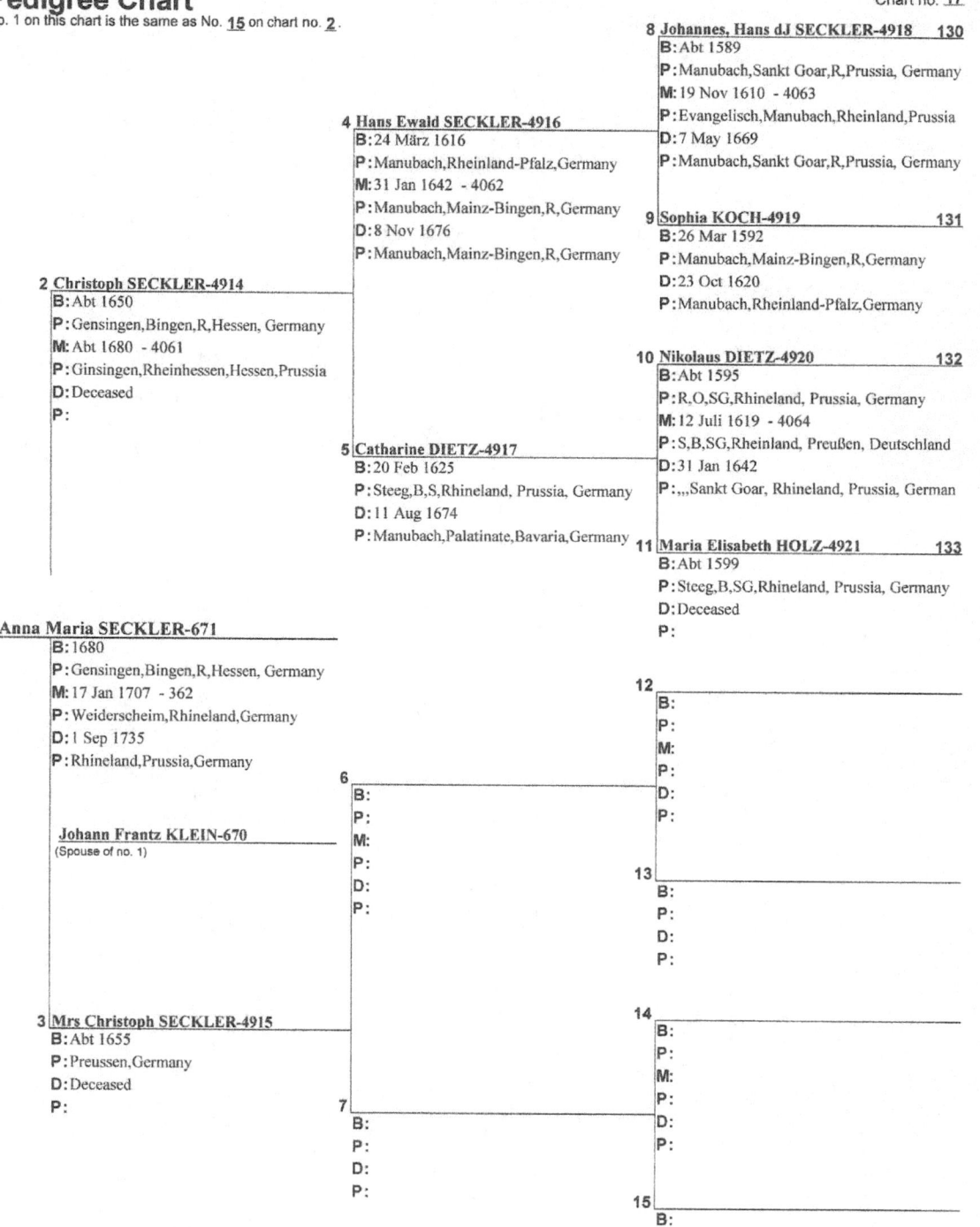

8 Johannes, Hans dJ SECKLER-4918   **130**
B: Abt 1589
P: Manubach,Sankt Goar,R,Prussia, Germany
M: 19 Nov 1610 - 4063
P: Evangelisch,Manubach,Rheinland,Prussia
D: 7 May 1669
P: Manubach,Sankt Goar,R,Prussia, Germany

4 Hans Ewald SECKLER-4916
B: 24 März 1616
P: Manubach,Rheinland-Pfalz,Germany
M: 31 Jan 1642 - 4062
P: Manubach,Mainz-Bingen,R,Germany
D: 8 Nov 1676
P: Manubach,Mainz-Bingen,R,Germany

9 Sophia KOCH-4919   **131**
B: 26 Mar 1592
P: Manubach,Mainz-Bingen,R,Germany
D: 23 Oct 1620
P: Manubach,Rheinland-Pfalz,Germany

2 Christoph SECKLER-4914
B: Abt 1650
P: Gensingen,Bingen,R,Hessen, Germany
M: Abt 1680 - 4061
P: Ginsingen,Rheinhessen,Hessen,Prussia
D: Deceased
P:

10 Nikolaus DIETZ-4920   **132**
B: Abt 1595
P: R,O,SG,Rhineland, Prussia, Germany
M: 12 Juli 1619 - 4064
P: S,B,SG,Rheinland, Preußen, Deutschland
D: 31 Jan 1642
P:,,,Sankt Goar, Rhineland, Prussia, German

5 Catharine DIETZ-4917
B: 20 Feb 1625
P: Steeg,B,S,Rhineland, Prussia, Germany
D: 11 Aug 1674
P: Manubach,Palatinate,Bavaria,Germany

11 Maria Elisabeth HOLZ-4921   **133**
B: Abt 1599
P: Steeg,B,SG,Rhineland, Prussia, Germany
D: Deceased
P:

1 Anna Maria SECKLER-671
B: 1680
P: Gensingen,Bingen,R,Hessen, Germany
M: 17 Jan 1707 - 362
P: Weiderscheim,Rhineland,Germany
D: 1 Sep 1735
P: Rhineland,Prussia,Germany

12
B:
P:
M:
P:
D:
P:

6
B:
P:
M:
P:
D:
P:

Johann Frantz KLEIN-670
(Spouse of no. 1)

13
B:
P:
D:
P:

3 Mrs Christoph SECKLER-4915
B: Abt 1655
P: Preussen,Germany
D: Deceased
P:

14
B:
P:
M:
P:
D:
P:

7
B:
P:
D:
P:

15
B:
P:
D:
P:

Pedigree Chart

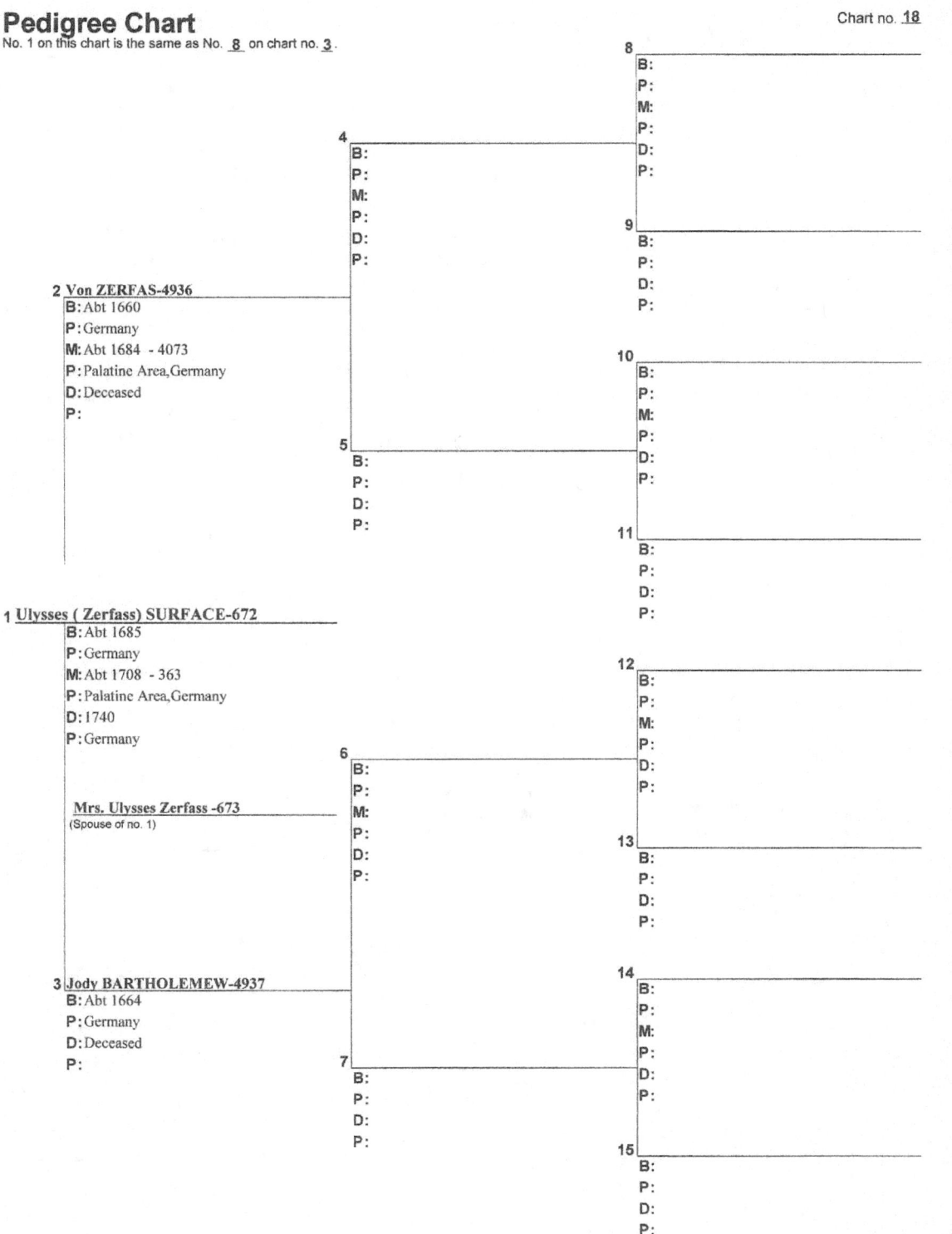

8
B:
P:
M:
P:
D:
P:

4
B:
P:
M:
P:
D:
P:

9
B:
P:
D:
P:

2 Von ZERFAS-4936
B: Abt 1660
P: Germany
M: Abt 1684 - 4073
P: Palatine Area, Germany
D: Deceased
P:

10
B:
P:
M:
P:
D:
P:

5
B:
P:
D:
P:

11
B:
P:
D:
P:

1 Ulysses (Zerfass) SURFACE-672
B: Abt 1685
P: Germany
M: Abt 1708 - 363
P: Palatine Area, Germany
D: 1740
P: Germany

Mrs. Ulysses Zerfass -673
(Spouse of no. 1)

12
B:
P:
M:
P:
D:
P:

6
B:
P:
M:
P:
D:
P:

13
B:
P:
D:
P:

3 Jody BARTHOLEMEW-4937
B: Abt 1664
P: Germany
D: Deceased
P:

14
B:
P:
M:
P:
D:
P:

7
B:
P:
D:
P:

15
B:
P:
D:
P:

07 Nov 2015

Pedigree Chart

8 Andreas SCHULER-4944   **170**
B: 6 Jan 1594
P: Kirchheim Unter Teck,D,W,Germany
M: 21 Apr 1617 - 4077
P: Calw,Schwarzwald,Württemberg
D: 23 Mar 1662
P: H,Calw,K,Baden-Württemberg, Germany

4 Hans Balthasar SCHULER-4940
B: Abt 1620
P: Kirchheim Unter Teck,D,W,Germany
M: 29 Jun 1647 - 4075
P: Haiterbach,S,Wuerttemberg
D: 3 Apr 1688
P: Haiterbach,Calw,B,Germany

9 Sara WEIßGERBER-4945   **171**
B: 1595
P: Calw,Schwarzwaldkreis,W,Germany
D: 1645
P: H,Calw,K,Baden-Württemberg, Germany

2 Martin SCHULER-4938
B: 17 Sep 1658
P: Wuerttemberg,Germany
M: 3 May 1681 - 4074
P: Haiterbach,Nagold,Württemberg
D: 25 Jan 1719
P:

10 Hans EISELIN-4946   **172**
B: 6 Mar 1591
P: Sulz,Nagold,S,Württemberg, Germany
M: 19 Apr 1616 - 4078
P: Deckenpfronn,C,S,Württemberg, Germany
D: Deceased
P:

5 Catarina EISELIN-4941
B: 16 Feb 1618
P: D,Calw,S,Württemberg, Germany
D: 15 Jan 1690
P: Haiterbach,Calw,B,Germany

11 Ursula WALTZ-4947   **173**
B: 27 Oct 1595
P: Merklingen,L,N,Württemberg, Germany
D: Deceased
P:

1 Hanss Adam SCHNEIDER-678
B: Abt 1694
P: Germany
M: 19 Jul 1722 - 366
P: Heselwangen,Heselwangen,W,Germany
D: 3 Nov 1769
P: Haiterbach,Calw,B,Germany

12
B:
P:
M:
P:
D:
P:

Anna HUNTZINGER-679
(Spouse of no. 1)

6 Andreas HOFFMANN-4942
B: Abt 1630
P: O,S,F,Baden-Württemberg, Germany
M: <1655> - 4076
P: Haiterbach,S,W,Deutschland
D: Deceased
P:

13
B:
P:
D:
P:

3 Elisabetha HOFFMANN-4939
B: 31 Jul 1656
P: Haiterbach,N,S,Württemberg, Germany
D: 19 Jun 1736
P:

14
B:
P:
M:
P:
D:
P:

7 Agathe -4943
B: Abt 1640
P: O,S,F,Baden-Württemberg, Germany
D: Deceased
P:

15
B:
P:
D:
P:

07 Nov 2015

Pedigree Chart

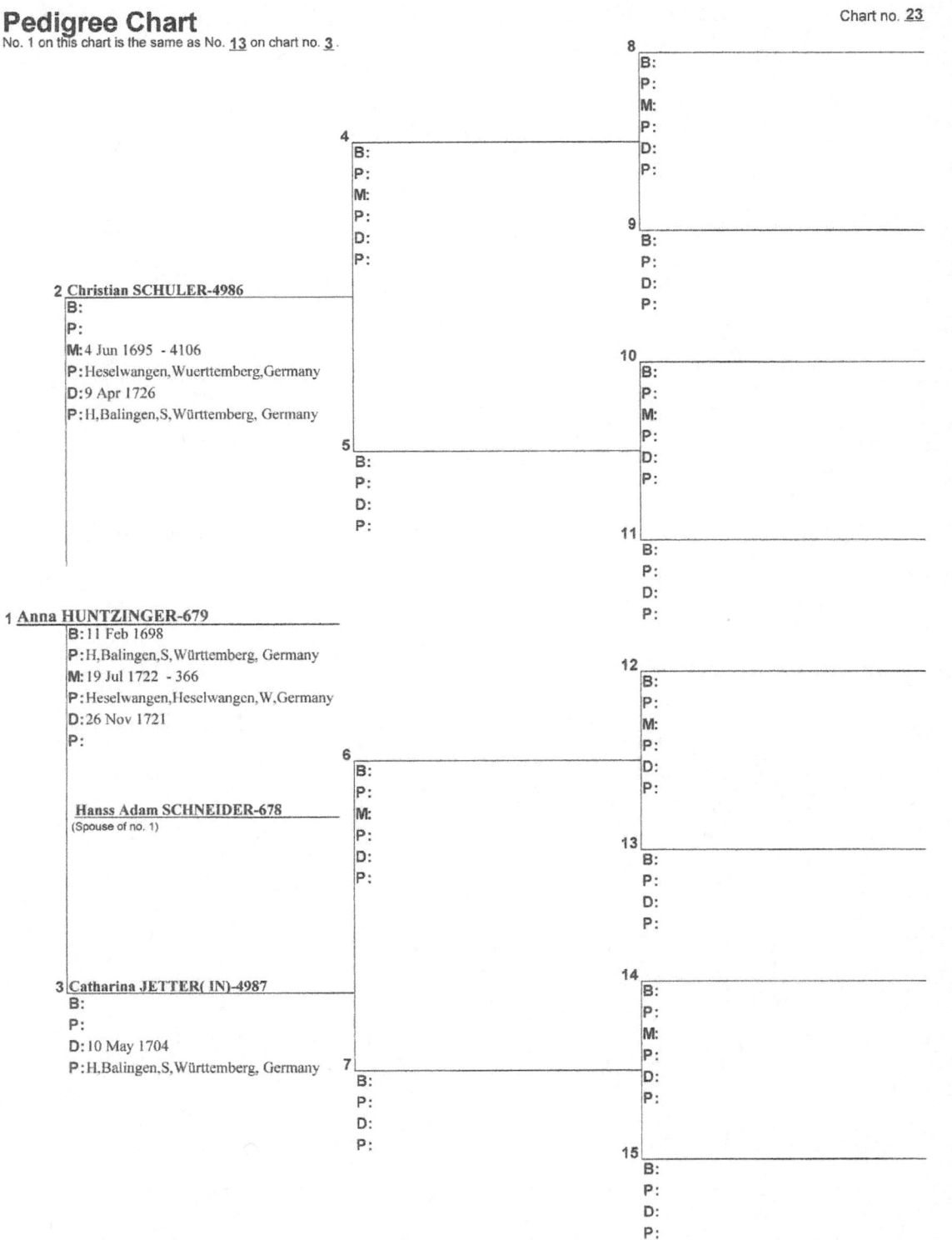

8
B:
P:
M:
P:
D:
P:

4
B:
P:
M:
P:
D:
P:

9
B:
P:
D:
P:

2 Christian SCHULER-4986
B:
P:
M: 4 Jun 1695 - 4106
P: Heselwangen, Wuerttemberg, Germany
D: 9 Apr 1726
P: H, Balingen, S, Württemberg, Germany

10
B:
P:
M:
P:
D:
P:

5
B:
P:
D:
P:

11
B:
P:
D:
P:

1 Anna HUNTZINGER-679
B: 11 Feb 1698
P: H, Balingen, S, Württemberg, Germany
M: 19 Jul 1722 - 366
P: Heselwangen, Heselwangen, W, Germany
D: 26 Nov 1721
P:

12
B:
P:
M:
P:
D:
P:

6
B:
P:
M:
P:
D:
P:

Hanss Adam SCHNEIDER-678
(Spouse of no. 1)

13
B:
P:
D:
P:

3 Catharina JETTER(IN)-4987
B:
P:
D: 10 May 1704
P: H, Balingen, S, Württemberg, Germany

14
B:
P:
M:
P:
D:
P:

7
B:
P:
D:
P:

15
B:
P:
D:
P:

Pedigree Chart

No. 1 on this chart is the same as No. **8** on chart no. **10** .

8
B:
P:
M:
P:
D:
P:

4 Martin VOLMAR-4766
B: Abt 1553
P: Ö,H,S,Württemberg, Germany
M: 27 Oct 1578 - 3978
P: Mötzingen,S,Württemberg,Germany
D:
P: Mötzingen,H,S,Württemberg, Germany

9
B:
P:
D:
P:

2 Conrad VOLMAR-4754
B: Abt 1581
P: ,,,Schwarzwaldkreis, Württemberg, Ger
M: Abt 1606 - 3972
P: Motzingen,Germany
D: Sep 1614
P: of Mötzingen,S,Württemberg,Germany

10 Johannes HARER-4774
B: Abt 1531
P: Mötzingen,H,S,Württemberg, Germany
M: Abt 1556 - 3982
P: Moetzingen,Schwarzwald,W,Germany
D: Deceased
P:

5 Maria HARER-4767
B: Abt 1557
P: Mötzingen,H,S,Württemberg, Germany
D:
P: Mötzingen,H,S,Württemberg, Germany

11 Wife of Johannes HARER-4775
B: Abt 1535
P: Mötzingen,H,S,Württemberg, Germany
D: Deceased
P:

1 Martin VOLLMAR-4748
B: 13 Jul 1606
P: Mötzingen,H,S,Württemberg, Germany
M: -- 3969
P:
D: 26 Sep 1635
P: Ö,Waiblingen,N,Württemberg, Germany

12
B:
P:
M:
P:
D:
P:

6
B:
P:
M:
P:
D:
P:

Margaretha BREINING-4749
(Spouse of no. 1)

13
B:
P:
D:
P:

3 Marga VOLMAR-4755
B: Abt 1586
P: Mötzingen,H,S,Württemberg, Germany
D: Sep 1614
P: Mötzingen,H,S,Württemberg, Germany

14
B:
P:
M:
P:
D:
P:

7
B:
P:
D:
P:

15
B:
P:
D:
P:

07 Nov 2015

Pedigree Chart

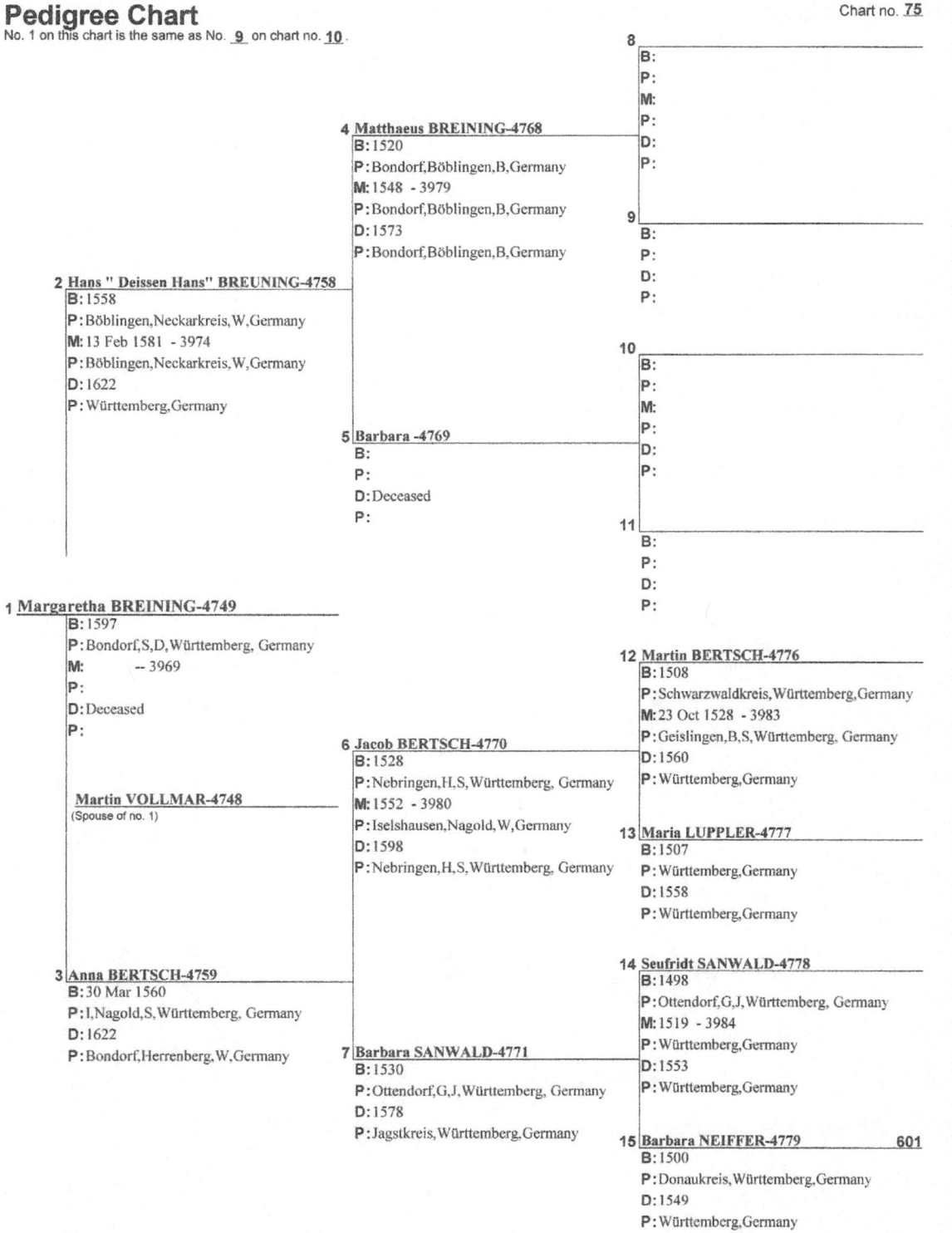

4 Matthaeus BREINING-4768
B: 1520
P: Bondorf,Böblingen,B,Germany
M: 1548 - 3979
P: Bondorf,Böblingen,B,Germany
D: 1573
P: Bondorf,Böblingen,B,Germany

2 Hans " Deissen Hans" BREUNING-4758
B: 1558
P: Böblingen,Neckarkreis,W,Germany
M: 13 Feb 1581 - 3974
P: Böblingen,Neckarkreis,W,Germany
D: 1622
P: Württemberg,Germany

5 Barbara -4769
B:
P:
D: Deceased
P:

8
B:
P:
M:
P:
D:
P:

9
B:
P:
D:
P:

10
B:
P:
M:
P:
D:
P:

11
B:
P:
D:
P:

1 Margaretha BREINING-4749
B: 1597
P: Bondorf,S,D,Württemberg, Germany
M: -- 3969
P:
D: Deceased
P:

Martin VOLLMAR-4748
(Spouse of no. 1)

3 Anna BERTSCH-4759
B: 30 Mar 1560
P: I,Nagold,S,Württemberg, Germany
D: 1622
P: Bondorf,Herrenberg,W,Germany

6 Jacob BERTSCH-4770
B: 1528
P: Nebringen,H,S,Württemberg, Germany
M: 1552 - 3980
P: Iselshausen,Nagold,W,Germany
D: 1598
P: Nebringen,H,S,Württemberg, Germany

7 Barbara SANWALD-4771
B: 1530
P: Ottendorf,G,J,Württemberg, Germany
D: 1578
P: Jagstkreis,Württemberg,Germany

12 Martin BERTSCH-4776
B: 1508
P: Schwarzwaldkreis,Württemberg,Germany
M: 23 Oct 1528 - 3983
P: Geislingen,B,S,Württemberg, Germany
D: 1560
P: Württemberg,Germany

13 Maria LUPPLER-4777
B: 1507
P: Württemberg,Germany
D: 1558
P: Württemberg,Germany

14 Seufridt SANWALD-4778
B: 1498
P: Ottendorf,G,J,Württemberg, Germany
M: 1519 - 3984
P: Württemberg,Germany
D: 1553
P: Württemberg,Germany

15 Barbara NEIFFER-4779   601
B: 1500
P: Donaukreis,Württemberg,Germany
D: 1549
P: Württemberg,Germany

Pedigree Chart

No. 1 on this chart is the same as No. **12** on chart no. **10** .

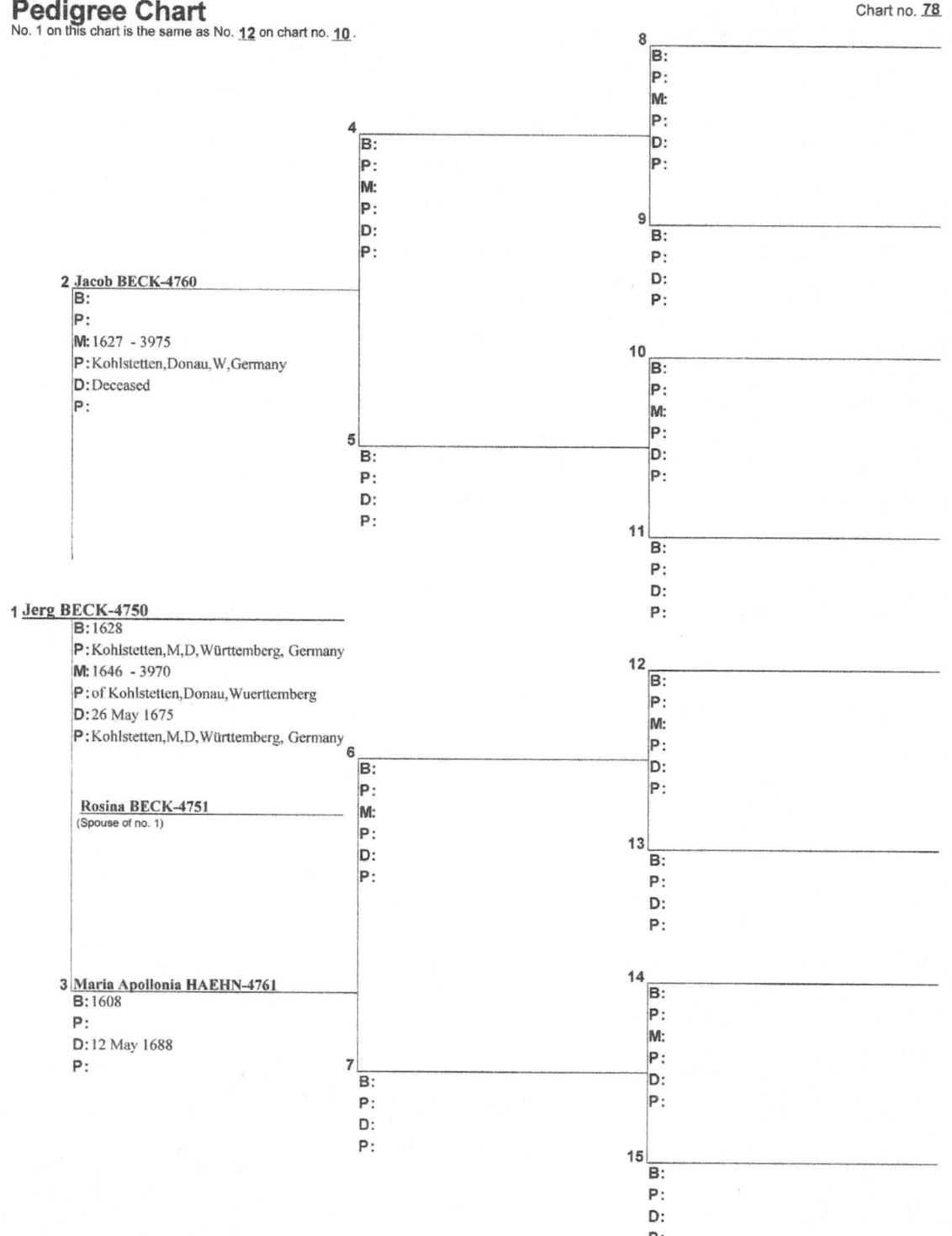

8
B:
P:
M:
P:
D:
P:

4
B:
P:
M:
P:
D:
P:

9
B:
P:
D:
P:

2 Jacob BECK-4760
B:
P:
M: 1627 - 3975
P: Kohlstetten,Donau,W,Germany
D: Deceased
P:

10
B:
P:
M:
P:
D:
P:

5
B:
P:
D:
P:

11
B:
P:
D:
P:

1 Jerg BECK-4750
B: 1628
P: Kohlstetten,M,D,Württemberg, Germany
M: 1646 - 3970
P: of Kohlstetten,Donau,Wuerttemberg
D: 26 May 1675
P: Kohlstetten,M,D,Württemberg, Germany

12
B:
P:
M:
P:
D:
P:

6
B:
P:
M:
P:
D:
P:

Rosina BECK-4751
(Spouse of no. 1)

13
B:
P:
D:
P:

3 Maria Apollonia HAEHN-4761
B: 1608
P:
D: 12 May 1688
P:

14
B:
P:
M:
P:
D:
P:

7
B:
P:
D:
P:

15
B:
P:
D:
P:

07 Nov 2015

Pedigree Chart

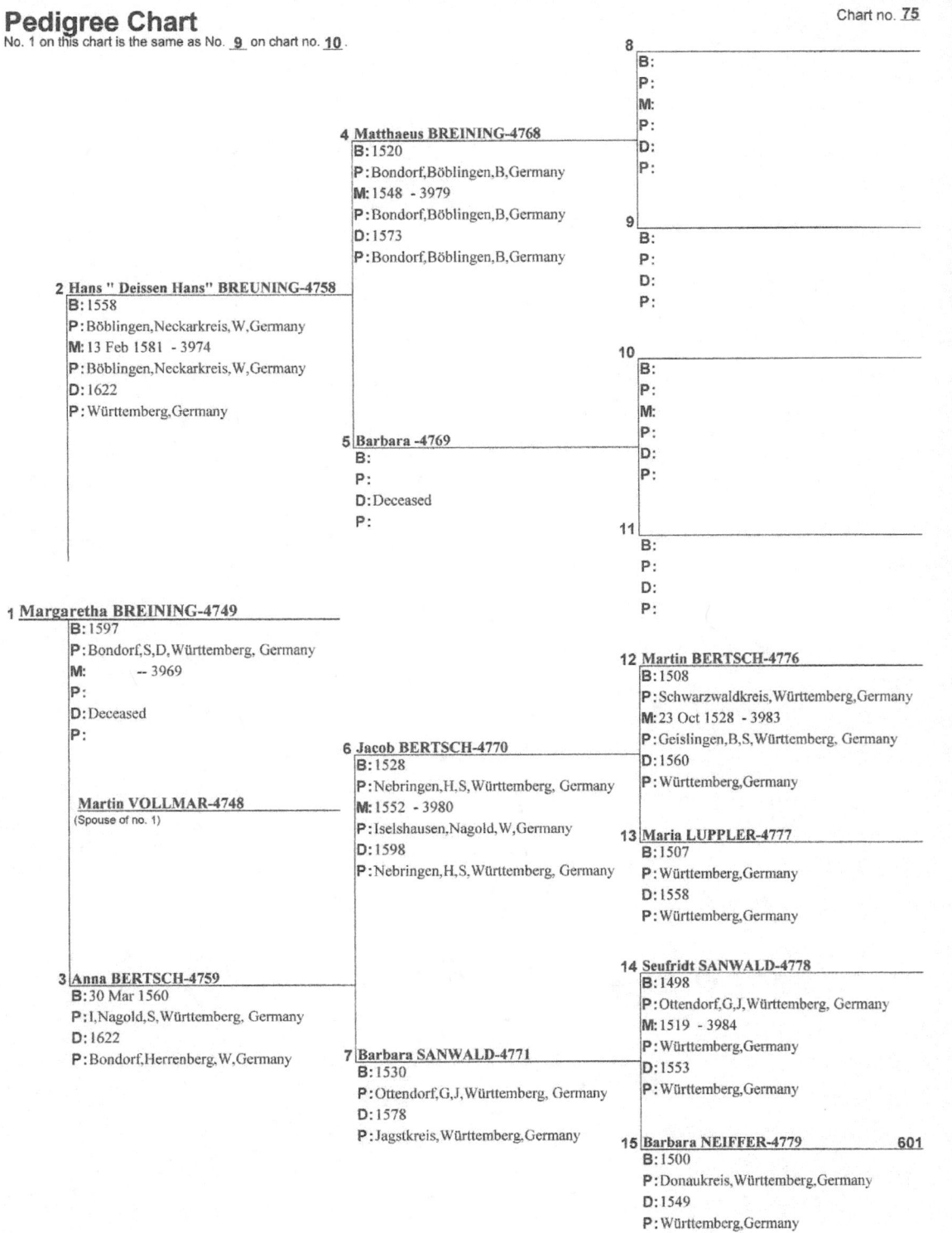

8
B:
P:
M:
P:
D:
P:

4 Matthaeus BREINING-4768
B: 1520
P: Bondorf,Böblingen,B,Germany
M: 1548 - 3979
P: Bondorf,Böblingen,B,Germany
D: 1573
P: Bondorf,Böblingen,B,Germany

9
B:
P:
D:
P:

2 Hans " Deissen Hans" BREUNING-4758
B: 1558
P: Böblingen,Neckarkreis,W,Germany
M: 13 Feb 1581 - 3974
P: Böblingen,Neckarkreis,W,Germany
D: 1622
P: Württemberg,Germany

10
B:
P:
M:
P:
D:
P:

5 Barbara -4769
B:
P:
D: Deceased
P:

11
B:
P:
D:
P:

1 Margaretha BREINING-4749
B: 1597
P: Bondorf,S,D,Württemberg, Germany
M: -- 3969
P:
D: Deceased
P:

12 Martin BERTSCH-4776
B: 1508
P: Schwarzwaldkreis,Württemberg,Germany
M: 23 Oct 1528 - 3983
P: Geislingen,B,S,Württemberg, Germany
D: 1560
P: Württemberg,Germany

6 Jacob BERTSCH-4770
B: 1528
P: Nebringen,H,S,Württemberg, Germany
M: 1552 - 3980
P: Iselshausen,Nagold,W,Germany
D: 1598
P: Nebringen,H,S,Württemberg, Germany

Martin VOLLMAR-4748
(Spouse of no. 1)

13 Maria LUPPLER-4777
B: 1507
P: Württemberg,Germany
D: 1558
P: Württemberg,Germany

14 Seufridt SANWALD-4778
B: 1498
P: Ottendorf,G,J,Württemberg, Germany
M: 1519 - 3984
P: Württemberg,Germany
D: 1553
P: Württemberg,Germany

3 Anna BERTSCH-4759
B: 30 Mar 1560
P: I,Nagold,S,Württemberg, Germany
D: 1622
P: Bondorf,Herrenberg,W,Germany

7 Barbara SANWALD-4771
B: 1530
P: Ottendorf,G,J,Württemberg, Germany
D: 1578
P: Jagstkreis,Württemberg,Germany

15 Barbara NEIFFER-4779   601
B: 1500
P: Donaukreis,Württemberg,Germany
D: 1549
P: Württemberg,Germany

Pedigree Chart

No. 1 on this chart is the same as No. 12 on chart no. 10 .

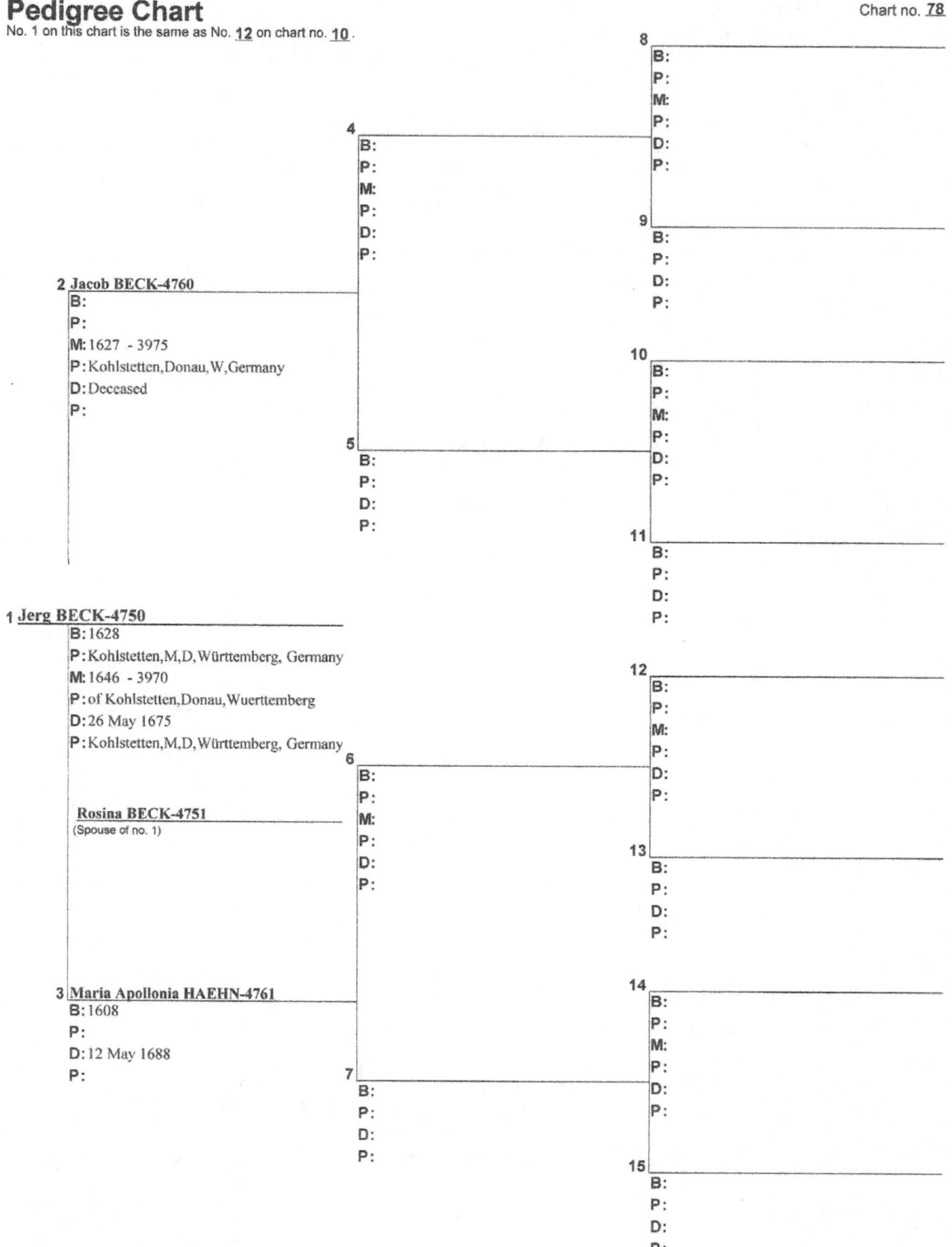

2 Jacob BECK-4760
B:
P:
M: 1627 - 3975
P: Kohlstetten, Donau, W, Germany
D: Deceased
P:

1 Jerg BECK-4750
B: 1628
P: Kohlstetten, M, D, Württemberg, Germany
M: 1646 - 3970
P: of Kohlstetten, Donau, Wuerttemberg
D: 26 May 1675
P: Kohlstetten, M, D, Württemberg, Germany

Rosina BECK-4751
(Spouse of no. 1)

3 Maria Apollonia HAEHN-4761
B: 1608
P:
D: 12 May 1688
P:

4
B:
P:
M:
P:
D:
P:

5
B:
P:
D:
P:

6
B:
P:
M:
P:
D:
P:

7
B:
P:
D:
P:

8
B:
P:
M:
P:
D:
P:

9
B:
P:
D:
P:

10
B:
P:
M:
P:
D:
P:

11
B:
P:
D:
P:

12
B:
P:
M:
P:
D:
P:

13
B:
P:
D:
P:

14
B:
P:
M:
P:
D:
P:

15
B:
P:
D:
P:

Pedigree Chart

No. 1 on this chart is the same as No. **14** on chart no. **10** .

Chart no. **80**

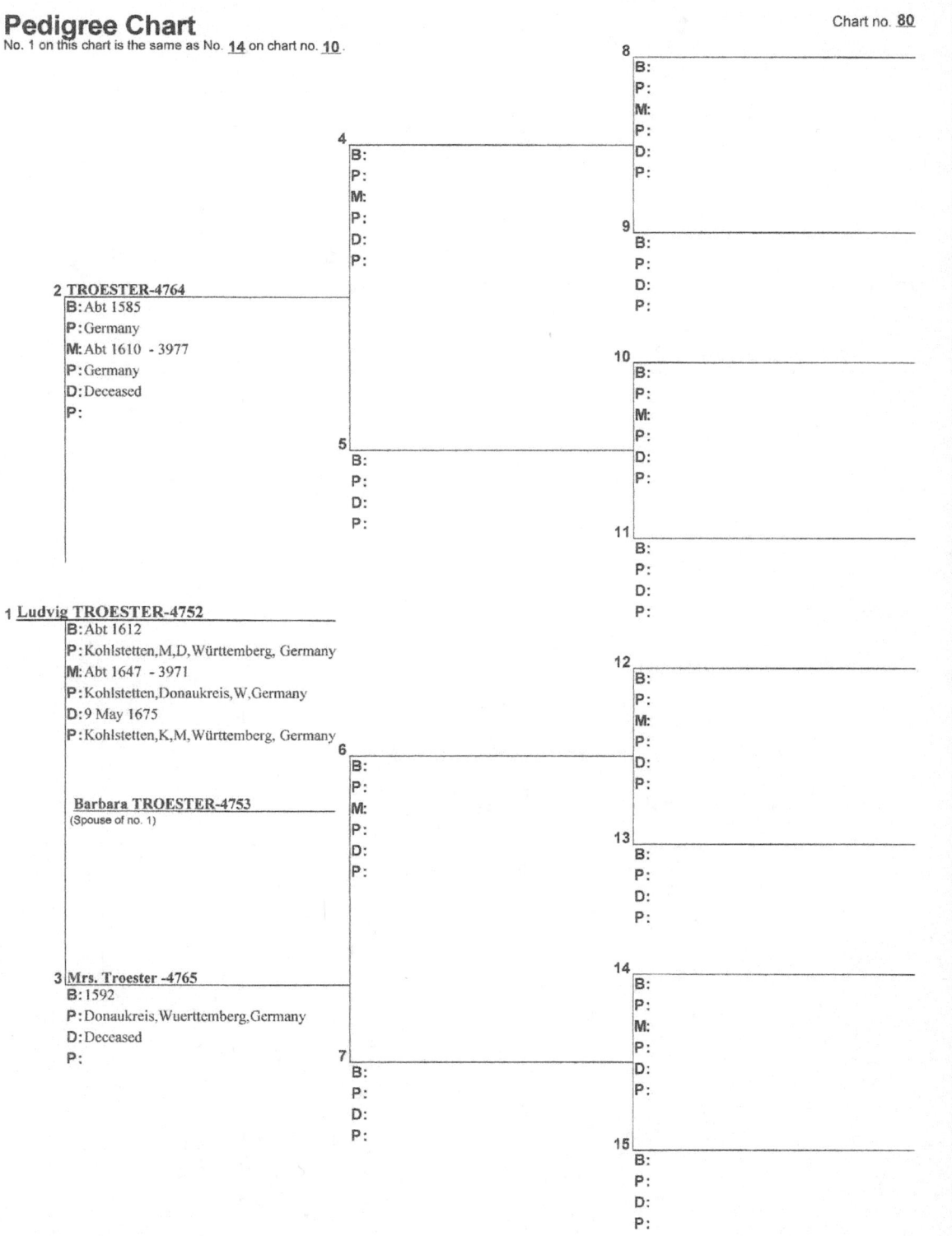

2 TROESTER-4764
B: Abt 1585
P: Germany
M: Abt 1610 - 3977
P: Germany
D: Deceased
P:

1 Ludvig TROESTER-4752
B: Abt 1612
P: Kohlstetten, M, D, Württemberg, Germany
M: Abt 1647 - 3971
P: Kohlstetten, Donaukreis, W, Germany
D: 9 May 1675
P: Kohlstetten, K, M, Württemberg, Germany

Barbara TROESTER-4753
(Spouse of no. 1)

3 Mrs. Troester -4765
B: 1592
P: Donaukreis, Wuerttemberg, Germany
D: Deceased
P:

4
B:
P:
M:
P:
D:
P:

5
B:
P:
D:
P:

6
B:
P:
M:
P:
D:
P:

7
B:
P:
D:
P:

8
B:
P:
M:
P:
D:
P:

9
B:
P:
D:
P:

10
B:
P:
M:
P:
D:
P:

11
B:
P:
D:
P:

12
B:
P:
M:
P:
D:
P:

13
B:
P:
D:
P:

14
B:
P:
M:
P:
D:
P:

15
B:
P:
D:
P:

07 Nov 2015

Pedigree Chart

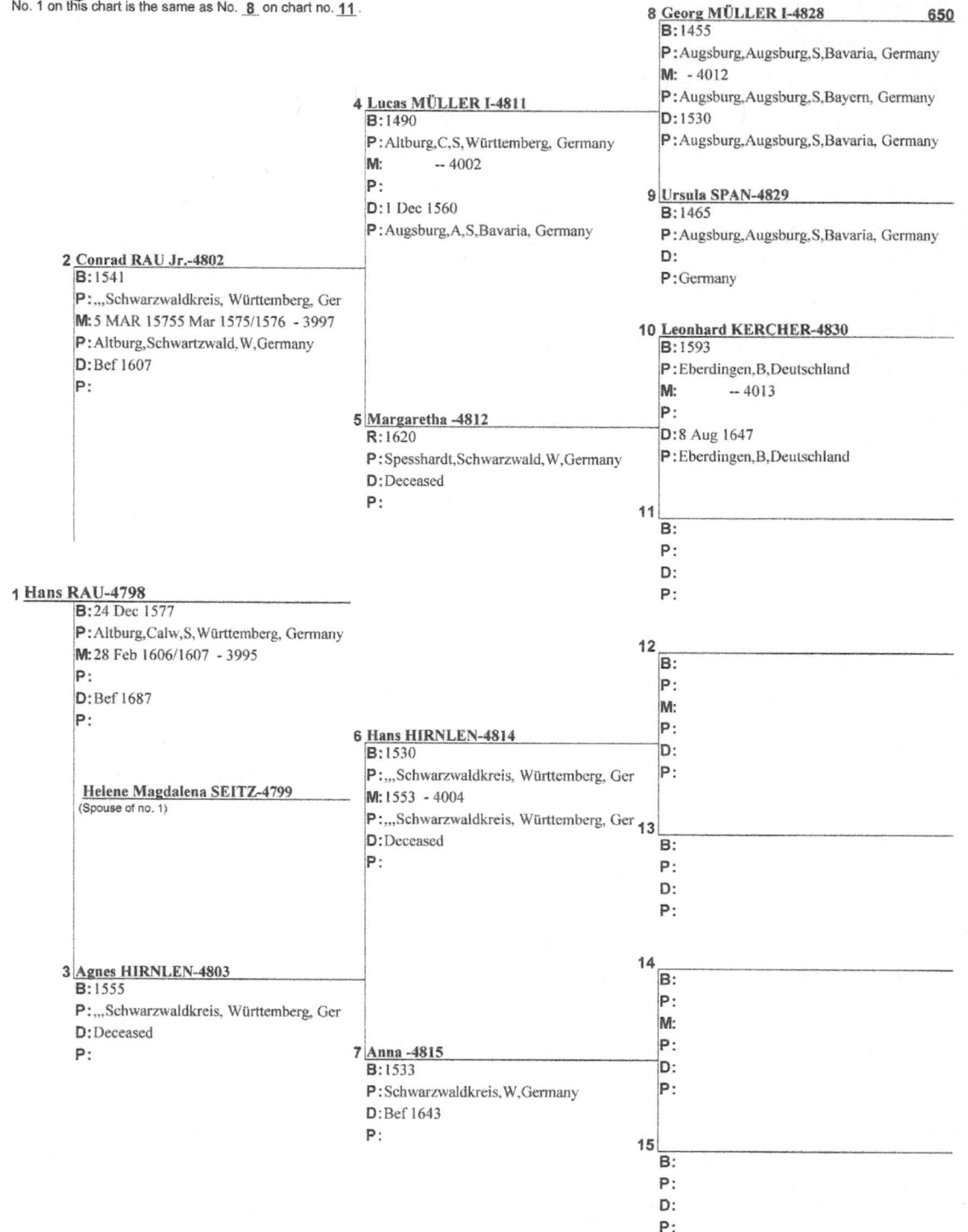

8 Georg MÜLLER I-4828   650
B: 1455
P: Augsburg,Augsburg,S,Bavaria, Germany
M: - 4012
P: Augsburg,Augsburg,S,Bayern, Germany
D: 1530
P: Augsburg,Augsburg,S,Bavaria, Germany

4 Lucas MÜLLER I-4811
B: 1490
P: Altburg,C,S,Württemberg, Germany
M: -- 4002
P:
D: 1 Dec 1560
P: Augsburg,A,S,Bavaria, Germany

9 Ursula SPAN-4829
B: 1465
P: Augsburg,Augsburg,S,Bavaria, Germany
D:
P: Germany

2 Conrad RAU Jr.-4802
B: 1541
P: ,,,Schwarzwaldkreis, Württemberg, Ger
M: 5 MAR 15755 Mar 1575/1576 - 3997
P: Altburg,Schwartzwald,W,Germany
D: Bef 1607
P:

10 Leonhard KERCHER-4830
B: 1593
P: Eberdingen,B,Deutschland
M: -- 4013
P:
D: 8 Aug 1647
P: Eberdingen,B,Deutschland

5 Margaretha -4812
R: 1620
P: Spesshardt,Schwarzwald,W,Germany
D: Deceased
P:

11
B:
P:
D:
P:

1 Hans RAU-4798
B: 24 Dec 1577
P: Altburg,Calw,S,Württemberg, Germany
M: 28 Feb 1606/1607 - 3995
P:
D: Bef 1687
P:

12
B:
P:
M:
P:

6 Hans HIRNLEN-4814
B: 1530
P: ,,,Schwarzwaldkreis, Württemberg, Ger
M: 1553 - 4004
P: ,,,Schwarzwaldkreis, Württemberg, Ger
D: Deceased
P:

D:
P:

Helene Magdalena SEITZ-4799
(Spouse of no. 1)

13
B:
P:
D:
P:

3 Agnes HIRNLEN-4803
B: 1555
P: ,,,Schwarzwaldkreis, Württemberg, Ger
D: Deceased
P:

14
B:
P:
M:
P:

7 Anna -4815
B: 1533
P: Schwarzwaldkreis,W,Germany
D: Bef 1643
P:

D:
P:

15
B:
P:
D:
P:

07 Nov 2015

Pedigree Chart

No. 1 on this chart is the same as No. **9** on chart no. **11**.

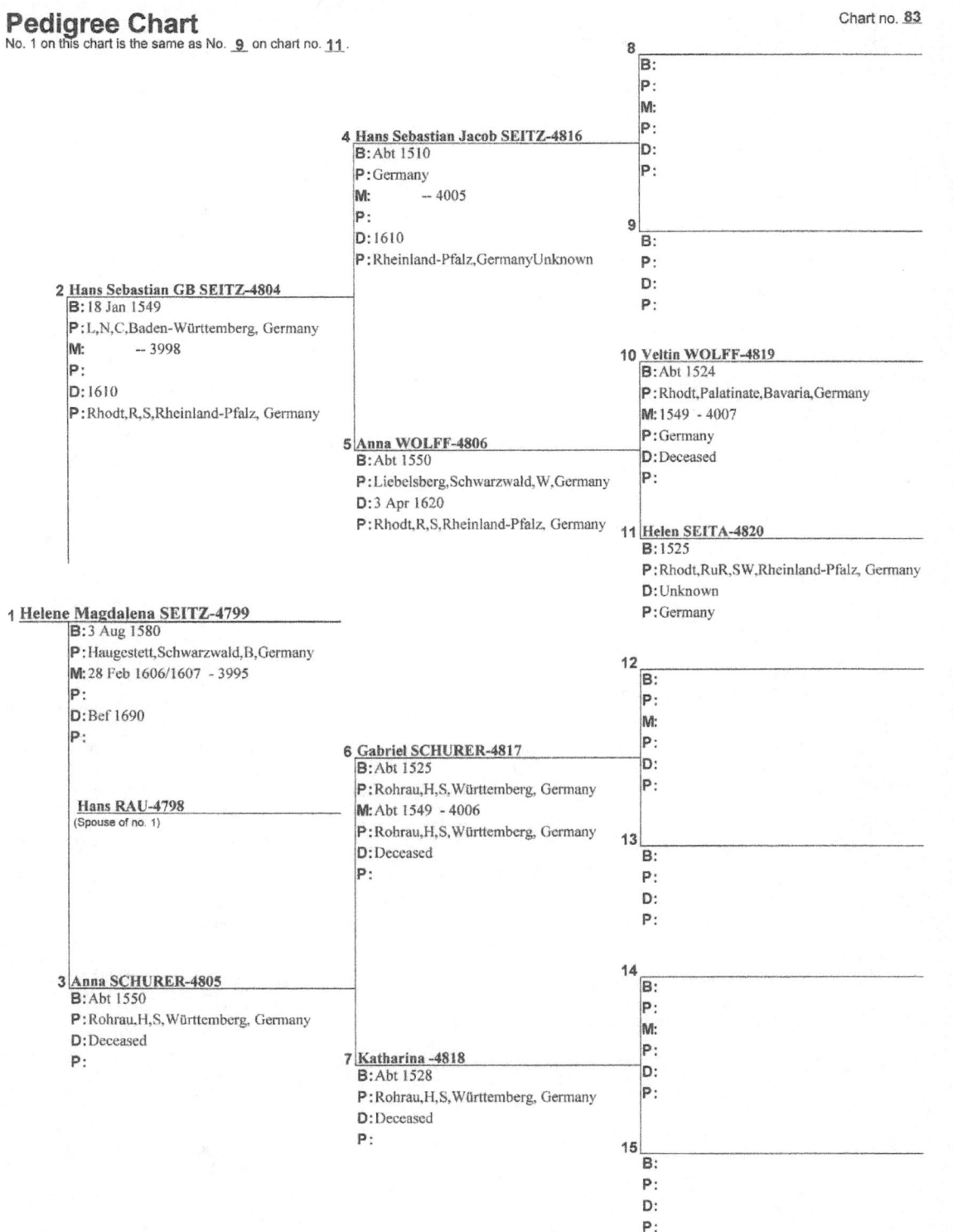

4 Hans Sebastian Jacob SEITZ-4816
B: Abt 1510
P: Germany
M: -- 4005
P:
D: 1610
P: Rheinland-Pfalz, Germany Unknown

2 Hans Sebastian GB SEITZ-4804
B: 18 Jan 1549
P: L,N,C, Baden-Württemberg, Germany
M: -- 3998
P:
D: 1610
P: Rhodt,R,S, Rheinland-Pfalz, Germany

5 Anna WOLFF-4806
B: Abt 1550
P: Liebelsberg, Schwarzwald, W, Germany
D: 3 Apr 1620
P: Rhodt,R,S, Rheinland-Pfalz, Germany

8
B:
P:
M:
P:
D:
P:

9
B:
P:
D:
P:

10 Veltin WOLFF-4819
B: Abt 1524
P: Rhodt, Palatinate, Bavaria, Germany
M: 1549 - 4007
P: Germany
D: Deceased
P:

11 Helen SEITA-4820
B: 1525
P: Rhodt, RuR, SW, Rheinland-Pfalz, Germany
D: Unknown
P: Germany

1 Helene Magdalena SEITZ-4799
B: 3 Aug 1580
P: Haugestett, Schwarzwald, B, Germany
M: 28 Feb 1606/1607 - 3995
P:
D: Bef 1690
P:

Hans RAU-4798
(Spouse of no. 1)

6 Gabriel SCHURER-4817
B: Abt 1525
P: Rohrau,H,S, Württemberg, Germany
M: Abt 1549 - 4006
P: Rohrau,H,S, Württemberg, Germany
D: Deceased
P:

12
B:
P:
M:
P:
D:
P:

13
B:
P:
D:
P:

3 Anna SCHURER-4805
B: Abt 1550
P: Rohrau,H,S, Württemberg, Germany
D: Deceased
P:

7 Katharina -4818
B: Abt 1528
P: Rohrau,H,S, Württemberg, Germany
D: Deceased
P:

14
B:
P:
M:
P:
D:
P:

15
B:
P:
D:
P:

07 Nov 2015

Pedigree Chart

8 **Cyriakus TREIBER-4831**   666
B: 1534
P: Nagold,Schwarzwaldkreis,W,Germany
M: -- 4014
P:
D: Bef 1592
P:

4 **Hans Michael TREIBER-4821**
B: 8 Sep 1560
P: Nagold,Schwarzwaldkreis,W,Germany
M: 5 Jul 1581 - 4008
P: Wildbad,N,S,Württemberg, Germany
D: Deceased
P:

9 **Maria -4832**
B:
P:
D: Deceased
P:

2 **Johannes TREIBER-4807**
B: 22 Jan 1583
P: Nagold,Schwarzwaldkreis,W,Germany
M: 1605 - 4000
P: Wildbad,Schwarzw,W,Germany
D: Deceased
P:

10 **Blasius Stephan GASSENMUELLER-4833**
B: 1534
P: Wildbad,N,S,Württemberg, Germany
M: Abt 1558 - 4015
P: Germany
D: Abt 1600
P: Germany

5 **Margaretha GASSENMUELLER-4822**
B: 12 Feb 1560
P: Wildbad,N,S,Württemberg, Germany
D: Deceased
P:

11 **Anna -4834**
B: Abt 1538
P: Wildbad,N,S,Württemberg, Germany
D: Abt 1600
P: Germany

1 **Hans Jacob TREIBER-4800**
B: 16 Sep 1613
P: Wildbach,Schwarzw,W,Germany
M: 24 Jan 1631 - 3996
P: Wildbad,N,S,Württemberg, Germany
D: 21 Sep 1682
P:

12 **Balthas HOEFFEL-4835**   670
B: 1530
P: Ehningen,B,N,Württemberg, Germany
M: 1555 - 4016
P: Ehningen,B,N,Württemberg, Germany
D: 1579
P: Württemberg,Germany

6 **Hans HOEFFEL-4823**
B: 1555
P:,,,Schwarzwaldkreis, Württemberg, Ger
M: 1581 - 4009
P:,,,Schwarzwaldkreis, Württemberg, Ger
D: 1617
P: Württemberg,Germany

Dorethea LANG-4801
(Spouse of no. 1)

13 **Maria Salome FEYERABEND-4836**   671
B: 1537
P: SH,Hall,Jagstkreis,Württemberg, Germany
D: 1579
P: Württemberg,Germany

14 **Gallus KEPPELER-4837**   672
B: 1525
P: Württemberg,Germany
M: 10 Mar 1545 - 4017
P: Ebingen,B,S,Württemberg, Germany
D: 1577
P: Württemberg,Germany

3 **Catharina HOEFFEL OR HEFEL-4808**
B: 31 Dec 1582
P: Ehningen,B,N,Württemberg, Germany
D: Deceased
P:

7 **Barbara KEPPELER-4824**
B: 7 Jun 1555
P: Bitz,Balingen,Württemberg,Germany
D: 1603
P: Württemberg,Germany

15 **Magdalena KAUFMAN-4838**
B: 1527
P: Württemberg,Germany
D: 1580
P: Württemberg,Germany

07 Nov 2015

Pedigree Chart

No. 1 on this chart is the same as No. 11 on chart no. 11 .

8 LANG-4839
B: Abt 1510
P: Germany
M: Abt 1535 - 4018
P: Germany
D: Deceased
P:

4 Peter LANG-4826
B: Abt 1540
P: Wildbad,N,S,Württemberg, Germany
M: 3 Sep 1565 - 4011
P: Wildbad,Schwarzwald,W,Germany
D: Deceased
P:

9 Mrs. Lang -4840
B: Abt 1515
P: Germany
D: Deceased
P:

2 Stephen Oswald LANG-4809
B: 5 Aug 1568
P: Wildbad,N,S,Württemberg, Germany
M: Abt 1591 - 4001
P: Wildbad,N,S,Wuerttemberg, Germany
D: Deceased
P:

10 KUCH-4841
B: Abt 1515
P: Germany
M: Abt 1540 - 4019
P: Germany
D: Deceased
P:

5 Margaretha KUCH-4827
B: Abt 1544
P: Wildbad,N,S,Württemberg, Germany
D: Deceased
P:

11 Mrs. Kuch -4842
B: Abt 1520
P: Germany
D: Deceased
P:

1 Dorethea LANG-4801
B: 1607
P: Wildbad,N,S,Wuerttemberg, Germany
M: 24 Jan 1631 - 3996
P: Wildbad,N,S,Württemberg, Germany
D: UNKNOWN
P:

12
B:
P:
M:
P:
D:
P:

6
B:
P:
M:
P:
D:
P:

Hans Jacob TREIBER-4800
(Spouse of no. 1)

13
B:
P:
D:
P:

14
B:
P:
M:
P:
D:
P:

3 Barbara -4810
B: 1570
P: Wildbad,N,S,Württemberg, Germany
D: Deceased
P:

7
B:
P:
D:
P:

15
B:
P:
D:
P:

07 Nov 2015

Pedigree Chart

No. 1 on this chart is the same as No. **12** on chart no. **12** .

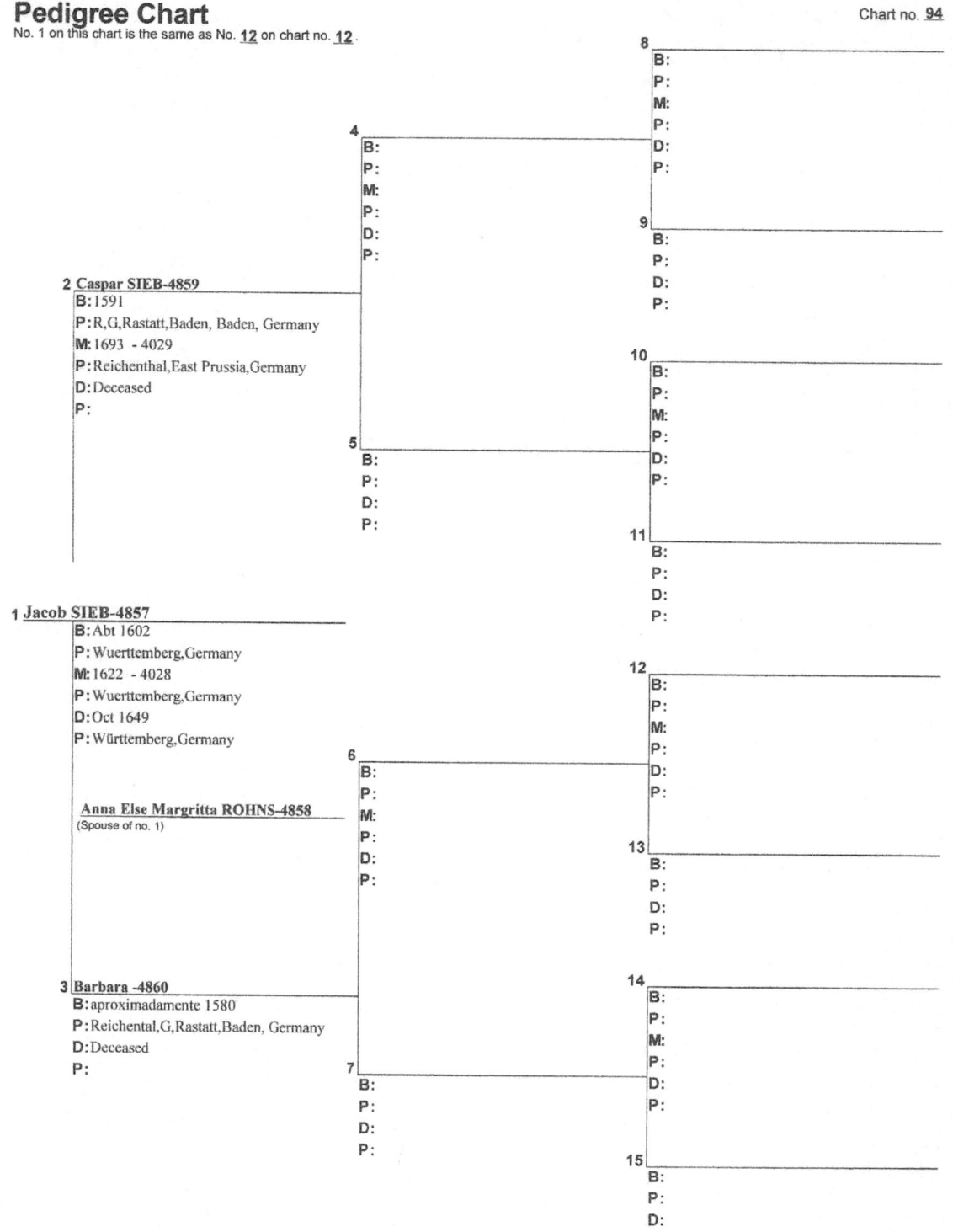

2 Caspar SIEB-4859
B: 1591
P: R,G,Rastatt,Baden, Baden, Germany
M: 1693 - 4029
P: Reichenthal,East Prussia,Germany
D: Deceased
P:

1 Jacob SIEB-4857
B: Abt 1602
P: Wuerttemberg,Germany
M: 1622 - 4028
P: Wuerttemberg,Germany
D: Oct 1649
P: Württemberg,Germany

Anna Else Margritta ROHNS-4858
(Spouse of no. 1)

3 Barbara -4860
B: aproximadamente 1580
P: Reichental,G,Rastatt,Baden, Germany
D: Deceased
P:

4
B:
P:
M:
P:
D:
P:

5
B:
P:
D:
P:

6
B:
P:
M:
P:
D:
P:

7
B:
P:
D:
P:

8
B:
P:
M:
P:
D:
P:

9
B:
P:
D:
P:

10
B:
P:
M:
P:
D:
P:

11
B:
P:
D:
P:

12
B:
P:
M:
P:
D:
P:

13
B:
P:
D:
P:

14
B:
P:
M:
P:
D:
P:

15
B:
P:
D:
P:

07 Nov 2015

Pedigree Chart

No. 1 on this chart is the same as No. **10** on chart no. **13** .

Chart no. **100**

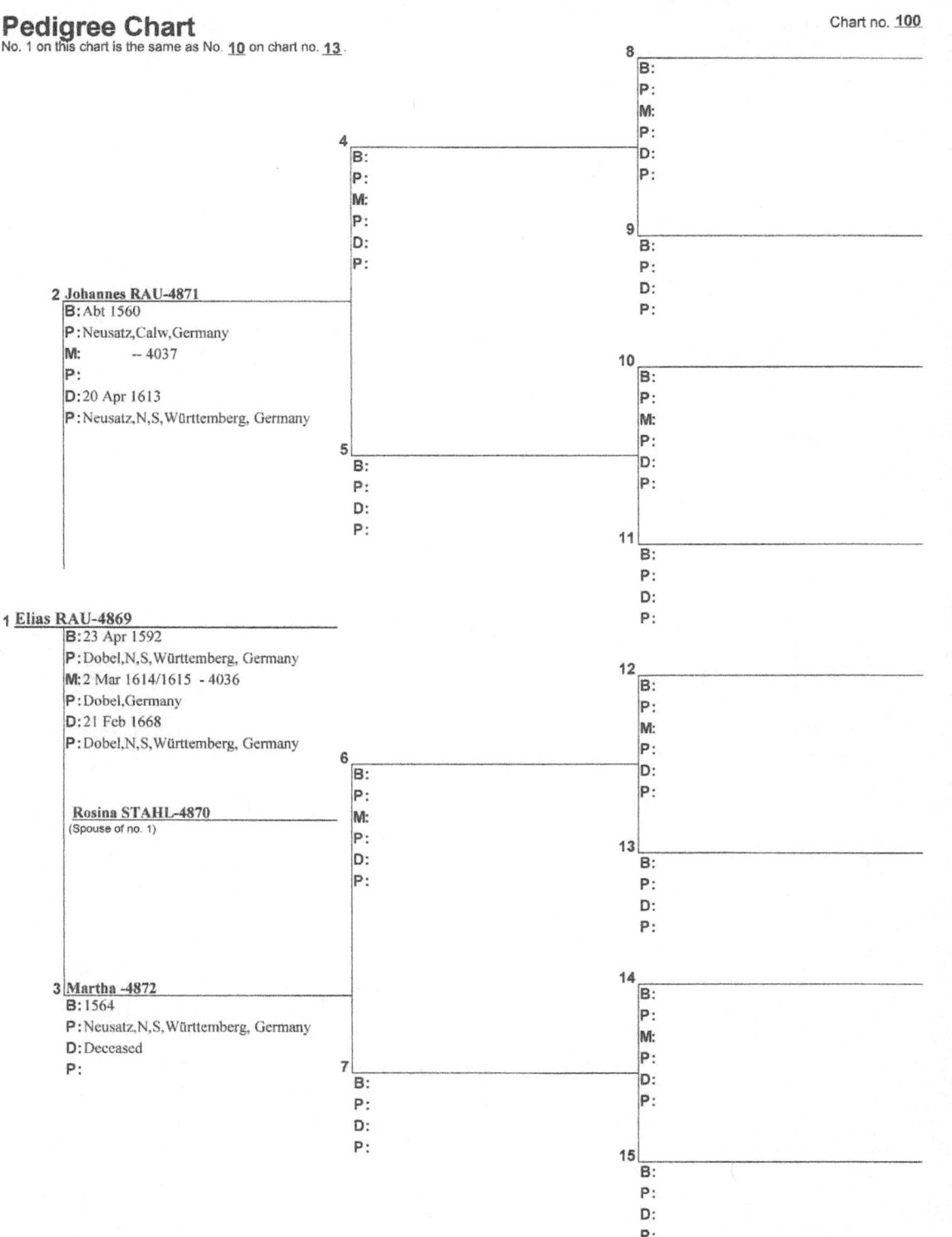

2 Johannes RAU-4871
B: Abt 1560
P: Neusatz,Calw,Germany
M: -- 4037
P:
D: 20 Apr 1613
P: Neusatz,N,S,Württemberg, Germany

1 Elias RAU-4869
B: 23 Apr 1592
P: Dobel,N,S,Württemberg, Germany
M: 2 Mar 1614/1615 - 4036
P: Dobel,Germany
D: 21 Feb 1668
P: Dobel,N,S,Württemberg, Germany

Rosina STAHL-4870
(Spouse of no. 1)

3 Martha -4872
B: 1564
P: Neusatz,N,S,Württemberg, Germany
D: Deceased
P:

4
B:
P:
M:
P:
D:
P:

5
B:
P:
D:
P:

6
B:
P:
M:
P:
D:
P:

7
B:
P:
D:
P:

8
B:
P:
M:
P:
D:
P:

9
B:
P:
D:
P:

10
B:
P:
M:
P:
D:
P:

11
B:
P:
D:
P:

12
B:
P:
M:
P:
D:
P:

13
B:
P:
D:
P:

14
B:
P:
M:
P:
D:
P:

15
B:
P:
D:
P:

07 Nov 2015

Pedigree Chart

No. 1 on this chart is the same as No. <u>11</u> on chart no. <u>13</u>.

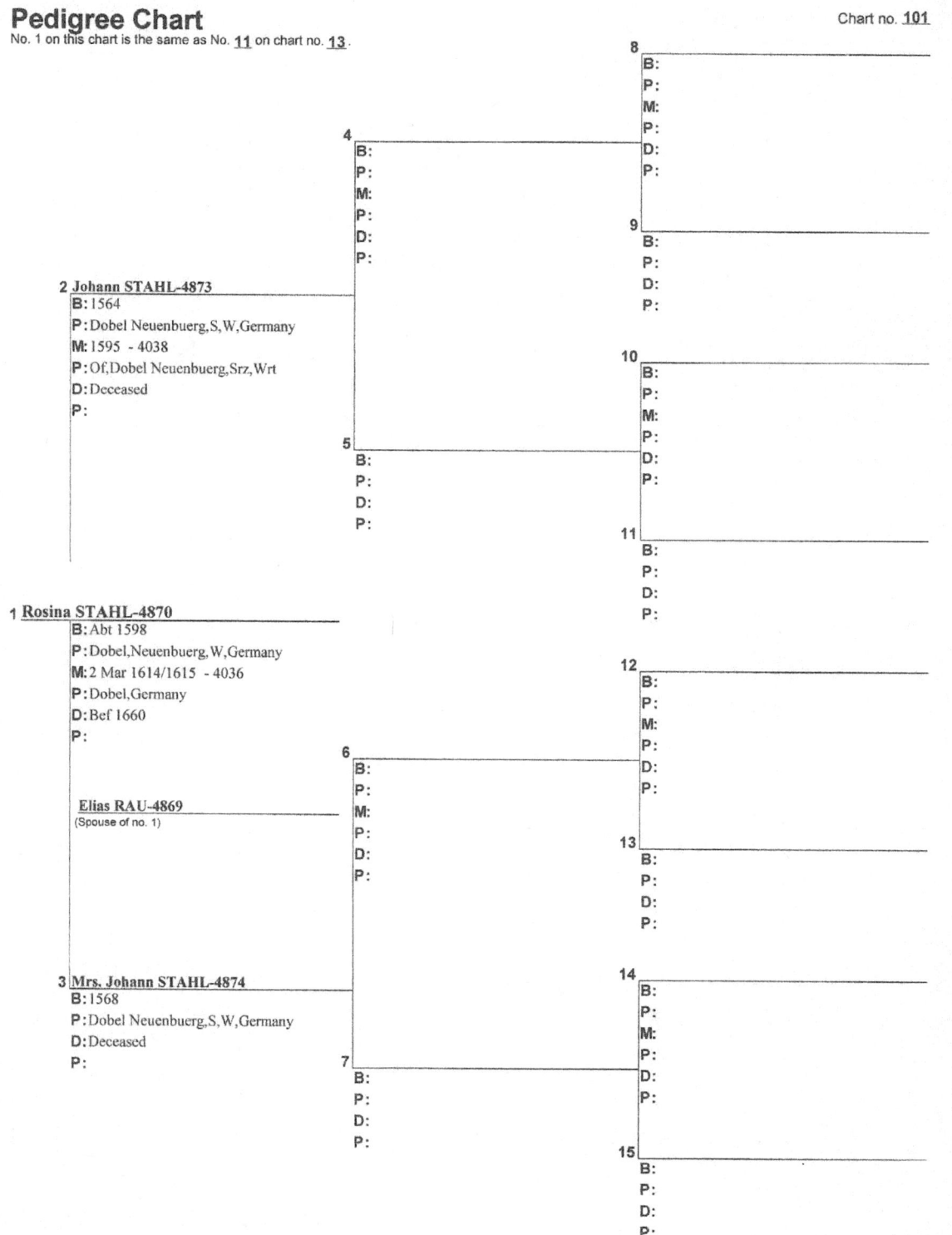

2 Johann STAHL-4873
B: 1564
P: Dobel Neuenbuerg,S,W,Germany
M: 1595 - 4038
P: Of,Dobel Neuenbuerg,Srz,Wrt
D: Deceased
P:

1 Rosina STAHL-4870
B: Abt 1598
P: Dobel,Neuenbuerg,W,Germany
M: 2 Mar 1614/1615 - 4036
P: Dobel,Germany
D: Bef 1660
P:

Elias RAU-4869
(Spouse of no. 1)

3 Mrs. Johann STAHL-4874
B: 1568
P: Dobel Neuenbuerg,S,W,Germany
D: Deceased
P:

4
B:
P:
M:
P:
D:
P:

5
B:
P:
D:
P:

6
B:
P:
M:
P:
D:
P:

7
B:
P:
D:
P:

8
B:
P:
M:
P:
D:
P:

9
B:
P:
D:
P:

10
B:
P:
M:
P:
D:
P:

11
B:
P:
D:
P:

12
B:
P:
M:
P:
D:
P:

13
B:
P:
D:
P:

14
B:
P:
M:
P:
D:
P:

15
B:
P:
D:
P:

07 Nov 2015

Pedigree Chart

No. 1 on this chart is the same as No. 8 on chart no. 16 .

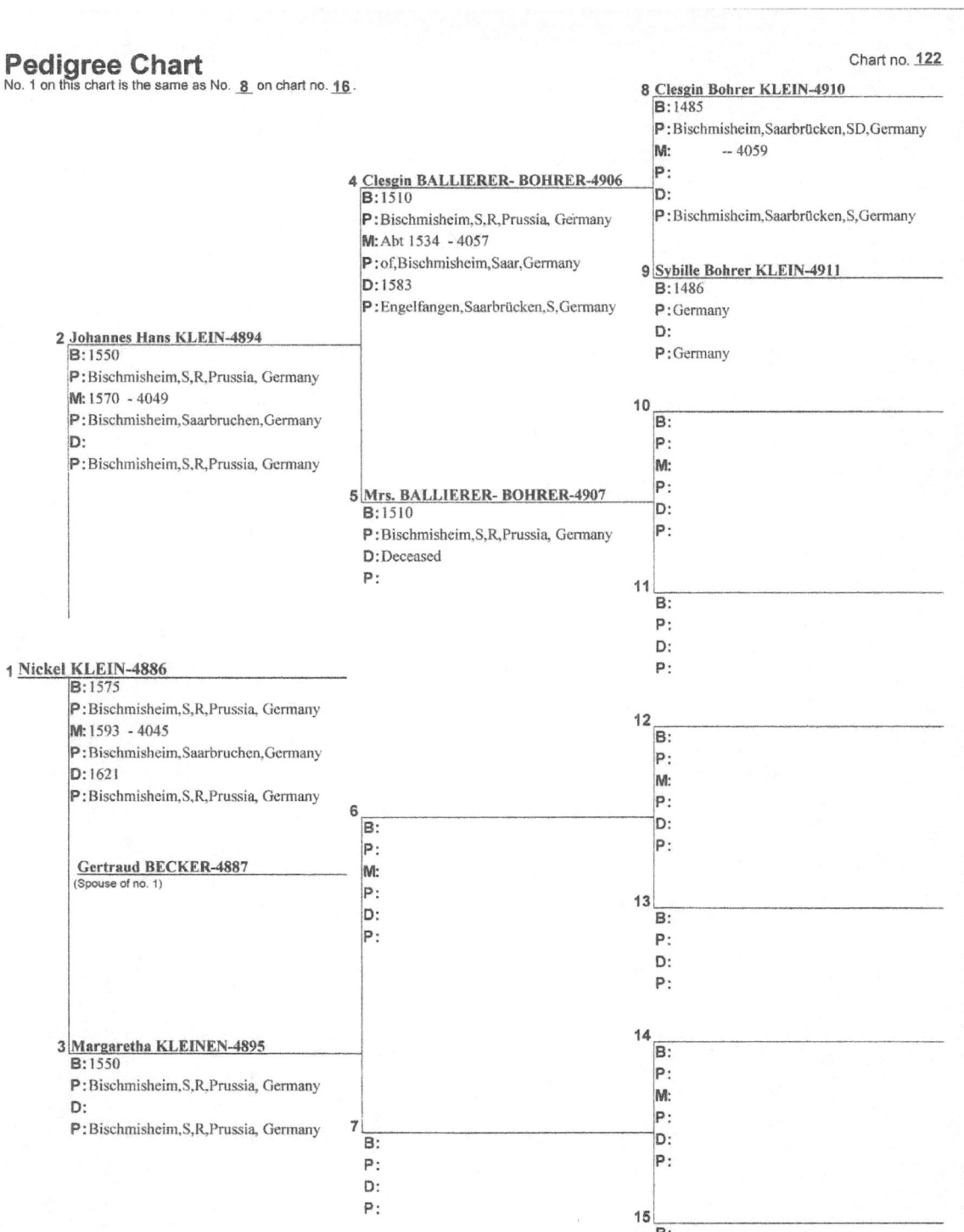

8 Clesgin Bohrer KLEIN-4910
B: 1485
P: Bischmisheim,Saarbrücken,SD,Germany
M: -- 4059
P:
D:
P: Bischmisheim,Saarbrücken,S,Germany

4 Clesgin BALLIERER- BOHRER-4906
B: 1510
P: Bischmisheim,S,R,Prussia, Germany
M: Abt 1534 - 4057
P: of,Bischmisheim,Saar,Germany
D: 1583
P: Engelfangen,Saarbrücken,S,Germany

9 Sybille Bohrer KLEIN-4911
B: 1486
P: Germany
D:
P: Germany

2 Johannes Hans KLEIN-4894
B: 1550
P: Bischmisheim,S,R,Prussia, Germany
M: 1570 - 4049
P: Bischmisheim,Saarbruchen,Germany
D:
P: Bischmisheim,S,R,Prussia, Germany

10
B:
P:
M:
P:
D:
P:

5 Mrs. BALLIERER- BOHRER-4907
B: 1510
P: Bischmisheim,S,R,Prussia, Germany
D: Deceased
P:

11
B:
P:
D:
P:

1 Nickel KLEIN-4886
B: 1575
P: Bischmisheim,S,R,Prussia, Germany
M: 1593 - 4045
P: Bischmisheim,Saarbruchen,Germany
D: 1621
P: Bischmisheim,S,R,Prussia, Germany

12
B:
P:
M:
P:
D:
P:

6
B:
P:
M:
P:
D:
P:

Gertraud BECKER-4887
(Spouse of no. 1)

13
B:
P:
D:
P:

14
B:
P:
M:
P:
D:
P:

3 Margaretha KLEINEN-4895
B: 1550
P: Bischmisheim,S,R,Prussia, Germany
D:
P: Bischmisheim,S,R,Prussia, Germany

7
B:
P:
D:
P:

15
B:
P:
D:
P:

07 Nov 2015

Pedigree Chart

No. 1 on this chart is the same as No. **9** on chart no. **16** .

8 Jacob BECKER-4912
B: 1530
P: Bischmisheim,Saarbrücken,SD,Germany
M: -- 4060
P:
D: 13 Feb 1616
P: Schwerte,Unna,N,Germany

4 Jacob BECKER-4908
B: 1553
P: Bischmisheim,Saarbrücken,S,Germany
M: -- 4058
P:
D: 27 Feb 1622
P: Bischmisheim,Saarbrücken,S,Germany

9 Harriet BAKER-4913
B: 1530
P: Bischmisheim,Saarbrücken,SD,Germany
D: 27 Feb 1622
P: Bischmisheim,Saarbrücken,S,Germany

2 Nickel BECKER-4896
B: Abt 1549
P: Bischmisheim,S,R,Prussia, Germany
M: -- 4050
P:
D: Abt 1625
P: Bischmisheim,S,R,Prussia, Germany

10
B:
P:
M:
P:
D:
P:

5 Catharina BECKER-4909
B: 1550
P: Germany
D: 27 Feb 1624
P: Germany

11
B:
P:
D:
P:

1 Gertraud BECKER-4887
B: 1576
P: Germany
M: 1593 - 4045
P: Bischmisheim,Saarbruchen,Germany
D: 1621
P: Bischmisheim,S,R,Prussia, Germany

Nickel KLEIN-4886
(Spouse of no. 1)

12
B:
P:
M:
P:
D:
P:

6
B:
P:
M:
P:
D:
P:

13
B:
P:
D:
P:

3
B:
P:
D:
P:

14
B:
P:
M:
P:
D:
P:

7
B:
P:
D:
P:

15
B:
P:
D:
P:

Pedigree Chart

No. 1 on this chart is the same as No. **10** on chart no. **16** .

Chart no. **124**

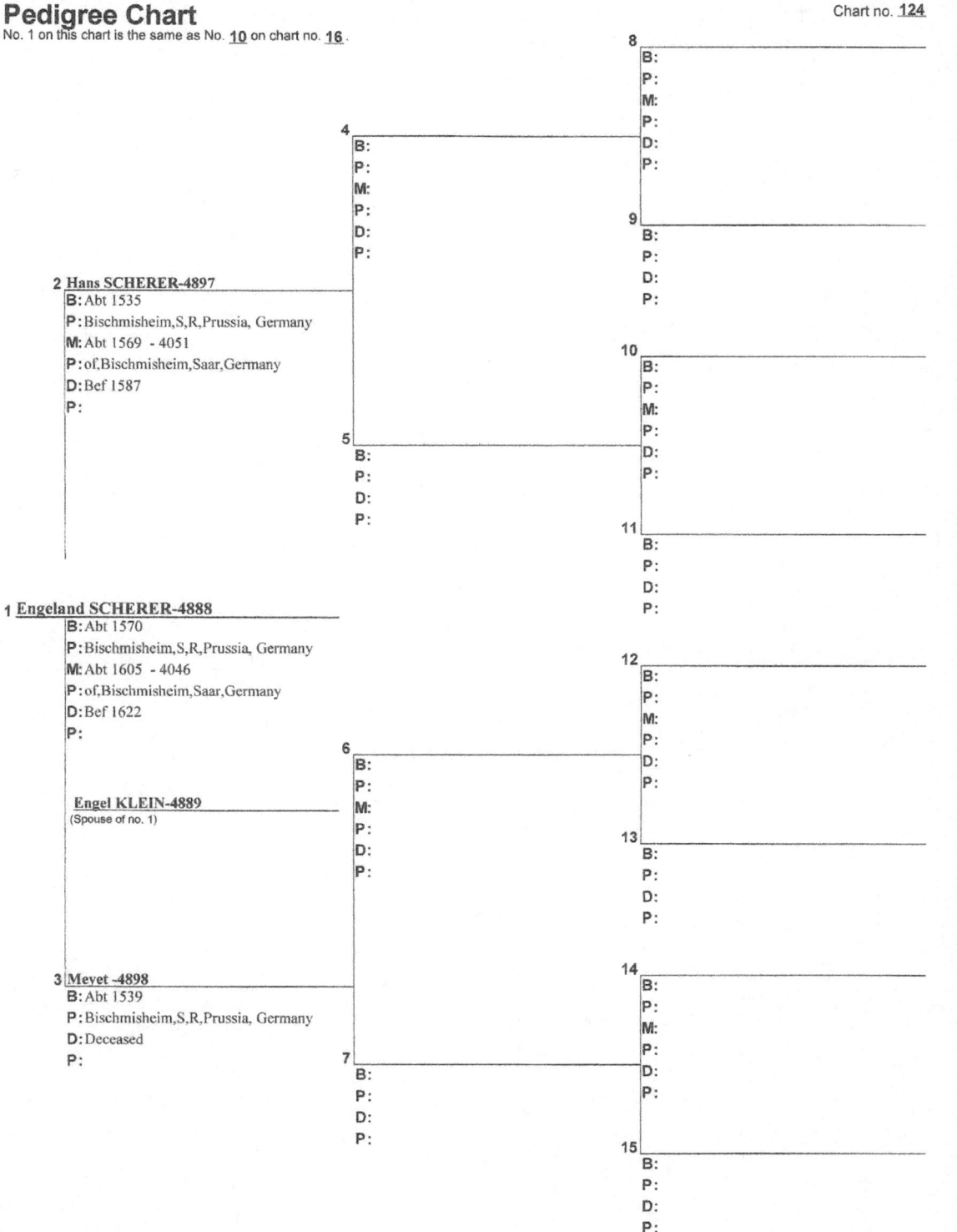

2 Hans SCHERER-4897
B: Abt 1535
P: Bischmisheim,S,R,Prussia, Germany
M: Abt 1569 - 4051
P: of,Bischmisheim,Saar,Germany
D: Bef 1587
P:

1 Engeland SCHERER-4888
B: Abt 1570
P: Bischmisheim,S,R,Prussia, Germany
M: Abt 1605 - 4046
P: of,Bischmisheim,Saar,Germany
D: Bef 1622
P:

Engel KLEIN-4889
(Spouse of no. 1)

3 Meyet -4898
B: Abt 1539
P: Bischmisheim,S,R,Prussia, Germany
D: Deceased
P:

4
B:
P:
M:
P:
D:
P:

5
B:
P:
D:
P:

6
B:
P:
M:
P:
D:
P:

7
B:
P:
D:
P:

8
B:
P:
M:
P:
D:
P:

9
B:
P:
D:
P:

10
B:
P:
M:
P:
D:
P:

11
B:
P:
D:
P:

12
B:
P:
M:
P:
D:
P:

13
B:
P:
D:
P:

14
B:
P:
M:
P:
D:
P:

15
B:
P:
D:
P:

07 Nov 2015

Pedigree Chart

No. 1 on this chart is the same as No. **11** on chart no. **16** .

2 Meyets Hans KLEIN-4899
B: Abt 1534
P: Bischmisheim,S,R,Prussia, Germany
M: Bef 25 Jan 1591 - 4052
P: of,Bischmisheim,Saar,Germany
D: 1622/1626
P:

1 Engel KLEIN-4889
B: Abt 1570
P: Bischmisheim,S,R,Prussia, Germany
M: Abt 1605 - 4046
P: of,Bischmisheim,Saar,Germany
D: Bef 11 Jun 1624
P:

Engeland SCHERER-4888
(Spouse of no. 1)

3 Gertrud -4900
B: Abt 1540
P: Bischmisheim,S,R,Prussia, Germany
D: Bef 6 May 1616
P:

4
B:
P:
M:
P:
D:
P:

5
B:
P:
D:
P:

6
B:
P:
M:
P:
D:
P:

7
B:
P:
D:
P:

8
B:
P:
M:
P:
D:
P:

9
B:
P:
D:
P:

10
B:
P:
M:
P:
D:
P:

11
B:
P:
D:
P:

12
B:
P:
M:
P:
D:
P:

13
B:
P:
D:
P:

14
B:
P:
M:
P:
D:
P:

15
B:
P:
D:
P:

07 Nov 2015

Pedigree Chart

No. 1 on this chart is the same as No. **12** on chart no. **16** .

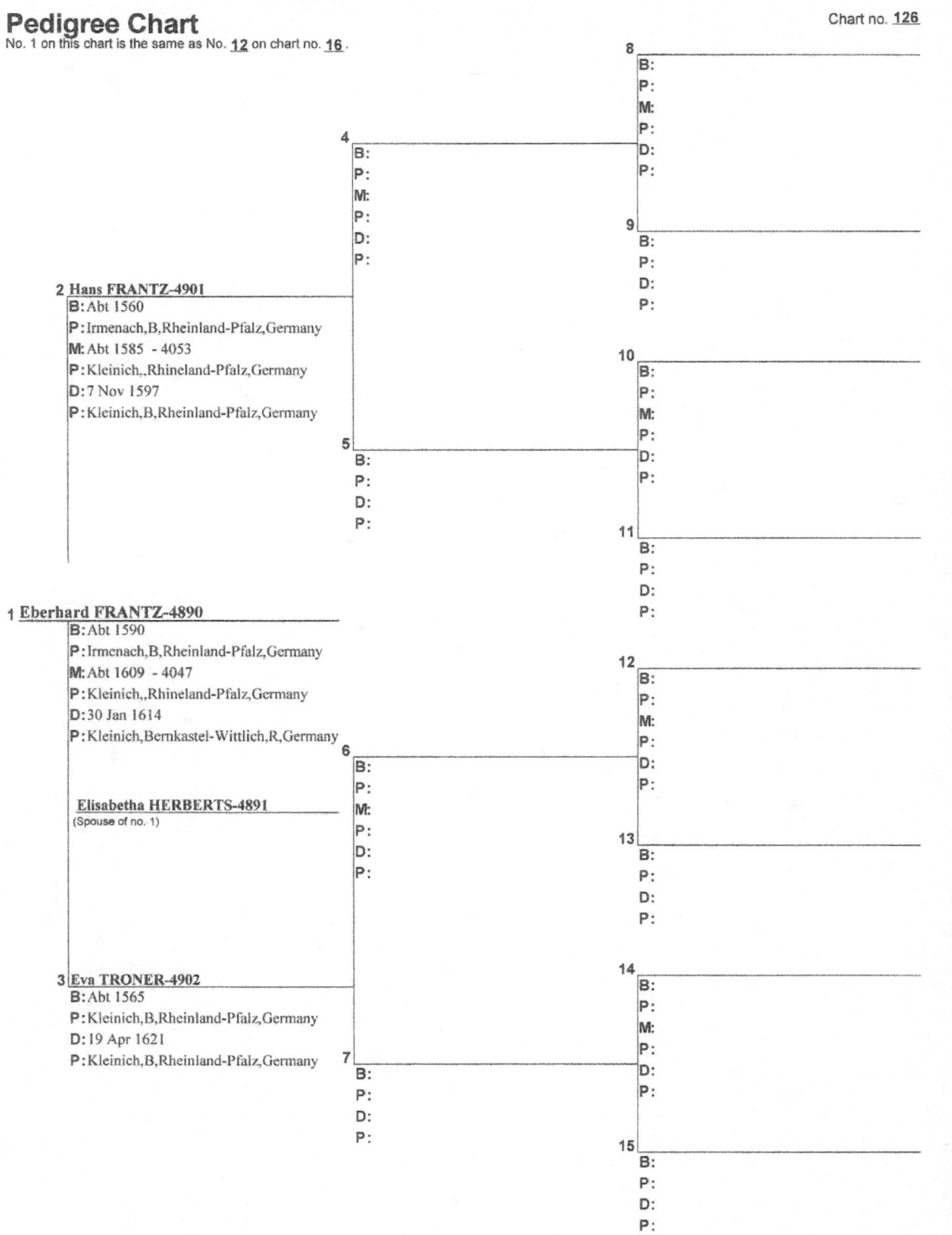

8
B:
P:
M:
P:
D:
P:

4
B:
P:
M:
P:
D:
P:

9
B:
P:
D:
P:

2 Hans FRANTZ-4901
B: Abt 1560
P: Irmenach,B,Rheinland-Pfalz,Germany
M: Abt 1585 - 4053
P: Kleinich,,Rhineland-Pfalz,Germany
D: 7 Nov 1597
P: Kleinich,B,Rheinland-Pfalz,Germany

10
B:
P:
M:
P:
D:
P:

5
B:
P:
D:
P:

11
B:
P:
D:
P:

1 Eberhard FRANTZ-4890
B: Abt 1590
P: Irmenach,B,Rheinland-Pfalz,Germany
M: Abt 1609 - 4047
P: Kleinich,,Rhineland-Pfalz,Germany
D: 30 Jan 1614
P: Kleinich,Bernkastel-Wittlich,R,Germany

12
B:
P:
M:
P:
D:
P:

6
B:
P:
M:
P:
D:
P:

Elisabetha HERBERTS-4891
(Spouse of no. 1)

13
B:
P:
D:
P:

14
B:
P:
M:
P:
D:
P:

3 Eva TRONER-4902
B: Abt 1565
P: Kleinich,B,Rheinland-Pfalz,Germany
D: 19 Apr 1621
P: Kleinich,B,Rheinland-Pfalz,Germany

7
B:
P:
D:
P:

15
B:
P:
D:
P:

07 Nov 2015

Pedigree Chart

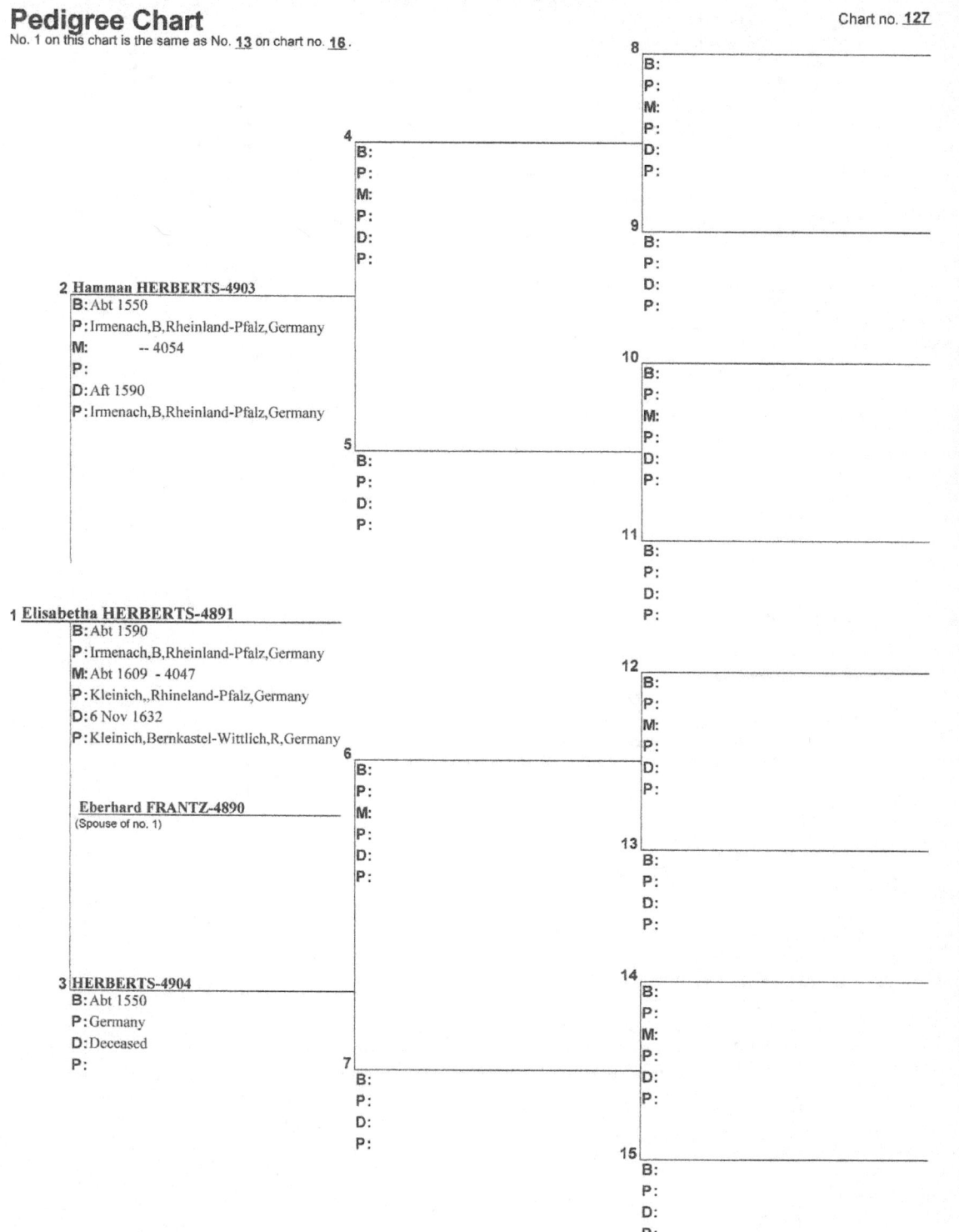

8
B:
P:
M:
P:
D:
P:

4
B:
P:
M:
P:
D:
P:

9
B:
P:
D:
P:

2 Hamman HERBERTS-4903
B: Abt 1550
P: Irmenach,B,Rheinland-Pfalz,Germany
M: -- 4054
P:
D: Aft 1590
P: Irmenach,B,Rheinland-Pfalz,Germany

10
B:
P:
M:
P:
D:
P:

5
B:
P:
D:
P:

11
B:
P:
D:
P:

1 Elisabetha HERBERTS-4891
B: Abt 1590
P: Irmenach,B,Rheinland-Pfalz,Germany
M: Abt 1609 - 4047
P: Kleinich,,Rhineland-Pfalz,Germany
D: 6 Nov 1632
P: Kleinich,Bernkastel-Wittlich,R,Germany

12
B:
P:
M:
P:
D:
P:

Eberhard FRANTZ-4890
(Spouse of no. 1)

6
B:
P:
M:
P:
D:
P:

13
B:
P:
D:
P:

3 HERBERTS-4904
B: Abt 1550
P: Germany
D: Deceased
P:

14
B:
P:
M:
P:
D:
P:

7
B:
P:
D:
P:

15
B:
P:
D:
P:

07 Nov 2015

Pedigree Chart

8 Hans SECKLER-4934
B: gegen 1503
P: Manubach,SG,R,Preußen, Deutschland
M: vor 1528 - 4072
P:
D:
P: Manubach,SG,R,Preußen, Deutschland

4 Jacob SECKLER-4928
B: 1528
P: Manubach,Rheinland,Germany
M: gegen 1562 - 4069
P: Manubach,Rheinland-Pfalz,Alemanha
D: 19 março 1608
P: Manubach,Rheinland,Germany

9 Mrs. SECKLER-4935
B: gegen 1507
P:
D:
P: Manubach,SG,R,Preußen, Deutschland

2 Hans (dit Roosen Hans) SECKLER-4922
B: Abt 1564
P: Manubach,SG,R,Prussia, Germany
M: 22 Jan 1588 - 4065
P: Manubach,SG,R,Preußen, Deutschland
D: 19 Jun 1634
P: Manubach,SG,R,Prussia, Germany

10
B:
P:
M:
P:
D:
P:

5 Elisabetha -4929
B: gegen 1541
P: Manubach,M,R,Deutschland
D: Deceased
P:

11
B:
P:
D:
P:

1 Johannes, Hans der Jüngste SECKLER-4918
B: Abt 1589
P: Manubach,SG,R,Prussia, Germany
M: 19 Nov 1610 - 4063
P: Evangelisch,Manubach,R,Prussia
D: 7 May 1669
P: Manubach,SG,R,Prussia, Germany

Sophia KOCH-4919
(Spouse of no. 1)

12
B:
P:
M:
P:
D:
P:

6 Hans ROOS-4930
B: gegen 1538
P: Manubach,SG,R,Preußen, Deutschland
M: gegen 1560 - 4070
P: Manubach,SG,R,Preußen, Deutschland
D: 27 Jan 1595
P: Manubach,SG,R,Preußen, Deutschland

13
B:
P:
D:
P:

3 Elizabeth ROOS-4923
B: Abt 1565
P: Manubach,SG,R,Prussia, Germany
D: 24 Jun 1602
P: Manubach,SG,R,Prussia, Germany

14
B:
P:
M:
P:
D:
P:

7 Catharina -4931
B: gegen 1540
P:
D: 6 Aug 1601
P: Manubach,SG,R,Preußen, Deutschland

15
B:
P:
D:
P:

07 Nov 2015

Pedigree Chart

No. 1 on this chart is the same as No. __9__ on chart no. __17__ .

8
B:
P:
M:
P:
D:
P:

4 Hans KOCH-4932
B: aproximadamente 1525
P: Oberdiebach,M,R,Alemanha
M: Abt 1553 - 4071
P: Manubach,Rheinland,Prussia
D:
P: Alemanha

9
B:
P:
D:
P:

2 Heinrich KOCH-4924
B:
P: Oberdiebach,M,R,Germany
M: 19 Jan 1579 - 4066
P: Manubach,Rhineland,Germany
D: 23 Jan 1604
P: Manubach,Mainz-Bingen,R,Germany

10
B:
P:
M:
P:
D:
P:

5 Mrs Hans KOCH-4933
B: Abt 1533
P: Manubach,Rheinland,Prussia
D: Deceased
P:

11
B:
P:
D:
P:

1 Sophia KOCH-4919
B: 26 Mar 1592
P: Manubach,Mainz-Bingen,R,Germany
M: 19 Nov 1610 - 4063
P: Evangelisch,Manubach,R,Prussia
D: 23 Oct 1620
P: Manubach,Rheinland-Pfalz,Germany

12
B:
P:
M:
P:
D:
P:

6
B:
P:
M:
P:
D:
P:

Johannes, Hans dJ SECKLER-4918
(Spouse of no. 1)

13
B:
P:
D:
P:

3 Katharina -4925
B: Abt 1556
P: Oberdiebach,M,R,Germany
D: 21 Oct 1608
P: Oberdiebach,M,R,Germany

14
B:
P:
M:
P:
D:
P:

7
B:
P:
D:
P:

15
B:
P:
D:
P:

07 Nov 2015

Pedigree Chart

No. 1 on this chart is the same as No. **10** on chart no. **17** .

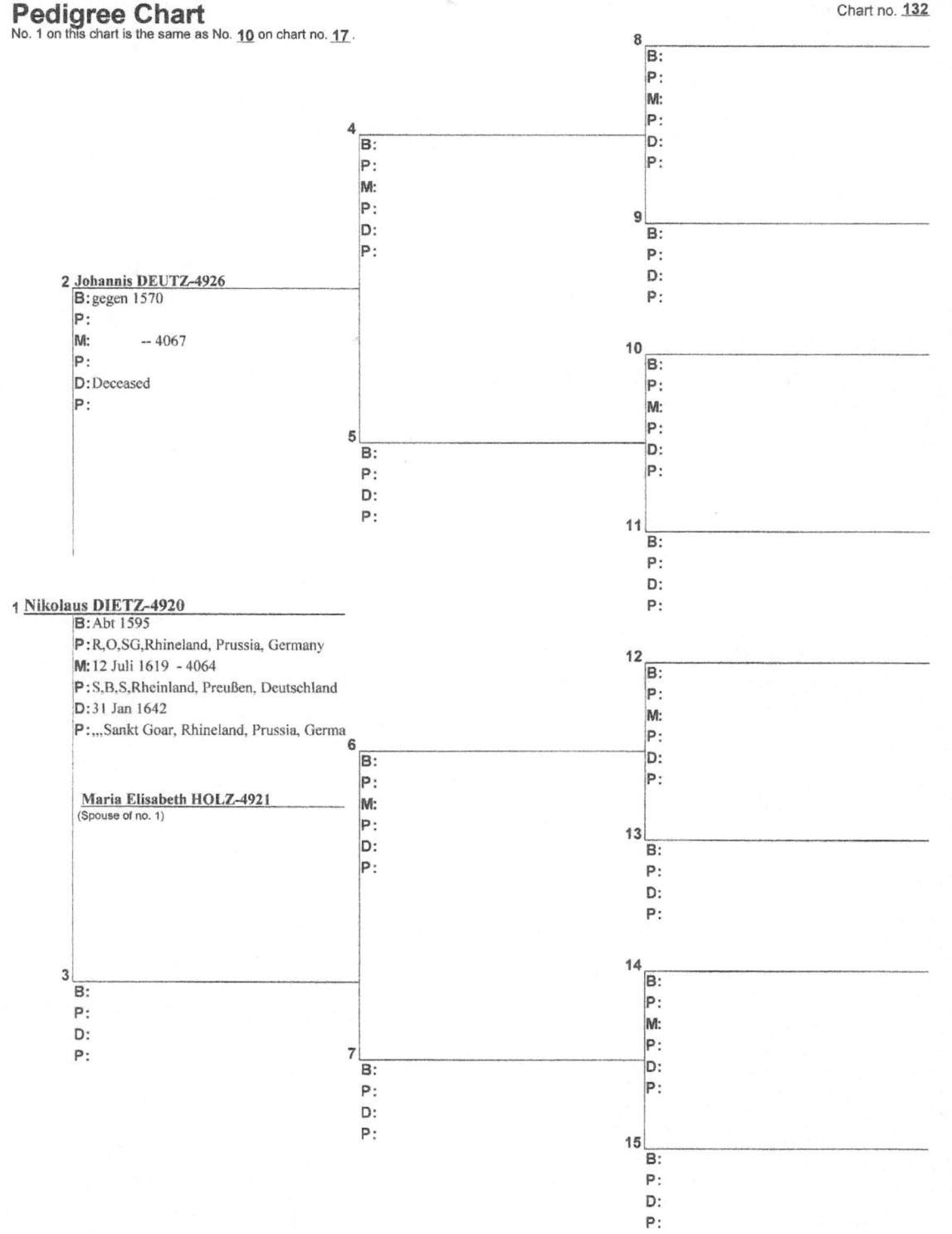

8
B:
P:
M:
P:
D:
P:

4
B:
P:
M:
P:
D:
P:

9
B:
P:
D:
P:

2 Johannis DEUTZ-4926
B: gegen 1570
P:
M: -- 4067
P:
D: Deceased
P:

10
B:
P:
M:
P:
D:
P:

5
B:
P:
D:
P:

11
B:
P:
D:
P:

1 Nikolaus DIETZ-4920
B: Abt 1595
P: R,O,SG,Rhineland, Prussia, Germany
M: 12 Juli 1619 - 4064
P: S,B,S,Rheinland, Preußen, Deutschland
D: 31 Jan 1642
P: ,,,Sankt Goar, Rhineland, Prussia, Germa

12
B:
P:
M:
P:
D:
P:

6
B:
P:
M:
P:
D:
P:

Maria Elisabeth HOLZ-4921
(Spouse of no. 1)

13
B:
P:
D:
P:

14
B:
P:
M:
P:
D:
P:

3
B:
P:
D:
P:

7
B:
P:
D:
P:

15
B:
P:
D:
P:

07 Nov 2015

Pedigree Chart

No. 1 on this chart is the same as No. __11__ on chart no. __17__ .

Chart no. __133__

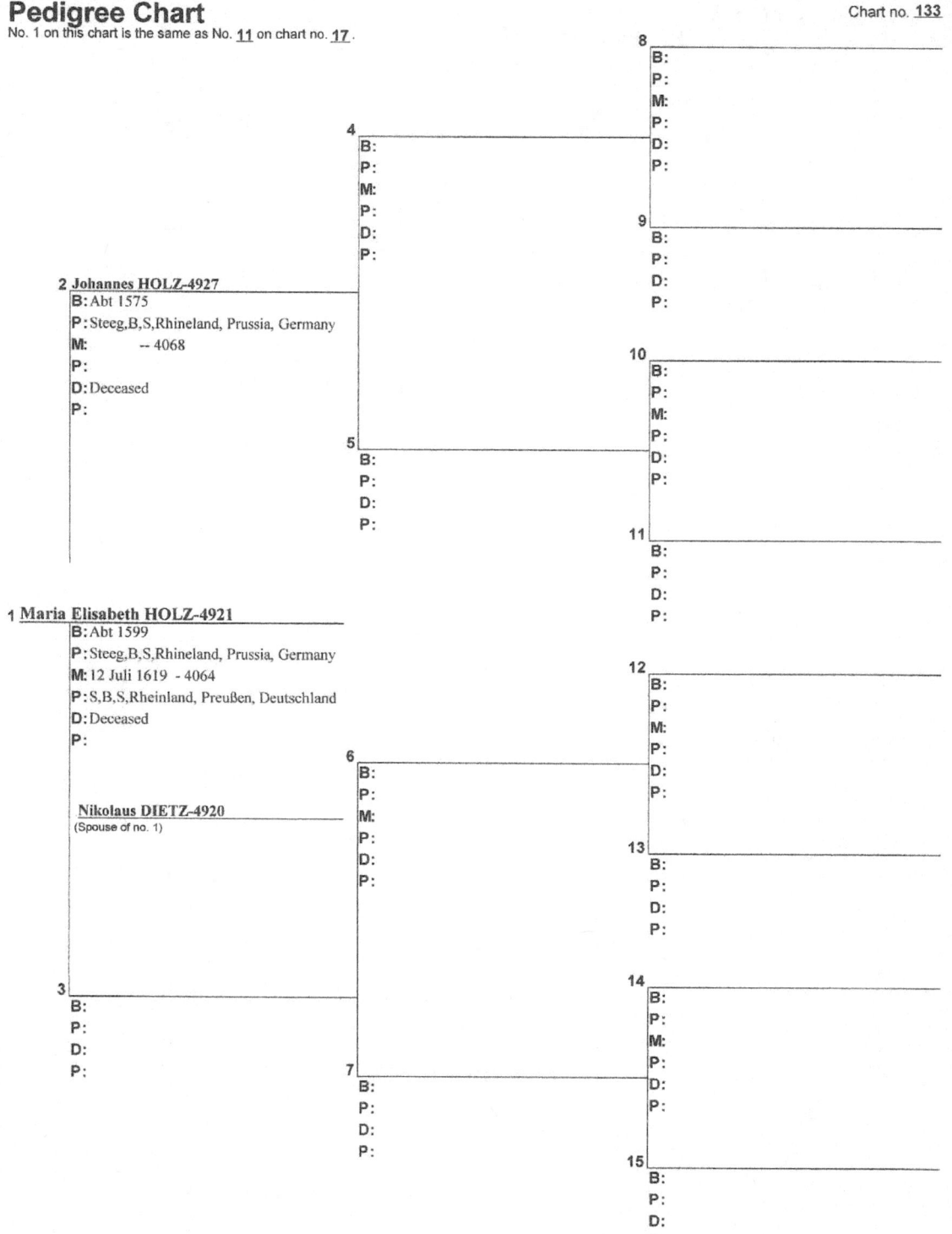

2 Johannes HOLZ-4927
B: Abt 1575
P: Steeg,B,S,Rhineland, Prussia, Germany
M: -- 4068
P:
D: Deceased
P:

1 Maria Elisabeth HOLZ-4921
B: Abt 1599
P: Steeg,B,S,Rhineland, Prussia, Germany
M: 12 Juli 1619 - 4064
P: S,B,S,Rheinland, Preußen, Deutschland
D: Deceased
P:

Nikolaus DIETZ-4920
(Spouse of no. 1)

4
B:
P:
M:
P:
D:
P:

5
B:
P:
D:
P:

3
B:
P:
D:
P:

6
B:
P:
M:
P:
D:
P:

7
B:
P:
D:
P:

8
B:
P:
M:
P:
D:
P:

9
B:
P:
D:
P:

10
B:
P:
M:
P:
D:
P:

11
B:
P:
D:
P:

12
B:
P:
M:
P:
D:
P:

13
B:
P:
D:
P:

14
B:
P:
M:
P:
D:
P:

15
B:
P:
D:
P:

07 Nov 2015

Pedigree Chart

No. 1 on this chart is the same as No. __8__ on chart no. __22__.

8
- B:
- P:
- M:
- P:
- D:
- P:

4 Peter SCHULER-4956
- B: Abt 1520
- P: Goppingen,Donaukreis,W,Germany
- M: Abt 1550 - 4083
- P: Goeppingen,B,Germany
- D: Deceased
- P:

9
- B:
- P:
- D:
- P:

2 Johann SCHULER-4948
- B: 1554
- P: Göppingen,Göppingen,B,Germany
- M: 9 Apr 1578 - 4079
- P: SCC,Stuttgart,Württemberg
- D: 1616
- P: K,E,S,Baden-Württemberg, Germany

10
- B:
- P:
- M:
- P:
- D:
- P:

5 Mrs. Peter SCHULER-4957
- B: Abt 1530
- P: Göppingen,B,Germany
- D: Deceased
- P:

11
- B:
- P:
- D:
- P:

1 Andreas SCHULER-4944
- B: 6 Jan 1594
- P: Kirchheim Unter Teck,D,W,Germany
- M: 21 Apr 1617 - 4077
- P: Calw,Schwarzwald,Württemberg
- D: 23 Mar 1662
- P: H,C,K,Baden-Württemberg, Germany

12 Andreas OSIANDER-4965   1358
- B: 19 Dec 1498
- P: Gunzenhausen,MF,Bavaria,Germany
- M: 2 Nov 1525 - 4088
- P: Nuernberg Stadt,Mittelfranken,Bavaria
- D: 17 Oct 1552
- P: Koenigsberg,Prussia

6 Lucas OSIANDER-4958
- B: 16 Dec 1534
- P: Nürnberg,N,MF,Bavaria, Germany
- M: 1555 - 4084
- P: Tubingen,B,Germany
- D: 17 Sep 1604
- P: Stuttgart,Stuttgart,B,Germany

Sara WEIßGERBER-4945
(Spouse of no. 1)

13 Katharina PREU-4966   1359
- B: 1502
- P: Weißenburg,Middle Franconia,B,Germany
- D: 14 Jul 1537
- P: Nuremberg,Bavern,Germany

14 Johann ENTRINGER-4967   1360
- B: Abt 1503
- P: Tubingen,Schwarzwaldkreis,W,Germany
- M: -- 4089
- P:
- D: Deceased
- P:

3 Monica OSIANDER-4949
- B: 1559
- P: Blaubeuren,A,B,Germany
- D: 23 Jul 1611
- P:

7 Margarete ENTRINGER-4959
- B: Jun 1524
- P: Tübingen,Tubingen,B,Germany
- D: 16 Jan 1566
- P: Stuttgart,Baden-Württemberg,Germany

15 Anna PALM-4968   1361
- B: Abt 1500
- P: Rottenburg Am Neckar,B,Germany
- D: Deceased
- P:

07 Nov 2015

Pedigree Chart

No. 1 on this chart is the same as No. **9** on chart no. **22** .

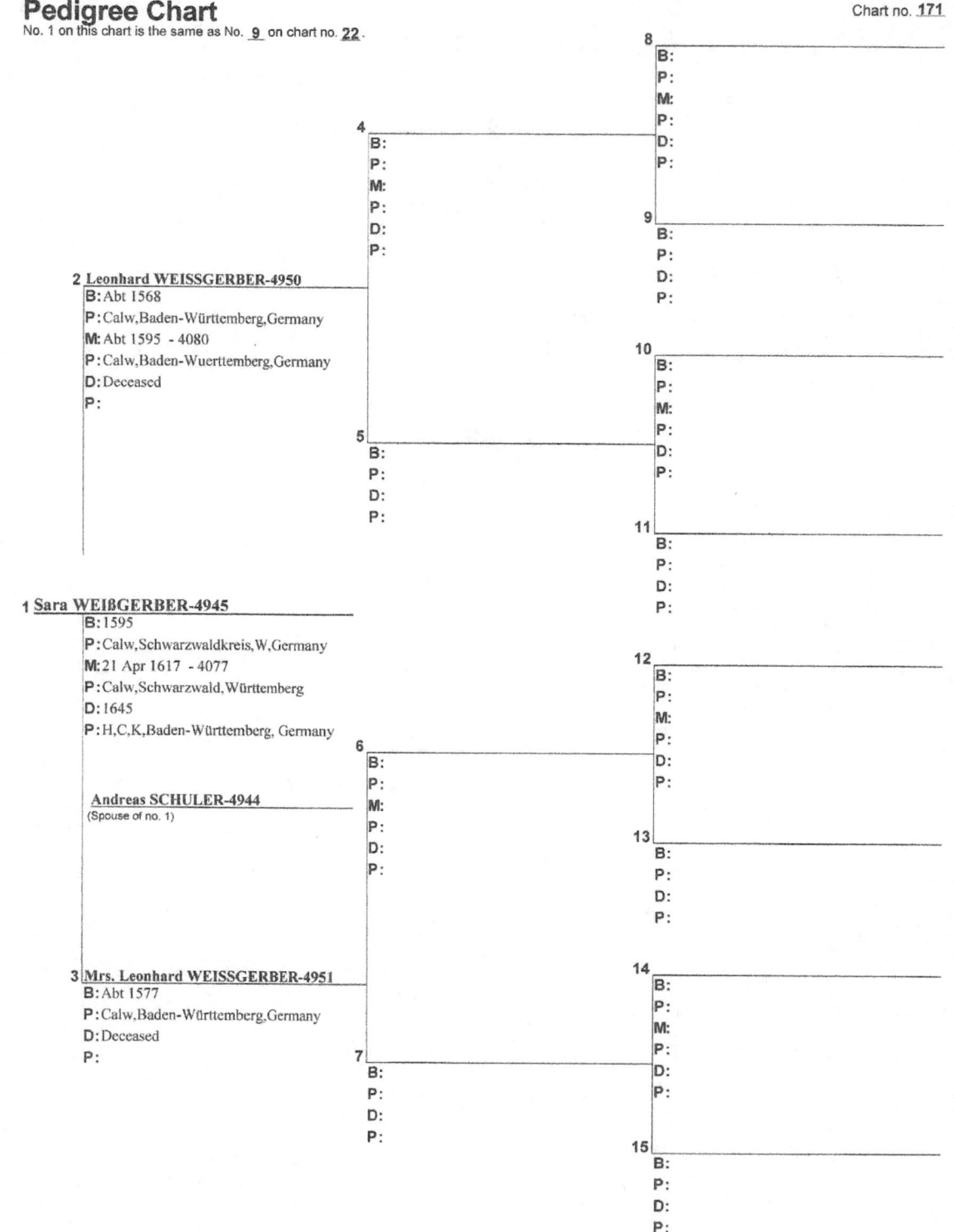

2 Leonhard WEISSGERBER-4950
B: Abt 1568
P: Calw,Baden-Württemberg,Germany
M: Abt 1595 - 4080
P: Calw,Baden-Wuerttemberg,Germany
D: Deceased
P:

1 Sara WEIßGERBER-4945
B: 1595
P: Calw,Schwarzwaldkreis,W,Germany
M: 21 Apr 1617 - 4077
P: Calw,Schwarzwald,Württemberg
D: 1645
P: H,C,K,Baden-Württemberg, Germany

Andreas SCHULER-4944
(Spouse of no. 1)

3 Mrs. Leonhard WEISSGERBER-4951
B: Abt 1577
P: Calw,Baden-Württemberg,Germany
D: Deceased
P:

4
B:
P:
M:
P:
D:
P:

5
B:
P:
D:
P:

6
B:
P:
M:
P:
D:
P:

7
B:
P:
D:
P:

8
B:
P:
M:
P:
D:
P:

9
B:
P:
D:
P:

10
B:
P:
M:
P:
D:
P:

11
B:
P:
D:
P:

12
B:
P:
M:
P:
D:
P:

13
B:
P:
D:
P:

14
B:
P:
M:
P:
D:
P:

15
B:
P:
D:
P:

07 Nov 2015

Pedigree Chart

No. 1 on this chart is the same as No. **10** on chart no. **22** .

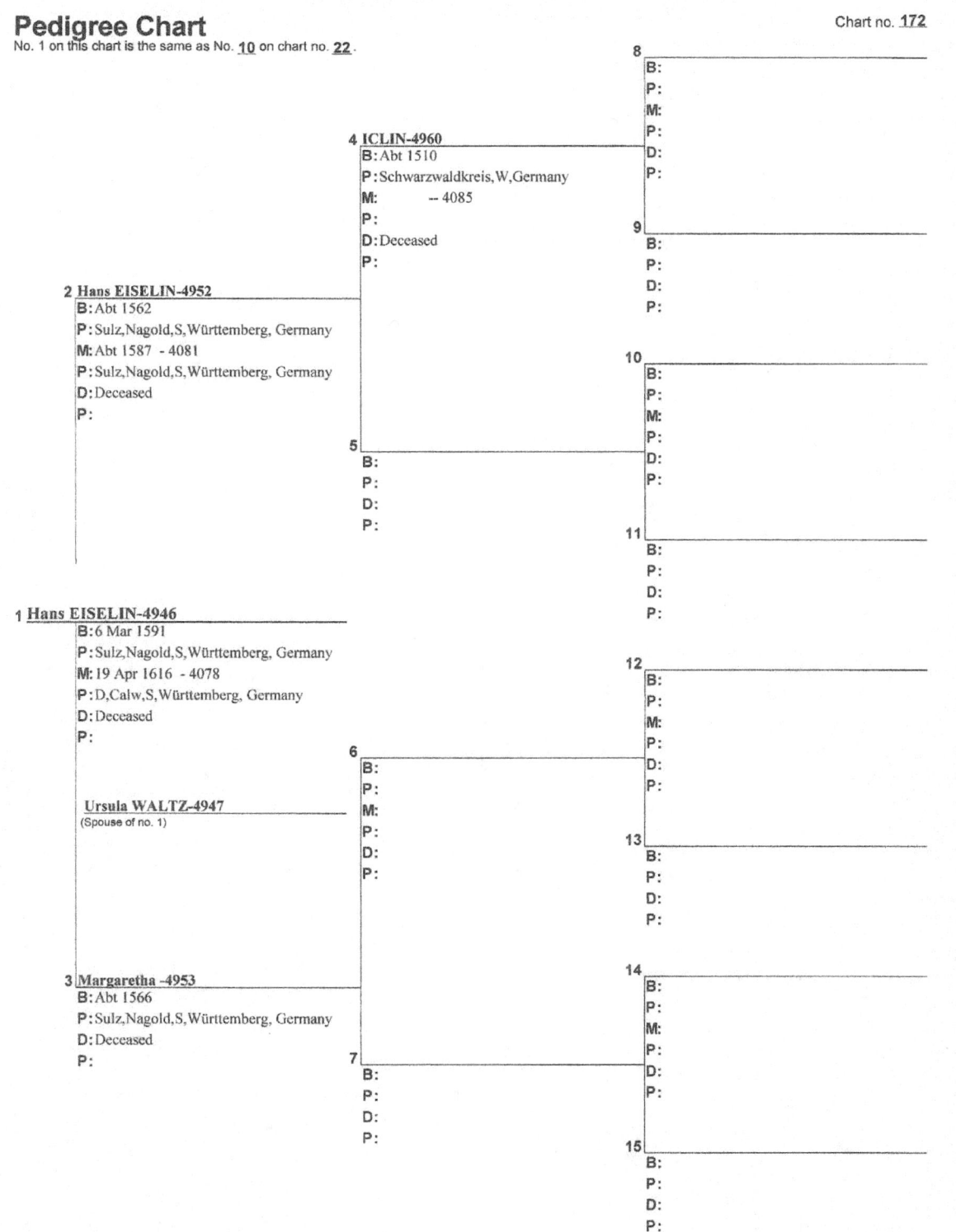

4 ICLIN-4960
B: Abt 1510
P: Schwarzwaldkreis,W,Germany
M: -- 4085
P:
D: Deceased
P:

2 Hans EISELIN-4952
B: Abt 1562
P: Sulz,Nagold,S,Württemberg, Germany
M: Abt 1587 - 4081
P: Sulz,Nagold,S,Württemberg, Germany
D: Deceased
P:

5
B:
P:
D:
P:

1 Hans EISELIN-4946
B: 6 Mar 1591
P: Sulz,Nagold,S,Württemberg, Germany
M: 19 Apr 1616 - 4078
P: D,Calw,S,Württemberg, Germany
D: Deceased
P:

Ursula WALTZ-4947
(Spouse of no. 1)

6
B:
P:
M:
P:
D:
P:

3 Margaretha -4953
B: Abt 1566
P: Sulz,Nagold,S,Württemberg, Germany
D: Deceased
P:

7
B:
P:
D:
P:

8
B:
P:
M:
P:
D:
P:

9
B:
P:
D:
P:

10
B:
P:
M:
P:
D:
P:

11
B:
P:
D:
P:

12
B:
P:
M:
P:
D:
P:

13
B:
P:
D:
P:

14
B:
P:
M:
P:
D:
P:

15
B:
P:
D:
P:

07 Nov 2015

Pedigree Chart

No. 1 on this chart is the same as No. <u>11</u> on chart no. <u>22</u>.

8
B:
P:
M:

4 <u>Caspar WALTZ-4961</u>
B: Abt 1540
P: Haslach,H,S,Württemberg, Germany
M: Abt 1565 - 4086
P: Haslach,H,S,Württemberg, Germany
D: Deceased
P:

P:
D:
P:

9
B:
P:
D:
P:

2 <u>Jacob WALTZ-4954</u>
B: Abt 1566
P: Haslach,H,S,Württemberg, Germany
M: 23 Aug 1591 - 4082
P: M,Leonberg,N,Württemberg, Germany
D: Deceased
P:

10
B:
P:
M:

5 <u>Mrs Ursula WALTZ-4962</u>
B: Abt 1544
P: Haslach,H,S,Württemberg, Germany
D: Deceased
P:

P:
D:
P:

11
B:
P:
D:
P:

1 <u>Ursula WALTZ-4947</u>
B: 27 Oct 1595
P: Merklingen,L,N,Württemberg, Germany
M: 19 Apr 1616 - 4078
P: D,Calw,S,Württemberg, Germany
D: Deceased
P:

12
B:
P:
M:

6 <u>Jacob HILTPURG-4963</u>
B: Abt 1529
P: M,Leonberg,N,Württemberg, Germany
M: Abt 1554 - 4087
P: M,Leonberg,N,Württemberg, Germany
D: 26 Dec 1580
P: M,Leonberg,N,Württemberg, Germany

P:
D:
P:

13
B:
P:
D:
P:

Hans EISELIN-4946
(Spouse of no. 1)

14
B:
P:
M:

3 <u>Barbara HILTPURG-4955</u>
B: Abt 1570
P: M,Leonberg,N,Württemberg, Germany
D: Deceased
P:

7 <u>Mrs. Jacob HILTPURG-4964</u>
B: Abt 1533
P: M,Leonberg,N,Württemberg, Germany
D: Deceased
P:

P:
D:
P:

15
B:
P:
D:
P:

07 Nov 2015

Pedigree Chart

No. 1 on this chart is the same as No. **15** on chart no. **75** .

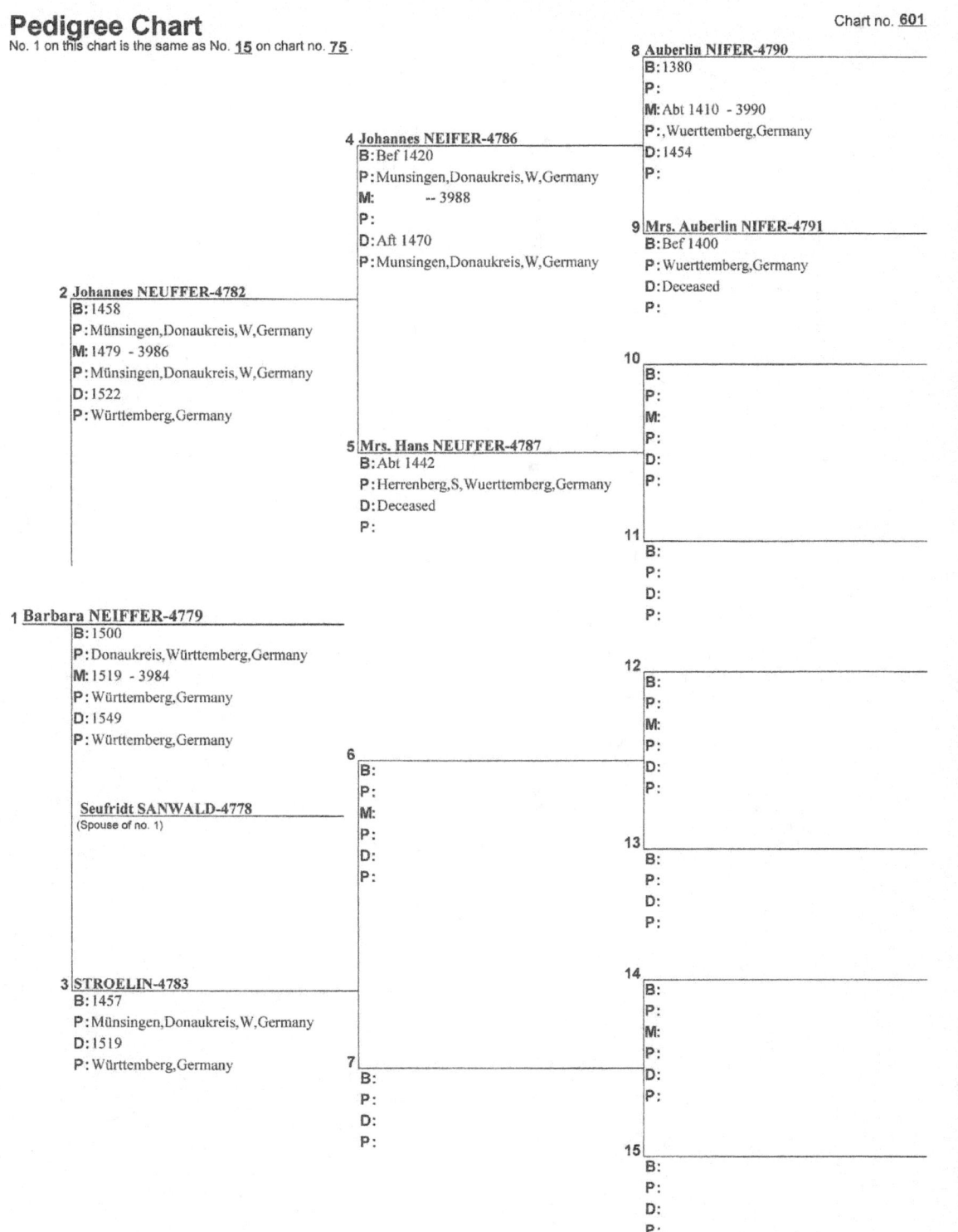

8 Auberlin NIFER-4790
B:1380
P:
M:Abt 1410 - 3990
P:,Wuerttemberg,Germany
D:1454
P:

4 Johannes NEIFER-4786
B:Bef 1420
P:Munsingen,Donaukreis,W,Germany
M: -- 3988
P:
D:Aft 1470
P:Munsingen,Donaukreis,W,Germany

9 Mrs. Auberlin NIFER-4791
B:Bef 1400
P:Wuerttemberg,Germany
D:Deceased
P:

2 Johannes NEUFFER-4782
B:1458
P:Münsingen,Donaukreis,W,Germany
M:1479 - 3986
P:Münsingen,Donaukreis,W,Germany
D:1522
P:Württemberg,Germany

10
B:
P:
M:
P:
D:
P:

5 Mrs. Hans NEUFFER-4787
B:Abt 1442
P:Herrenberg,S,Wuerttemberg,Germany
D:Deceased
P:

11
B:
P:
D:
P:

1 Barbara NEIFFER-4779
B:1500
P:Donaukreis,Württemberg,Germany
M:1519 - 3984
P:Württemberg,Germany
D:1549
P:Württemberg,Germany

12
B:
P:
M:
P:
D:
P:

Seufridt SANWALD-4778
(Spouse of no. 1)

6
B:
P:
M:
P:
D:
P:

13
B:
P:
D:
P:

3 STROELIN-4783
B:1457
P:Münsingen,Donaukreis,W,Germany
D:1519
P:Württemberg,Germany

14
B:
P:
M:
P:
D:
P:

7
B:
P:
D:
P:

15
B:
P:
D:
P:

07 Nov 2015

Pedigree Chart

No. 1 on this chart is the same as No. **8** on chart no. **82** .

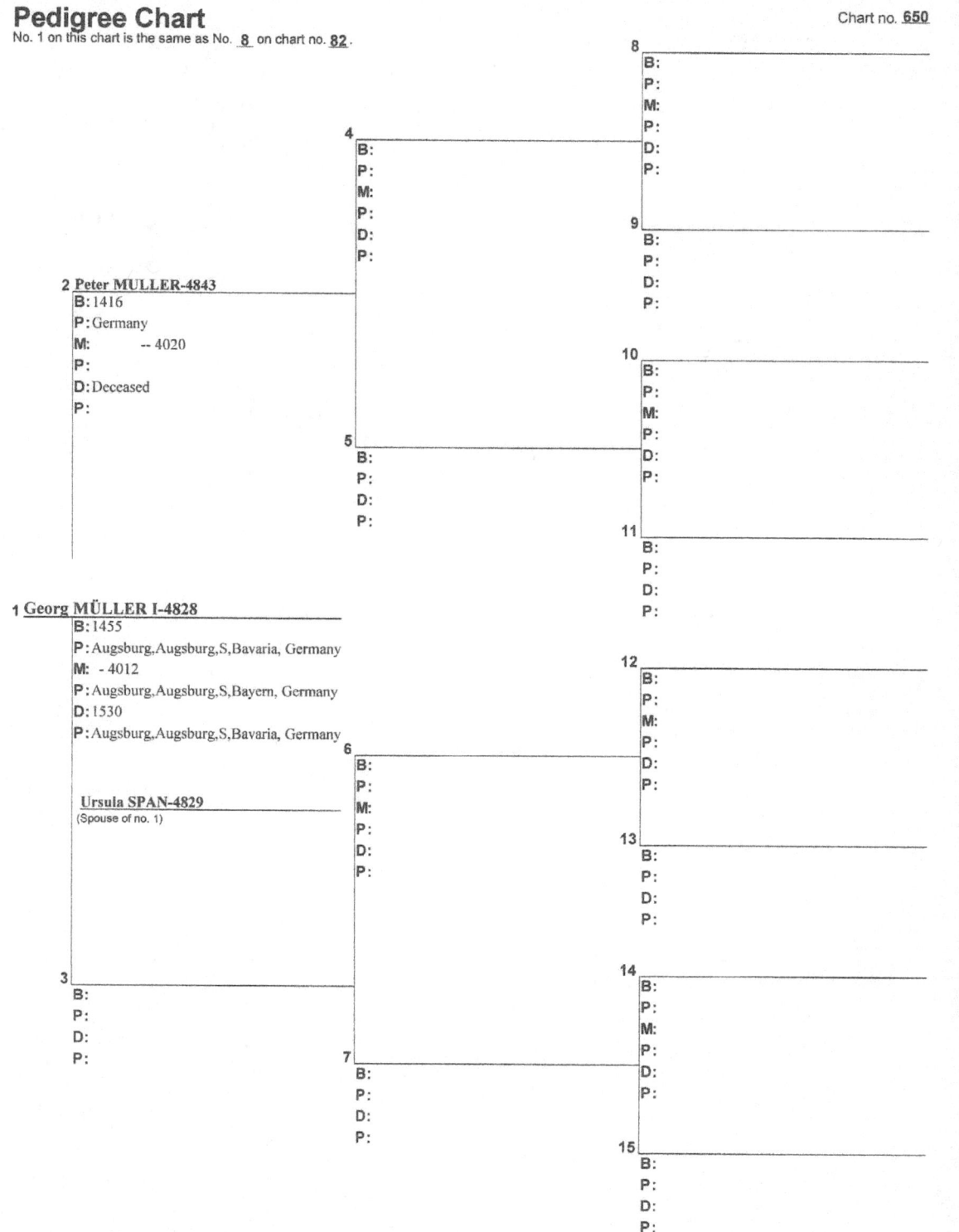

2 Peter MULLER-4843
B: 1416
P: Germany
M: -- 4020
P:
D: Deceased
P:

1 Georg MÜLLER I-4828
B: 1455
P: Augsburg,Augsburg,S,Bavaria, Germany
M: - 4012
P: Augsburg,Augsburg,S,Bayern, Germany
D: 1530
P: Augsburg,Augsburg,S,Bavaria, Germany

Ursula SPAN-4829
(Spouse of no. 1)

3
B:
P:
D:
P:

4
B:
P:
M:
P:
D:
P:

5
B:
P:
D:
P:

6
B:
P:
M:
P:
D:
P:

7
B:
P:
D:
P:

8
B:
P:
M:
P:
D:
P:

9
B:
P:
D:
P:

10
B:
P:
M:
P:
D:
P:

11
B:
P:
D:
P:

12
B:
P:
M:
P:
D:
P:

13
B:
P:
D:
P:

14
B:
P:
M:
P:
D:
P:

15
B:
P:
D:
P:

07 Nov 2015

Pedigree Chart

No. 1 on this chart is the same as No. __8__ on chart no. __84__.

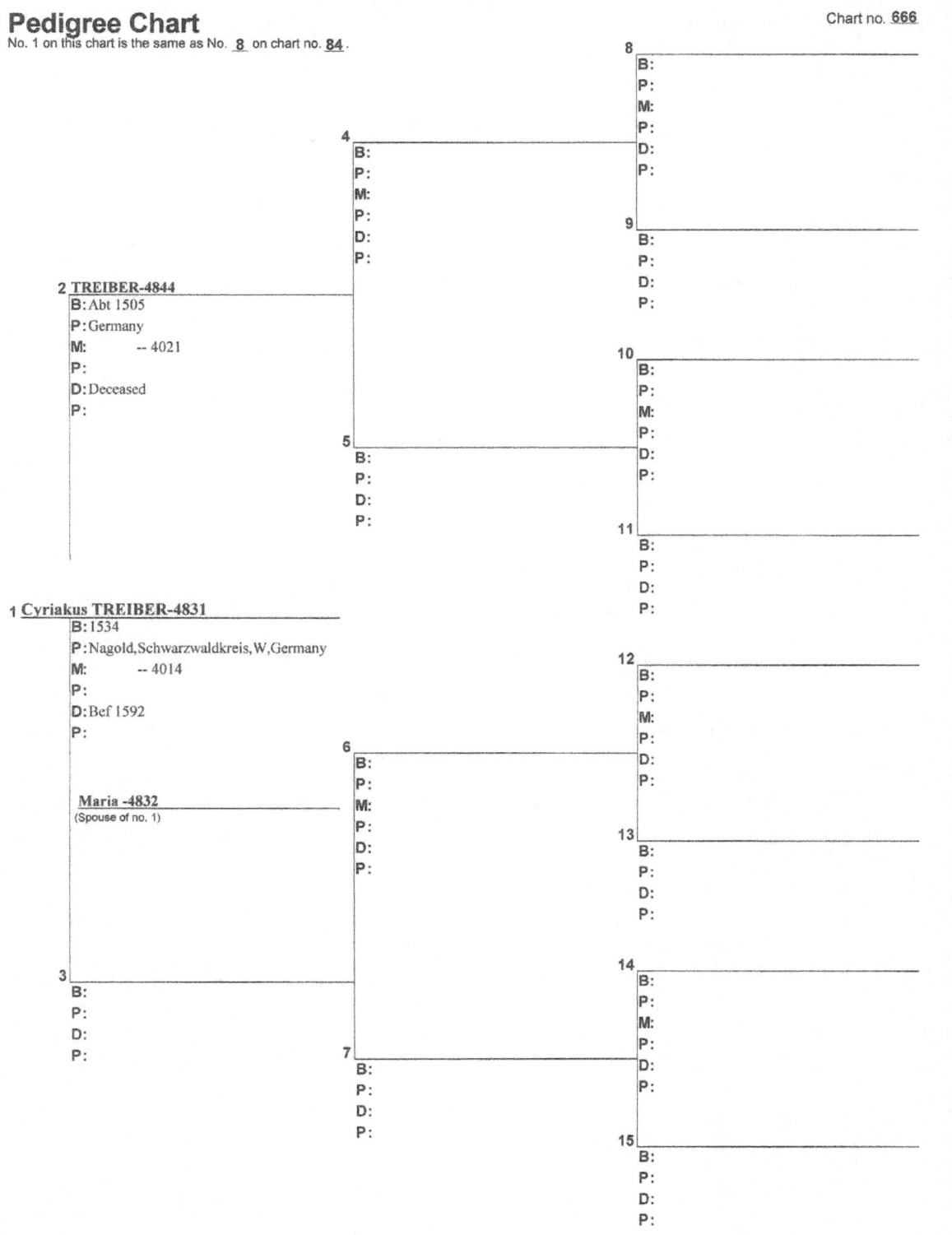

8
B:
P:
M:
P:
D:
P:

4
B:
P:
M:
P:
D:
P:

9
B:
P:
D:
P:

2 TREIBER-4844
B: Abt 1505
P: Germany
M: -- 4021
P:
D: Deceased
P:

10
B:
P:
M:
P:
D:
P:

5
B:
P:
D:
P:

11
B:
P:
D:
P:

1 Cyriakus TREIBER-4831
B: 1534
P: Nagold, Schwarzwaldkreis, W, Germany
M: -- 4014
P:
D: Bef 1592
P:

12
B:
P:
M:
P:
D:
P:

6
B:
P:
M:
P:
D:
P:

13
B:
P:
D:
P:

Maria -4832
(Spouse of no. 1)

14
B:
P:
M:
P:
D:
P:

3
B:
P:
D:
P:

7
B:
P:
D:
P:

15
B:
P:
D:
P:

07 Nov 2015

Pedigree Chart

No. 1 on this chart is the same as No. **12** on chart no. **84** .

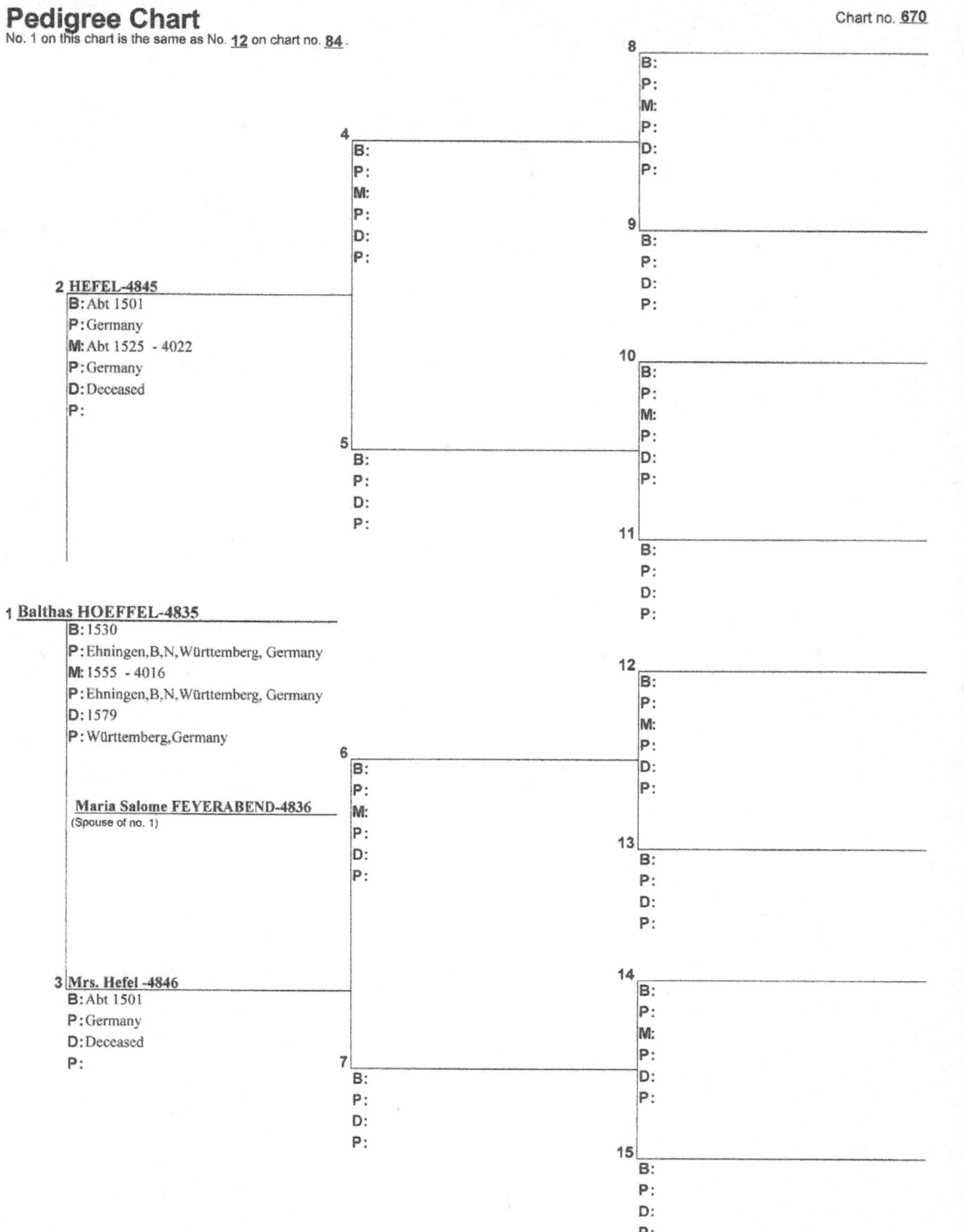

8
B:
P:
M:
P:
D:
P:

4
B:
P:
M:
P:
D:
P:

9
B:
P:
D:
P:

2 HEFEL-4845
B: Abt 1501
P: Germany
M: Abt 1525 - 4022
P: Germany
D: Deceased
P:

10
B:
P:
M:
P:
D:
P:

5
B:
P:
D:
P:

11
B:
P:
D:
P:

1 Balthas HOEFFEL-4835
B: 1530
P: Ehningen,B,N,Württemberg, Germany
M: 1555 - 4016
P: Ehningen,B,N,Württemberg, Germany
D: 1579
P: Württemberg,Germany

12
B:
P:
M:
P:
D:
P:

6
B:
P:
M:
P:
D:
P:

Maria Salome FEYERABEND-4836
(Spouse of no. 1)

13
B:
P:
D:
P:

3 Mrs. Hefel -4846
B: Abt 1501
P: Germany
D: Deceased
P:

14
B:
P:
M:
P:
D:
P:

7
B:
P:
D:
P:

15
B:
P:
D:
P:

07 Nov 2015

Pedigree Chart

No. 1 on this chart is the same as No. **13** on chart no. **84** .

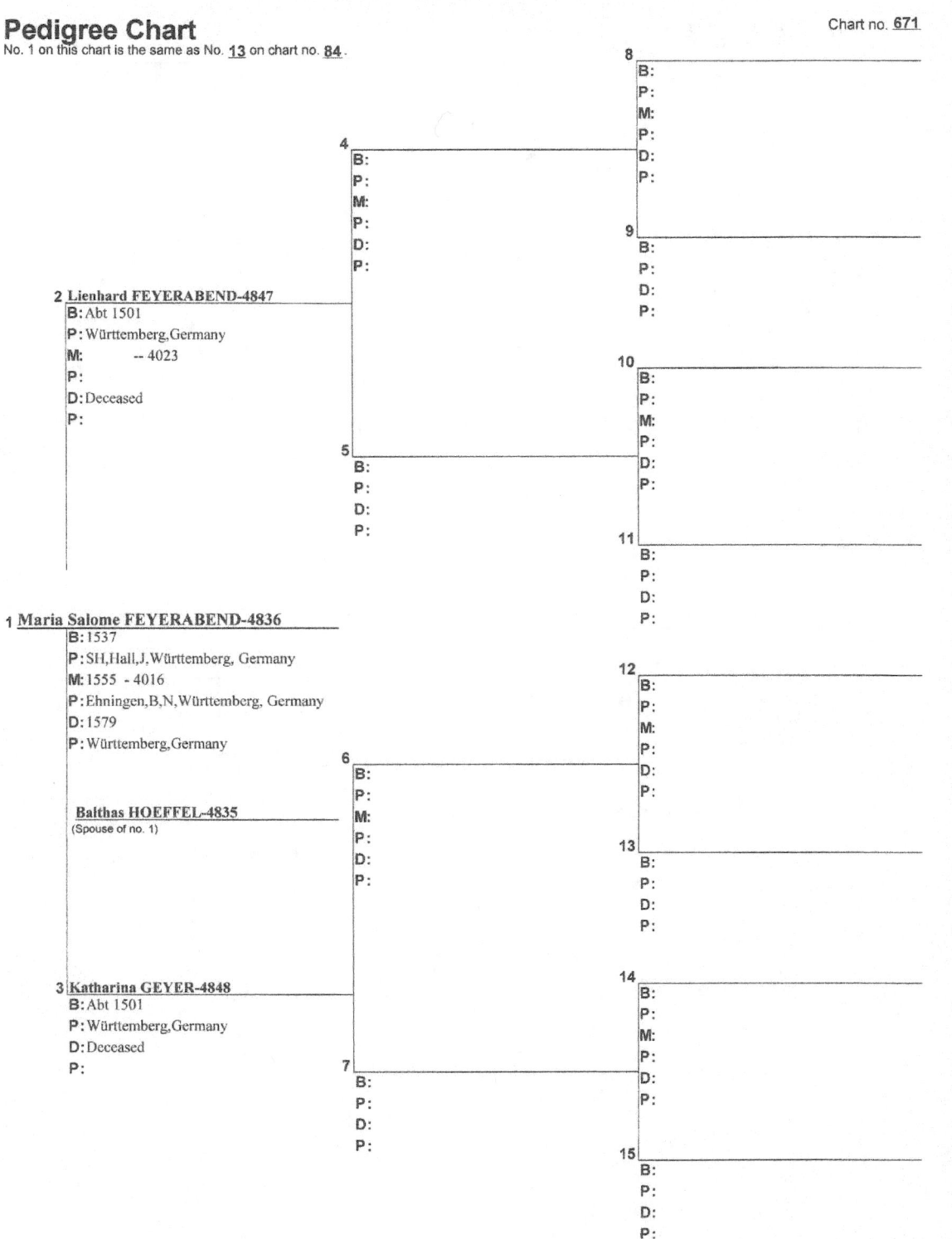

2 Lienhard FEYERABEND-4847
B: Abt 1501
P: Württemberg, Germany
M: -- 4023
P:
D: Deceased
P:

1 Maria Salome FEYERABEND-4836
B: 1537
P: SH, Hall, J, Württemberg, Germany
M: 1555 - 4016
P: Ehningen, B, N, Württemberg, Germany
D: 1579
P: Württemberg, Germany

Balthas HOEFFEL-4835
(Spouse of no. 1)

3 Katharina GEYER-4848
B: Abt 1501
P: Württemberg, Germany
D: Deceased
P:

4
B:
P:
M:
P:
D:
P:

5
B:
P:
D:
P:

6
B:
P:
M:
P:
D:
P:

7
B:
P:
D:
P:

8
B:
P:
M:
P:
D:
P:

9
B:
P:
D:
P:

10
B:
P:
M:
P:
D:
P:

11
B:
P:
D:
P:

12
B:
P:
M:
P:
D:
P:

13
B:
P:
D:
P:

14
B:
P:
M:
P:
D:
P:

15
B:
P:
D:
P:

07 Nov 2015

Pedigree Chart

No. 1 on this chart is the same as No. <u>14</u> on chart no. <u>84</u>.

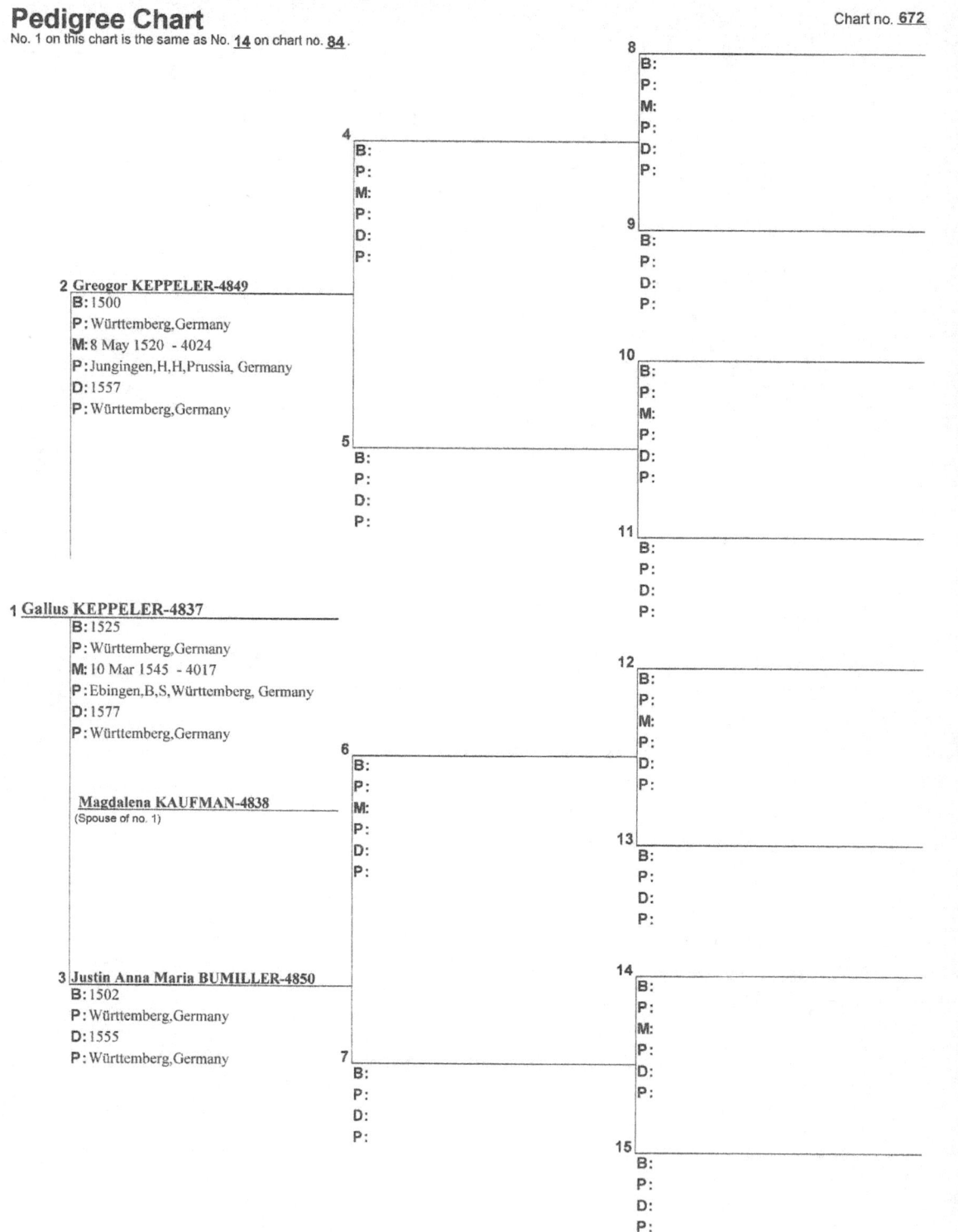

2 <u>Greogor KEPPELER-4849</u>
B: 1500
P: Württemberg, Germany
M: 8 May 1520 - 4024
P: Jungingen, H, H, Prussia, Germany
D: 1557
P: Württemberg, Germany

1 <u>Gallus KEPPELER-4837</u>
B: 1525
P: Württemberg, Germany
M: 10 Mar 1545 - 4017
P: Ebingen, B, S, Württemberg, Germany
D: 1577
P: Württemberg, Germany

Magdalena KAUFMAN-4838
(Spouse of no. 1)

3 <u>Justin Anna Maria BUMILLER-4850</u>
B: 1502
P: Württemberg, Germany
D: 1555
P: Württemberg, Germany

4
B:
P:
M:
P:
D:
P:

5
B:
P:
D:
P:

6
B:
P:
M:
P:
D:
P:

7
B:
P:
D:
P:

8
B:
P:
M:
P:
D:
P:

9
B:
P:
D:
P:

10
B:
P:
M:
P:
D:
P:

11
B:
P:
D:
P:

12
B:
P:
M:
P:
D:
P:

13
B:
P:
D:
P:

14
B:
P:
M:
P:
D:
P:

15
B:
P:
D:
P:

07 Nov 2015

Pedigree Chart

No. 1 on this chart is the same as No. **12** on chart no. **170** .

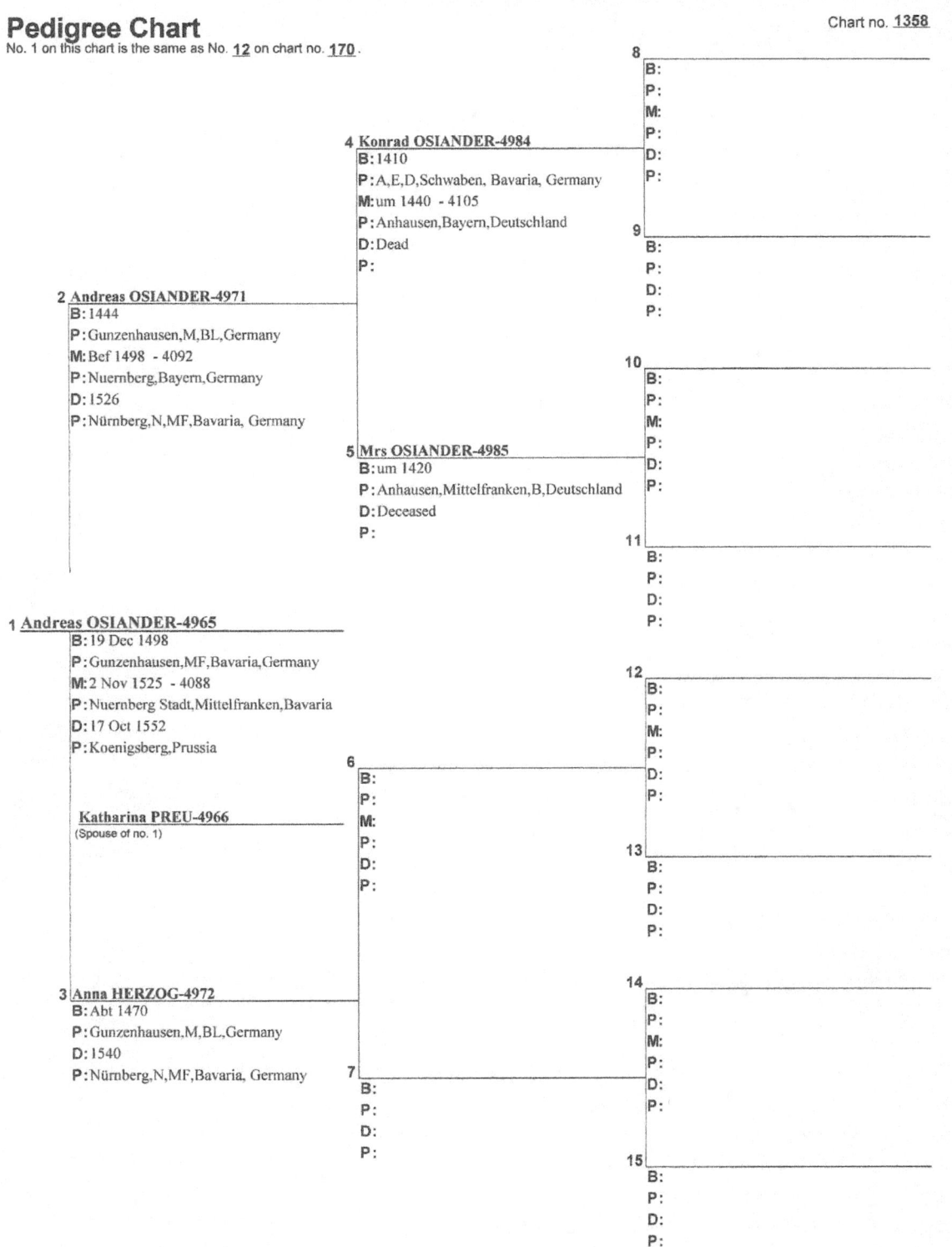

8
B:
P:
M:
P:
D:
P:

4 Konrad OSIANDER-4984
B: 1410
P: A,E,D,Schwaben, Bavaria, Germany
M: um 1440 - 4105
P: Anhausen,Bayern,Deutschland
D: Dead
P:

9
B:
P:
D:
P:

2 Andreas OSIANDER-4971
B: 1444
P: Gunzenhausen,M,BL,Germany
M: Bef 1498 - 4092
P: Nuernberg,Bayern,Germany
D: 1526
P: Nürnberg,N,MF,Bavaria, Germany

10
B:
P:
M:
P:
D:
P:

5 Mrs OSIANDER-4985
B: um 1420
P: Anhausen,Mittelfranken,B,Deutschland
D: Deceased
P:

11
B:
P:
D:
P:

1 Andreas OSIANDER-4965
B: 19 Dec 1498
P: Gunzenhausen,MF,Bavaria,Germany
M: 2 Nov 1525 - 4088
P: Nuernberg Stadt,Mittelfranken,Bavaria
D: 17 Oct 1552
P: Koenigsberg,Prussia

12
B:
P:
M:
P:
D:
P:

6
B:
P:
M:
P:
D:
P:

Katharina PREU-4966
(Spouse of no. 1)

13
B:
P:
D:
P:

3 Anna HERZOG-4972
B: Abt 1470
P: Gunzenhausen,M,BL,Germany
D: 1540
P: Nürnberg,N,MF,Bavaria, Germany

14
B:
P:
M:
P:
D:
P:

7
B:
P:
D:
P:

15
B:
P:
D:
P:

07 Nov 2015

No. 1 on this chart is the same as No. <u>13</u> on chart no. <u>170</u>.

2 Heinrich PREU-4973
B: 1464
P: Weissenburg,Mittelfranken,B,Germany
M: Abt 1500 - 4093
P: Nuernberg Stadt,Mittelfranken,Bayern
D: Bef 1525
P:

1 Katharina PREU-4966
B: 1502
P: Weißenburg,MF,Bavaria,Germany
M: 2 Nov 1525 - 4088
P: Nuernberg Stadt,Mittelfranken,Bavaria
D: 14 Jul 1537
P: Nuremberg,Bavern,Germany

Andreas OSIANDER-4965
(Spouse of no. 1)

3 Dorothea WOLFF-4974
B: Bef 1469
P: Weissenburg,Mittelfranken,B,Germany
D: 1533
P:

4
B:
P:
M:
P:
D:
P:

5
B:
P:
D:
P:

6
B:
P:
M:
P:
D:
P:

7
B:
P:
D:
P:

8
B:
P:
M:
P:
D:
P:

9
B:
P:
D:
P:

10
B:
P:
M:
P:
D:
P:

11
B:
P:
D:
P:

12
B:
P:
M:
P:
D:
P:

13
B:
P:
D:
P:

14
B:
P:
M:
P:
D:
P:

15
B:
P:
D:
P:

07 Nov 2015

Pedigree Chart

No. 1 on this chart is the same as No. **14** on chart no. **170** .

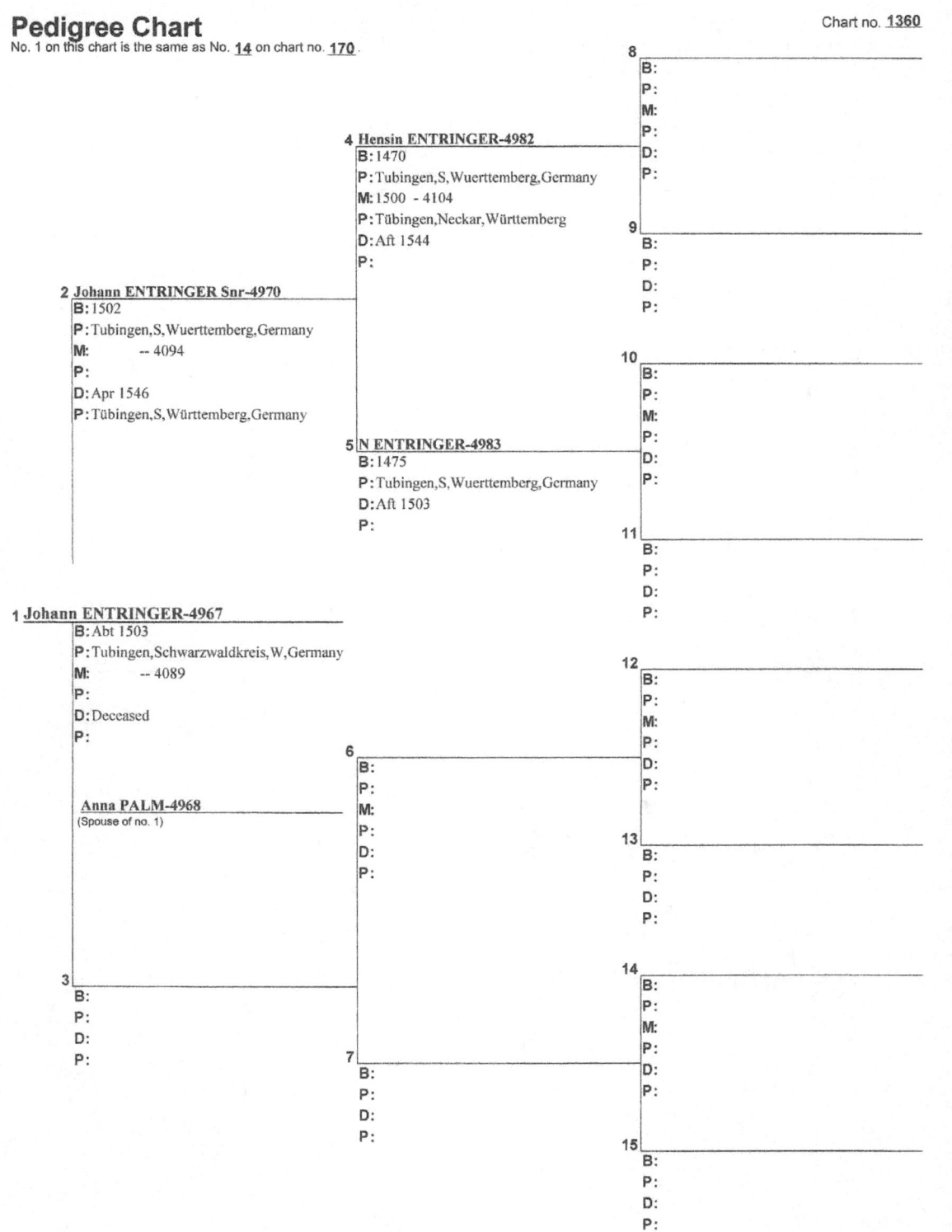

4 Hensin ENTRINGER-4982
B: 1470
P: Tubingen,S,Wuerttemberg,Germany
M: 1500 - 4104
P: Tübingen,Neckar,Württemberg
D: Aft 1544
P:

2 Johann ENTRINGER Snr-4970
B: 1502
P: Tubingen,S,Wuerttemberg,Germany
M: -- 4094
P:
D: Apr 1546
P: Tübingen,S,Württemberg,Germany

5 N ENTRINGER-4983
B: 1475
P: Tubingen,S,Wuerttemberg,Germany
D: Aft 1503
P:

1 Johann ENTRINGER-4967
B: Abt 1503
P: Tubingen,Schwarzwaldkreis,W,Germany
M: -- 4089
P:
D: Deceased
P:

Anna PALM-4968
(Spouse of no. 1)

6
B:
P:
M:
P:
D:
P:

3
B:
P:
D:
P:

7
B:
P:
D:
P:

8
B:
P:
M:
P:
D:
P:

9
B:
P:
D:
P:

10
B:
P:
M:
P:
D:
P:

11
B:
P:
D:
P:

12
B:
P:
M:
P:
D:
P:

13
B:
P:
D:
P:

14
B:
P:
M:
P:
D:
P:

15
B:
P:
D:
P:

Pedigree Chart

No. 1 on this chart is the same as No. **15** on chart no. **170** .

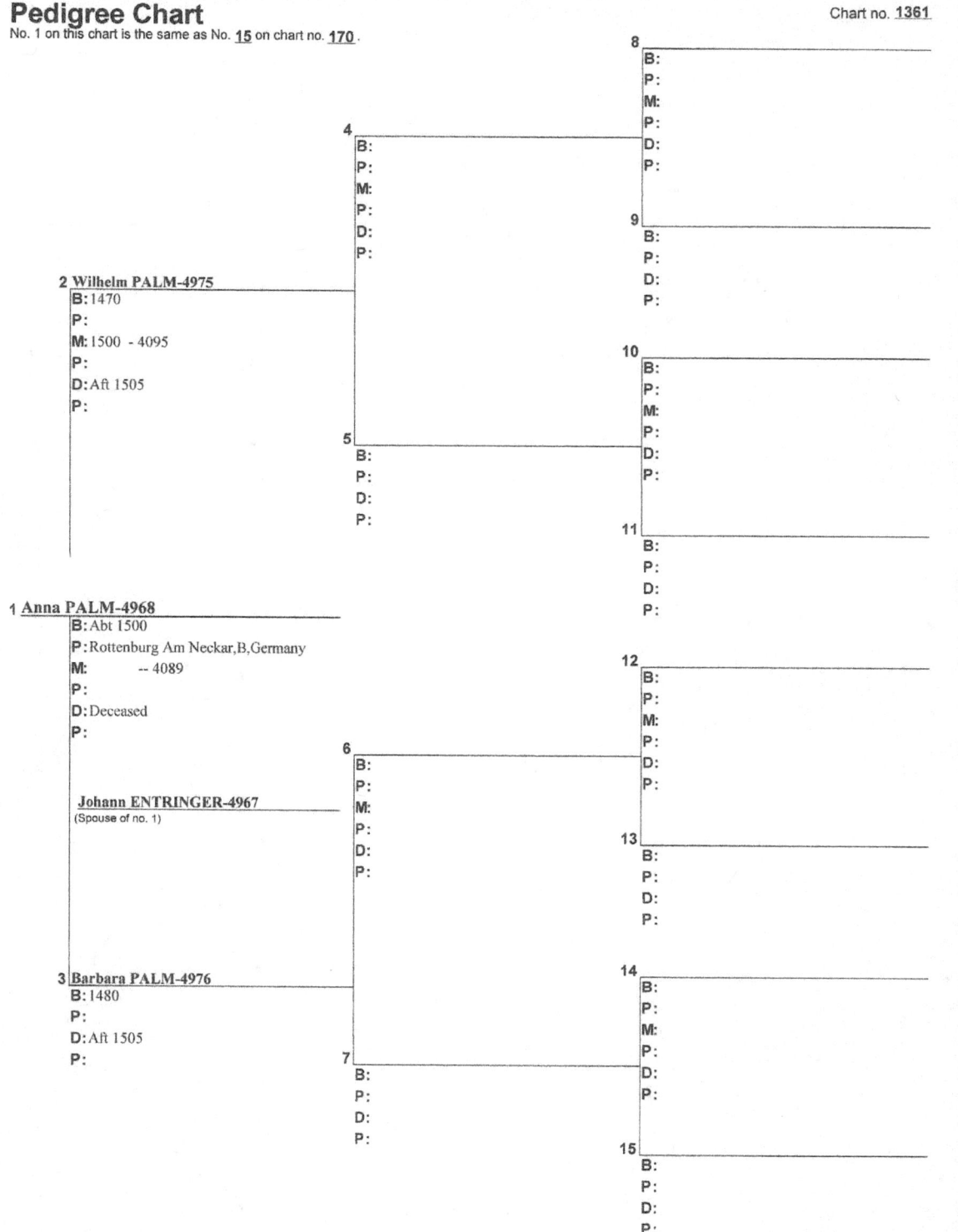

2 Wilhelm PALM-4975
B: 1470
P:
M: 1500 - 4095
P:
D: Aft 1505
P:

1 Anna PALM-4968
B: Abt 1500
P: Rottenburg Am Neckar,B,Germany
M: -- 4089
P:
D: Deceased
P:

Johann ENTRINGER-4967
(Spouse of no. 1)

3 Barbara PALM-4976
B: 1480
P:
D: Aft 1505
P:

4
B:
P:
M:
P:
D:
P:

5
B:
P:
D:
P:

6
B:
P:
M:
P:
D:
P:

7
B:
P:
D:
P:

8
B:
P:
M:
P:
D:
P:

9
B:
P:
D:
P:

10
B:
P:
M:
P:
D:
P:

11
B:
P:
D:
P:

12
B:
P:
M:
P:
D:
P:

13
B:
P:
D:
P:

14
B:
P:
M:
P:
D:
P:

15
B:
P:
D:
P:

07 Nov 2015

Pedigree Chart

Alphabetical Index

RIN	Name	Born /BR	Died /Bur	Found on Chart	Position
4943	, Agathe	Abt 1640	Deceased	22	7
4815	, Anna	1533	Bef 1643	82	7
4834	, Anna	Abt 1538	Abt 1600	84	11
4862	, Anna Maria	Abt 1661	1741	13	3
4769	, Barbara		Deceased	75	5
4810	, Barbara	1570	Deceased	85	3
4860	, Barbara	aproximadamente 1580	Deceased	94	3
4931	, Catharina	gegen 1540	6 Aug 1601	130	7
4929	, Elisabetha	gegen 1541	Deceased	130	5
4900	, Gertrud	Abt 1540	Bef 6 May 1616	125	3
4893	, Geze		Deceased	16	15
4846	, Hefel	Abt 1501	Deceased	670	3
4818	, Katharina	Abt 1528	Deceased	83	7
4925	, Katharina	Abt 1556	21 Oct 1608	131	3
4842	, Kuch	Abt 1520	Deceased	85	11
4840	, Lang	Abt 1515	Deceased	85	9
4866	, M	1594	Deceased	13	9
4812	, Margaretha	1620	Deceased	82	5
4953	, Margaretha	Abt 1566	Deceased	172	3
4832	, Maria		Deceased	84	9
4872	, Martha	1564	Deceased	100	3
4898	, Meyet	Abt 1539	Deceased	124	3
361	, Sarah Elizabeth Young	1724	Deceased	4	7
4765	, Troester	1592	Deceased	80	3
673	, Ulysses Zerfass	Abt 1689	Deceased	3	9
4913	BAKER, Harriet	1530	27 Feb 1622	123	9
4907	BALLIERER- BOHRER,	1510	Deceased	122	5
4906	BALLIERER- BOHRER, Clesgin	1510	1583	122	4
4937	BARTHOLEMEW, Jody	Abt 1664	Deceased	18	3
4892	BAUR, Hans		Deceased	16	14
4885	BAUR, Marie	7 Oct 1603	10 May 1635	16	7
4744	BECK, Anna	11 Mar 1671	1 Jan 1710	10	3
4746	BECK, Hans	31 Aug 1650	17 Jan 1729	10	6
4760	BECK, Jacob		Deceased	78	2
4750	BECK, Jerg	1628	26 May 1675	10	12
4751	BECK, Rosina	Dec 1628	26 May 1675	10	13
4909	BECKER, Catharina	1550	27 Feb 1624	123	5
4887	BECKER, Gertraud	1576	1621	16	9
4908	BECKER, Jacob	1553	27 Feb 1622	123	4
4912	BECKER, Jacob	1530	13 Feb 1616	123	8
4896	BECKER, Nickel	Abt 1549	Abt 1625	123	2
693	BENNETT, James	1706	Deceased	5	10
694	BENNETT, James	Abt 1710	Deceased	5	11
4759	BERTSCH, Anna	30 Mar 1560	1622	75	3
4770	BERTSCH, Jacob	1528	1598	75	6
4776	BERTSCH, Martin	1508	1560	75	12
373	BRADFORD, Anna	23 Jul 1732		7	5
713	BRADFORD, Joseph	9 Apr 1702	5 Jan 1778	7	10
4749	BREINING, Margaretha	1597	Deceased	10	9
4768	BREINING, Matthaeus	1520	1573	75	4
4758	BREUNING, Hans " Deissen Hans"	1558	1622	75	2
718	BROWN, Elizabeth	1736	25 Jan 1828	8	11
4850	BUMILLER, Justin Anna Maria	1502	1555	672	3
11	CAMERON, Rhoda Maie	15 Jan 1886	19 Nov 1951	1	Spouse
89	CLEMENTS, Albert N	19 Mar 1801	2 Apr 1883	1	14
43	CLEMENTS, Elizabeth	17 May 1836	1 Feb 1924	1	7
183	CLEMENTS, James H	1780	27 Aug 1866	8	2
715	CLEMENTS, Johannes Peter	8 Nov 1702	31 Oct 1780	8	8
374	CLEMENTS, Peter	12 Feb 1747	21 Dec 1834	8	4
684	COLLINS, Elizabeth	1704	21 Jun 1750	4	9
708	COOLEY, Zerviah	29 Feb 1708	23 Feb 1781	6	13
4926	DEUTZ, Johannis	gegen 1570	Deceased	132	2
4917	DIETZ, Catharine	20 Feb 1625	11 Aug 1674	17	5
4920	DIETZ, Nikolaus	Abt 1595	31 Jan 1642	17	10
4941	EISELIN, Catarina	16 Feb 1618	15 Jan 1690	22	5
4946	EISELIN, Hans	6 Mar 1591	Deceased	22	10

Pedigree Chart
Alphabetical Index

RIN	Name	Born /BR	Died /Bur	Found on Chart	Position
4952	EISELIN, Hans	Abt 1562	Deceased	172	2
686	ELLIOTT, Mary	Abt 1712	13 Feb 1764	4	11
4982	ENTRINGER, Hensin	1470	Aft 1544	1360	4
4967	ENTRINGER, Johann	Abt 1503	Deceased	170	14
4970	ENTRINGER, Johann Snr	1502	Apr 1546	1360	2
4959	ENTRINGER, Margarete	Jun 1524	16 Jan 1566	170	7
4983	ENTRINGER, N	1475	Aft 1503	1360	5
706	EVANS, Andrew	26 Jan 1708	18 Dec 1778	6	10
369	EVANS, Elizabeth	6 Jan 1732	22 Jun 1813	6	5
4847	FEYERABEND, Lienhard	Abt 1501	Deceased	671	2
4836	FEYERABEND, Maria Salome	1537	1579	84	13
170	FOLLMER, Johann Michael	29 Sep 1744	14 Mar 1817	2	2
4884	FRANTZ, Eberhard	Abt 1610	8 Mar 1690	16	6
4890	FRANTZ, Eberhard	Abt 1590	30 Jan 1614	16	12
4901	FRANTZ, Hans	Abt 1560	7 Nov 1597	126	2
4881	FRANTZ, Johanna	1633	Deceased	16	3
10	FULLMER, Edgar Osden	3 May 1884	11 Apr 1959	1	1
40	FULLMER, John Solomon	21 Jul 1807	8 Oct 1883	1	4
83	FULLMER, Peter	25 Feb 1774	6 Jan 1857	1	8
20	FULLMER, Samuel David	4 Nov 1856	29 Jul 1921	1	2
4833	GASSENMUELLER, Blasius Stephan	1534	Abt 1600	84	10
4822	GASSENMUELLER, Margaretha	12 Feb 1560	Deceased	84	5
4848	GEYER, Katharina	Abt 1501	Deceased	671	3
371	GILBERT, Elizabeth	16 Jun 1732	16 Sep 1785	6	7
709	GILBERT, Thomas IV	1 Aug 1695	13 Feb 1781	6	14
725	GIPSON, John	28 Sep 1708	24 Jul 1757	9	14
381	GIPSON, Martha	28 Sep 1736	15 Mar 1813	9	7
710	GOSS, Judith	10 Apr 1699	Deceased	6	15
4761	HAEHN, Maria Apollonia	1608	12 May 1688	78	3
702	HANCOCK, Sarah	1719	1769	5	15
4774	HARER, Johannes	Abt 1531	Deceased	74	10
4767	HARER, Maria	Abt 1557		74	5
4775	HARER, Wife of Johannes	Abt 1535	Deceased	74	11
4845	HEFEL,	Abt 1501	Deceased	670	2
674	HELWIG, Herman	Abt 1676	Deceased	3	10
351	HELWIG, Maria Elisabeth	1705	Abt 1742	3	5
4904	HERBERTS,	Abt 1550	Deceased	127	3
4891	HERBERTS, Elisabetha	Abt 1590	6 Nov 1632	16	13
4903	HERBERTS, Hamman	Abt 1550	Aft 1590	127	2
4972	HERZOG, Anna	Abt 1470	1540	1358	3
690	HILL, Mary	Abt 1694	Deceased	4	15
4955	HILTPURG, Barbara	Abt 1570	Deceased	173	3
4963	HILTPURG, Jacob	Abt 1529	26 Dec 1580	173	6
4964	HILTPURG, Jacob	Abt 1533	Deceased	173	7
4803	HIRNLEN, Agnes	1555	Deceased	82	3
4814	HIRNLEN, Hans	1530	Deceased	82	6
4875	HIRTZ, Anna Catharina		Deceased	14	3
4876	HIRTZ, Debelt	Abt 1620	1672	14	6
4877	HIRTZ, Debelt	Abt 1624	Deceased	14	7
4835	HOEFFEL, Balthas	1530	1579	84	12
4823	HOEFFEL, Hans	1555	1617	84	6
4808	HOEFFEL OR HEFEL, Catharina	31 Dec 1582	Deceased	84	3
4942	HOFFMANN, Andreas	Abt 1630	Deceased	22	6
4939	HOFFMANN, Elisabetha	31 Jul 1656	19 Jun 1736	22	3
4927	HOLZ, Johannes	Abt 1575	Deceased	133	2
4921	HOLZ, Maria Elisabeth	Abt 1599	Deceased	17	11
679	HUNTZINGER, Anna	11 Feb 1698	26 Nov 1721	3	13
685	HUTCHINGS, James Sr.	Abt 1715	1770	4	10
359	HUTCHINGS, Mary	1740		4	5
4960	ICLIN,	Abt 1510	Deceased	172	4
370	JENNINGS, Benjamin	16 Jul 1730	18 Dec 1796	6	6
180	JENNINGS, Hannah	1 Apr 1768	14 Jul 1811	6	3
4987	JETTER(IN), Catharina		10 May 1704	23	3
367	JONES, Johanna	1736	23 Mar 1797	5	7
701	JONES, Thomas	8 Jul 1715	1782	5	14
347	KAERCHER, Justina Catharina	Abt 1720	17 Jan 1820	2	5

Pedigree Chart
Alphabetical Index

RIN	Name	Born /BR	Died /Bur	Found on Chart	Position
4854	KARCHER, Anna Catharina	1604	1648	12	5
666	KARCHER, John Michael	Bef 22 Aug 1685	1787	2	10
4851	KARCHER, Moritz Jr	21 Aug 1655	8 Sep 1727	12	2
4853	KARCHER, Moritz	1600	18 Feb 1673	12	4
4838	KAUFMAN, Magdalena	1527	1580	84	15
360	KEENE, John Henry	27 Mar 1720	1785	4	6
176	KEENE, Letitia	11 Feb 1760	14 Sep 1832	4	3
687	KEENE, Richard	1689	1787	4	12
179	KENDALL, Andrew	17 Apr 1766	3 May 1829	6	2
368	KENDALL, Jesse	15 May 1727	14 Apr 1797	6	4
87	KENDALL, Levi	13 Jun 1798	19 Apr 1822	1	12
42	KENDALL, Levi Newell	19 Apr 1822	10 Mar 1903	1	6
21	KENDALL, Roxey Jane	21 Dec 1859	18 Jun 1934	1	3
703	KENDALL, Samuel	1529		6	8
4824	KEPPELER, Barbara	7 Jun 1555	1603	84	7
4837	KEPPELER, Gallus	1525	1577	84	14
4849	KEPPELER, Greogor	1500	1557	672	2
4830	KERCHER, Leonhard	1593	8 Aug 1647	82	10
171	KESSLER, Anna Juliana	16 May 1745	17 Jan 1820	2	3
668	KESSLER, Hanss Otto	17 Feb 1673	19 Sep 1749	2	12
348	KESSLER, Johann Georg	11 Oct 1711	1 Jul 1760	2	6
4910	KLEIN, Clesgin Bohrer	1485		122	8
4889	KLEIN, Engel	Abt 1570	Bef 11 Jun 1624	16	11
4882	KLEIN, Hans	1595	Bef 9 Nov 1655	16	4
670	KLEIN, Johann Frantz	1681	26 Jan 1733	2	14
4894	KLEIN, Johannes Hans	1550		122	2
4880	KLEIN, Joseph	1621	24 May 1708	16	2
4899	KLEIN, Meyets Hans	Abt 1534	1622/1626	125	2
4886	KLEIN, Nickel	1575	1621	16	8
4911	KLEIN, Sybille Bohrer	1486		122	9
4895	KLEINEN, Margaretha	1550		122	3
4861	KNOELLER, Hanns Ludwig	2 Jan 1657	2 May 1719	13	2
667	KNOELLER, Maria Catharina	23 Mar 1697	11 Feb 1802	2	11
4864	KNOELLER, Mathias	Jan 1622	31 May 1687	13	4
4932	KOCH, Hans	aproximadamente 1525		131	4
4933	KOCH, Hans	Abt 1533	Deceased	131	5
4924	KOCH, Heinrich		23 Jan 1604	131	2
4919	KOCH, Sophia	26 Mar 1592	23 Oct 1620	17	9
4841	KUCH,	Abt 1515	Deceased	85	10
4827	KUCH, Margaretha	Abt 1544	Deceased	85	5
4839	LANG,	Abt 1510	Deceased	85	8
4801	LANG, Dorethea	1607	UNKNOWN	11	11
4826	LANG, Peter	Abt 1540	Deceased	85	4
4809	LANG, Stephen Oswald	5 Aug 1568	Deceased	85	2
354	LORICH, Catherine	1724	16 Aug 1818	3	7
4794	LUDWIG, Anna Margaretha	Abt 1666	Abt 1730	11	3
4777	LUPPLER, Maria	1507	1558	75	13
182	LYMAN, Hannah	Abt 1776	Aft 1850	7	3
181	LYMAN, Joseph Bradford	1 Sep 1767	11 Dec 1847	7	2
88	LYMAN, Lorena (Laura)	27 Jul 1804	27 Dec 1860	1	13
711	LYMAN, Richard IV	Apr 1678	3 Jun 1746	7	8
372	LYMAN, Richard	23 Mar 1721/1722	Deceased	7	4
716	MEY, Maritie Mary	1706	Nov 1780	8	9
4828	MÜLLER, Georg I	1455	1530	82	8
4811	MÜLLER, Lucas I	1490	1 Dec 1560	82	4
4843	MULLER, Peter	1416	Deceased	650	2
4786	NEIFER, Johannes	Bef 1420	Aft 1470	601	4
4779	NEIFFER, Barbara	1500	1549	75	15
4787	NEUFFER, Hans	Abt 1442	Deceased	601	5
4782	NEUFFER, Johannes	1458	1522	601	2
720	NICKEL, Anna Margaretha	24 Sep 1713	24 Sep 1751	9	9
4790	NIFER, Auberlin	1380	1454	601	8
4791	NIFER, Mrs. Auberlin	Bef 1400	Deceased	601	9
4985	OSIANDER,	um 1420	Deceased	1358	5
4965	OSIANDER, Andreas	19 Dec 1498	17 Oct 1552	170	12
4971	OSIANDER, Andreas	1444	1526	1358	2

Pedigree Chart
Alphabetical Index

RIN	Name	Born /BR	Died /Bur	Found on Chart	Position
4984	OSIANDER, Konrad	1410	Dead	1358	4
4958	OSIANDER, Lucas	16 Dec 1534	17 Sep 1604	170	6
4949	OSIANDER, Monica	1559	23 Jul 1611	170	3
376	OWEN, Ananias	1756	Deceased	8	6
184	OWEN, Lucy	26 Jan 1781	26 Jan 1851	8	3
4968	PALM, Anna	Abt 1500	Deceased	170	15
4976	PALM, Barbara	1480	Aft 1505	1361	3
4975	PALM, Wilhelm	1470	Aft 1505	1361	2
704	PEIRCE, Elizabeth	1687	10 Jan 1742	6	9
692	PHILLIPS, Susannah Lloyd	1684	28 Aug 1742	5	9
688	POLLARD, Susan	Abt 1695	1794	4	13
4973	PREU, Heinrich	1464	Bef 1525	1359	2
4966	PREU, Katharina	1502	14 Jul 1537	170	13
175	PRICE, James Hutchings	1759	1811	4	2
358	PRICE, John	Abt 1732	Deceased	4	4
85	PRICE, John	23 Dec 1790	27 Dec 1848	1	10
41	PRICE, Mary Ann	16 Sep 1815	28 Mar 1897	1	5
683	PRICE, William	18 Sep 1699	17 Apr 1740	4	8
669	PURPUR, Elisabeth Maria	Abt 1676	Deceased	2	13
4878	PURPUR, Peter	Abt 1652	Deceased	15	2
4879	PURPUR, Peter	Abt 1656	Deceased	15	3
4802	RAU, Conrad Jr.	1541	Bef 1607	82	2
4869	RAU, Elias	23 Apr 1592	21 Feb 1668	13	10
4798	RAU, Hans	24 Dec 1577	Bef 1687	11	8
4795	RAU, Johannes	13 Apr 1610		11	4
4871	RAU, Johannes	Abt 1560	20 Apr 1613	100	2
664	RAU, Marie Agnes	16 Nov 1695	6 Apr 1735	2	9
4865	RAU, Martha	20 Nov 1620	24 Nov 1687	13	5
4793	RAU, Michael	9 Apr 1665	10 Mar 1696	11	2
697	READE, John	Abt 1708	1739	5	12
178	READE, Nancy Ann	12 May 1765	3 Nov 1843	5	3
366	READE, William	Aft 1729	24 Sep 1798	5	6
707	RICHARDSON, Mary	13 Mar 1710	31 Aug 1781	6	11
4858	ROHNS, Anna Else Margritta	Abt 1603	Deceased	12	13
4923	ROOS, Elizabeth	Abt 1565	24 Jun 1602	130	3
4930	ROOS, Hans	gegen 1538	27 Jan 1595	130	6
362	RUCKER, Benjamin	Abt 1730	1 Feb 1810	5	4
177	RUCKER, James	4 Sep 1758	10 Sep 1819	5	2
86	RUCKER, Johanna	19 Apr 1786	6 Feb 1822	1	11
691	RUCKER, John	1699	Jan 1743	5	8
726	SAGE, Marcy	20 Jan 1711	24 Mar 1761	9	15
377	SALES, Lucy	1758	Deceased	8	7
4771	SANWALD, Barbara	1530	1578	75	7
4778	SANWALD, Seufridt	1498	1553	75	14
186	SAVAGE, Eva	Oct 1770	1841	9	3
380	SAVAGE, John	1733	1809	9	6
722	SAVAGE, Sarah	2 Sep 1700	10 Aug 1782	9	13
721	SAVAGE, William	18 Sep 1699	16 Apr 1774	9	12
4883	SCHERER, Catharina	1595	24 Apr 1686	16	5
4888	SCHERER, Engeland	Abt 1570	Bef 1622	16	10
4897	SCHERER, Hans	Abt 1535	Bef 1587	124	2
678	SCHNEIDER, Hanss Adam	Abt 1694	3 Nov 1769	3	12
4944	SCHULER, Andreas	6 Jan 1594	23 Mar 1662	22	8
4986	SCHULER, Christian		9 Apr 1726	23	2
4940	SCHULER, Hans Balthasar	Abt 1620	3 Apr 1688	22	4
4948	SCHULER, Johann	1554	1616	170	2
4938	SCHULER, Martin	17 Sep 1658	25 Jan 1719	22	2
4957	SCHULER, Mrs. Peter	Abt 1530	Deceased	170	5
4956	SCHULER, Peter	Abt 1520	Deceased	170	4
4805	SCHURER, Anna	Abt 1550	Deceased	83	3
4817	SCHURER, Gabriel	Abt 1525	Deceased	83	6
4935	SECKLER,	gegen 1507		130	9
671	SECKLER, Anna Maria	1680	1 Sep 1735	2	15
4914	SECKLER, Christoph	Abt 1650	Deceased	17	2
4915	SECKLER, Christoph	Abt 1655	Deceased	17	3
4934	SECKLER, Hans	gegen 1503		130	8

Pedigree Chart
Alphabetical Index

RIN	Name	Born /BR	Died /Bur	Chart	Found on Position
4922	SECKLER, Hans (dit Roosen Hans)	Abt 1564	19 Jun 1634	130	2
4916	SECKLER, Hans Ewald	24 März 1616	8 Nov 1676	17	4
4928	SECKLER, Jacob	1528	19 março 1608	130	4
4918	SECKLER, Johannes, Hans der Jüngste	Abt 1589	7 May 1669	17	8
375	SEELEY, Anna	Abt 1755	10 Mar 1813	8	5
717	SEELEY, James	Abt 1735	10 Feb 1819	8	10
4820	SEITA, Helen	1525	Unknown	83	11
4804	SEITZ, Hans Sebastian Georg Bernherd	18 Jan 1549	1610	83	2
4816	SEITZ, Hans Sebastian Jacob	Abt 1510	1610	83	4
4799	SEITZ, Helene Magdalena	3 Aug 1580	Bef 1690	11	9
174	SHAFER, Mary Elizabeth	11 Feb 1746	16 Mar 1800	3	3
353	SHAFER, Peter	1720	1825	3	6
4859	SIEB, Caspar	1591	Deceased	94	2
4857	SIEB, Jacob	Abt 1602	Oct 1649	12	12
4852	SIEB, Margaret	Abt 1653	31 May 1690	12	3
4855	SIEB, Valentin	Abt 1630	Aft 1694	12	6
4829	SPAN, Ursula	1465		82	9
4873	STAHL, Johann	1564	Deceased	101	2
4874	STAHL, Johann	1568	Deceased	101	3
4870	STAHL, Rosina	Abt 1598	Bef 1660	13	11
4783	STROELIN,	1457	1519	601	3
672	SURFACE, Ulysses (Zerfass)	Abt 1685	1740	3	8
714	SWIFT, Heniretta	1701	9 Oct 1758	7	11
379	TAYLER, Hannah	Abt 1729	Deceased	9	5
4844	TREIBER,	Abt 1505	Deceased	666	2
4796	TREIBER, Anna Maria	24 Feb 1634	4 Sep 1693	11	5
4831	TREIBER, Cyriakus	1534	Bef 1592	84	8
4800	TREIBER, Hans Jacob	16 Sep 1613	21 Sep 1682	11	10
4821	TREIBER, Hans Michael	8 Sep 1560	Deceased	84	4
4807	TREIBER, Johannes	22 Jan 1583	Deceased	84	2
4764	TROESTER,	Abt 1585	Deceased	80	2
4747	TROESTER, Anna Maria	1648	27 Oct 1678	10	7
4753	TROESTER, Barbara	Abt 1616	15 Apr 1674	10	15
4752	TROESTER, Ludvig	Abt 1612	9 May 1675	10	14
4902	TRONER, Eva	Abt 1565	19 Apr 1621	126	3
349	UNKNOWN,	1715	21 Oct 1762	2	7
363	UNKNOWN, Elizabeth	Abt 1725	Deceased	5	5
663	VOLLMAR, Hans Jacob	6 Mar 1697	25 Jan 1762	2	8
4745	VOLLMAR, Hans Jerg	1640	Bef 9 Jun 1696	10	4
346	VOLLMAR, Johann Jacob	2 Apr 1721	20 Sep 1758	2	4
4748	VOLLMAR, Martin	13 Jul 1606	26 Sep 1635	10	8
4743	VOLLMER, Hans Joerg	Abt 1665	22 Apr 1745	10	2
4754	VOLMAR, Conrad	Abt 1581	Sep 1614	74	2
4755	VOLMAR, Marga	Abt 1586	Sep 1614	74	3
4766	VOLMAR, Martin	Abt 1553		74	4
675	VON KIRSCHROTH, Sabina Elisabeth	Abt 1680	Bef 1779	3	11
4961	WALTZ, Caspar	Abt 1540	Deceased	173	4
4954	WALTZ, Jacob	Abt 1566	Deceased	173	2
4947	WALTZ, Ursula	27 Oct 1595	Deceased	22	11
4962	WALTZ, Ursula	Abt 1544	Deceased	173	5
4950	WEISSGERBER, Leonhard	Abt 1568	Deceased	171	2
4951	WEISSGERBER, Leonhard	Abt 1577	Deceased	171	3
4945	WEIßGERBER, Sara	1595	1645	22	9
719	WENTZEL, Johann Adam		Deceased	9	8
185	WINCHEL, Justus Jr.	7 Dec 1759	Feb 1838	9	2
90	WINCHELL, Ada	24 Dec 1801	4 Mar 1890	1	15
378	WINCHELL, Justus	Abt 1729	Deceased	9	4
4806	WOLFF, Anna	Abt 1550	3 Apr 1620	83	5
4974	WOLFF, Dorothea	Bef 1469	1533	1359	3
4819	WOLFF, Veltin	Abt 1524	Deceased	83	10
712	WOODWARD, Mary	26 Feb 1678	6 Jun 1746	7	9
689	YOUNG, Samuel	1692		4	14
4936	ZERFAS, Von	Abt 1660	Deceased	18	2
350	ZERFASS, Johan Nicholas	1709	1 Oct 1784	3	4
173	ZERFASS, Johann Adam	25 Jan 1742	18 Aug 1806	3	2
84	ZERFASS, Susannah	17 Sep 1783	11 Nov 1856	1	9

Pedigree Chart
Alphabetical Index

RIN	Name	Born /BR	Died /Bur	Found on Chart	Position
4922	SECKLER, Hans (dit Roosen Hans)	Abt 1564	19 Jun 1634	130	2
4916	SECKLER, Hans Ewald	24 März 1616	8 Nov 1676	17	4
4928	SECKLER, Jacob	1528	19 março 1608	130	4
4918	SECKLER, Johannes, Hans der Jüngste	Abt 1589	7 May 1669	17	8
375	SEELEY, Anna	Abt 1755	10 Mar 1813	8	5
717	SEELEY, James	Abt 1735	10 Feb 1819	8	10
4820	SEITA, Helen	1525	Unknown	83	11
4804	SEITZ, Hans Sebastian Georg Bernherd	18 Jan 1549	1610	83	2
4816	SEITZ, Hans Sebastian Jacob	Abt 1510	1610	83	4
4799	SEITZ, Helene Magdalena	3 Aug 1580	Bef 1690	11	9
174	SHAFER, Mary Elizabeth	11 Feb 1746	16 Mar 1800	3	3
353	SHAFER, Peter	1720	1825	3	6
4859	SIEB, Caspar	1591	Deceased	94	2
4857	SIEB, Jacob	Abt 1602	Oct 1649	12	12
4852	SIEB, Margaret	Abt 1653	31 May 1690	12	3
4855	SIEB, Valentin	Abt 1630	Aft 1694	12	6
4829	SPAN, Ursula	1465		82	9
4873	STAHL, Johann	1564	Deceased	101	2
4874	STAHL, Johann	1568	Deceased	101	3
4870	STAHL, Rosina	Abt 1598	Bef 1660	13	11
4783	STROELIN,	1457	1519	601	3
672	SURFACE, Ulysses (Zerfass)	Abt 1685	1740	3	8
714	SWIFT, Heniretta	1701	9 Oct 1758	7	11
379	TAYLER, Hannah	Abt 1729	Deceased	9	5
4844	TREIBER,	Abt 1505	Deceased	666	2
4796	TREIBER, Anna Maria	24 Feb 1634	4 Sep 1693	11	5
4831	TREIBER, Cyriakus	1534	Bef 1592	84	8
4800	TREIBER, Hans Jacob	16 Sep 1613	21 Sep 1682	11	10
4821	TREIBER, Hans Michael	8 Sep 1560	Deceased	84	4
4807	TREIBER, Johannes	22 Jan 1583	Deceased	84	2
4764	TROESTER,	Abt 1585	Deceased	80	2
4747	TROESTER, Anna Maria	1648	27 Oct 1678	10	7
4753	TROESTER, Barbara	Abt 1616	15 Apr 1674	10	15
4752	TROESTER, Ludvig	Abt 1612	9 May 1675	10	14
4902	TRONER, Eva	Abt 1565	19 Apr 1621	126	3
349	UNKNOWN,	1715	21 Oct 1762	2	7
363	UNKNOWN, Elizabeth	Abt 1725	Deceased	5	5
663	VOLLMAR, Hans Jacob	6 Mar 1697	25 Jan 1762	2	8
4745	VOLLMAR, Hans Jerg	1640	Bef 9 Jun 1696	10	4
346	VOLLMAR, Johann Jacob	2 Apr 1721	20 Sep 1758	2	4
4748	VOLLMAR, Martin	13 Jul 1606	26 Sep 1635	10	8
4743	VOLLMER, Hans Joerg	Abt 1665	22 Apr 1745	10	2
4754	VOLMAR, Conrad	Abt 1581	Sep 1614	74	2
4755	VOLMAR, Marga	Abt 1586	Sep 1614	74	3
4766	VOLMAR, Martin	Abt 1553		74	4
675	VON KIRSCHROTH, Sabina Elisabeth	Abt 1680	Bef 1779	3	11
4961	WALTZ, Caspar	Abt 1540	Deceased	173	4
4954	WALTZ, Jacob	Abt 1566	Deceased	173	2
4947	WALTZ, Ursula	27 Oct 1595	Deceased	22	11
4962	WALTZ, Ursula	Abt 1544	Deceased	173	5
4950	WEISSGERBER, Leonhard	Abt 1568	Deceased	171	2
4951	WEISSGERBER, Leonhard	Abt 1577	Deceased	171	3
4945	WEIßGERBER, Sara	1595	1645	22	9
719	WENTZEL, Johann Adam		Deceased	9	8
185	WINCHEL, Justus Jr.	7 Dec 1759	Feb 1838	9	2
90	WINCHELL, Ada	24 Dec 1801	4 Mar 1890	1	15
378	WINCHELL, Justus	Abt 1729	Deceased	9	4
4806	WOLFF, Anna	Abt 1550	3 Apr 1620	83	5
4974	WOLFF, Dorothea	Bef 1469	1533	1359	3
4819	WOLFF, Veltin	Abt 1524	Deceased	83	10
712	WOODWARD, Mary	26 Feb 1678	6 Jun 1746	7	9
689	YOUNG, Samuel	1692		4	14
4936	ZERFAS, Von	Abt 1660	Deceased	18	2
350	ZERFASS, Johan Nicholas	1709	1 Oct 1784	3	4
173	ZERFASS, Johann Adam	25 Jan 1742	18 Aug 1806	3	2
84	ZERFASS, Susannah	17 Sep 1783	11 Nov 1856	1	9

Pedigree Chart

Alphabetical Index

RIN	Name	Born /BR	Died /Bur	Found on Chart	Position
4856	ZU ROTENSOL NEUENBUERG, Christina	Abt 1636	5 Dec 1698	12	7

Ahnentafel Chart for Edgar Osden FULLMER-10

First Generation

1. **Edgar Osden FULLMER**-10 was born on 3 May 1884 in Mapleton, Utah, Utah, United States. He died on 11 Apr 1959 in Blackfoot, Bingham, Idaho, United States. He was buried on 15 Apr 1959 in Parker, Fremont, Idaho, United States.

   Edgar married (MRIN:5) **Rhoda Maie CAMERON**-11, daughter of William CAMERON-22 and Georganna SEVY-23 (MRIN:11), on 5 Jun 1913 in Cache, Utah, United States. Rhoda was born on 15 Jan 1886 in Panguitch, Garfield, Utah Territory, United States. She died on 19 Nov 1951 in St. Anthony, Fremont, Idaho, United States. She was buried on 20 Nov 1951 in Parker, Fremont, Idaho, United States.

Second Generation

2. **Samuel David FULLMER**-20 was born on 4 Nov 1856 in Salt Lake City, Salt Lake, Utah Territory, United States. He died on 29 Jul 1921 in Blackfoot, Bingham, Idaho, United States. He was buried on 31 Jul 1921 in Sugar City, Madison, Idaho, United States. Samuel married (MRIN:10) Roxey Jane KENDALL-21 on 24 Oct 1878 in of Springville, Utah, Utah, USA.

3. **Roxey Jane KENDALL**-21 was born on 21 Dec 1859 in Springville, Utah, Utah, United States. She died on 18 Jun 1934 in Rexburg, Madison, Idaho, United States. She was buried on 22 Jun 1934 in Sugar City, Madison, Idaho, United States.

Third Generation

4. **John Solomon FULLMER**-40 was born on 21 Jul 1807 in Huntington Mills, Luzerne, Pennsylvania, United States. He died on 8 Oct 1883 in Springville, Utah, Utah Territory, United States. He was buried on 10 Oct 1883 in Springville, Utah, Utah Territory, United States. John married (MRIN:20) Mary Ann PRICE-41 on 24 May 1837 in Nashville, Davidson, Tennessee, United States.

5. **Mary Ann PRICE**-41 was born on 16 Sep 1815 in Nashville, Davidson, Tennessee, United States. She was christened on 16 Sep 1815 in Nashville, Davidson, Tennessee, United States. She died on 28 Mar 1897 in Marysvale, Piute, Utah, United States. She was buried in Mar 1897 in Springville, Utah, Utah, United States.

6. **Levi Newell KENDALL**-42 was born on 19 Apr 1822 in Lockport, Niagara, New York, United States. He died on 10 Mar 1903 in Mapleton, Utah, Utah, United States. He was buried on 13 Mar 1903 in Evergreen Cemetery, Springville, Utah, Utah, United States. Levi married (MRIN:21) Elizabeth CLEMENTS-43 on 29 Nov 1852 in Salt Lake City, Salt Lake, Utah, United States.

7. **Elizabeth CLEMENTS**-43 was born on 17 May 1836 in Liberty, Clay, Missouri, United States. She died on 1 Feb 1924 in Oxford, Franklin, Idaho, United States. She was buried on 3 Feb 1924 in Oxford, Franklin, Idaho, United States.

Fourth Generation

8. **Peter FULLMER**-83 was born on 25 Feb 1774 in Reading, Berks, Pennsylvania, British America. He died on 6 Jan 1857 in Salt Lake City, Salt Lake, Utah Territory, United States. He was buried in Salt Lake City, Salt Lake, Utah Territory, United States. Peter married (MRIN:42) Susannah ZERFASS-84 on 2 Mar 1802 in Schuylkill Township, Schuylkill, Pennsylvania, United States.

9. **Susannah ZERFASS**-84 was born on 17 Sep 1783 in Whitehall, Allegheny, Pennsylvania, United States. She was christened on 27 Sep 1778 in Springfield Township, Bucks, Pennsylvania, United States. She died on 11 Nov 1856 in Salt Lake City, Salt Lake, Utah Territory, United States. She was buried on 14 Nov 1856 in Salt Lake City, Salt Lake, Utah Territory, United States.

10. **John PRICE**-85 was born on 23 Dec 1790 in Nashville, Davidson, Tennessee, United States. He died on 27 Dec 1848 in Vicksburg, Warren, Mississippi, United States. John married (MRIN:43) Johanna RUCKER-86 on 29 Dec 1814 in Rutherford, Tennessee, United States.

11. **Johanna RUCKER**-86 was born on 19 Apr 1786 in Shockoe, Richmond City, Virginia, United States. She died on 6 Feb 1822 in Nashville, Davidson, Tennessee, United States. She was buried in (See Notes).

12. **Levi KENDALL**-87 was born on 13 Jun 1798 in Royalston, Worcester, Massachusetts, United States. He died on 19 Apr 1822 in Lockport, Niagara, New York, United Staes. He was buried on Est 19 Apr 1822 in Lockport, Niagara, New York, United States. Levi married (MRIN:44) Lorena (Laura) LYMAN-88 on 10 Apr 1820 in Lockport, Niagara, New York, United States.

13. **Lorena (Laura) LYMAN**-88 was born on 27 Jul 1804 in Canada. She died on 27 Dec 1860. She was buried in Redford Cemetery, Wayne, Michigan, United States.

14. **Albert N CLEMENTS**-89 was born on 19 Mar 1801 in Fort Ann, Washington, New York, United States. He died on 2 Apr 1883 in Springville, Utah, Utah, United States. He was buried in Apr 1883 in Springville City Cemetery, Springville, Utah, Utah, United States. Albert married (MRIN:45) Ada WINCHELL-90 on 21 Jan 1821 in Fort Ann, Washington, New York, United States.

15. **Ada WINCHELL**-90 was born on 24 Dec 1801 in Hebron, Washington, New York, United States. She died on 4 Mar 1890 in Oxford, Franklin, Idaho, United States. She was buried on 7 Mar 1890 in Oxford Cemetery, Franklin, Idaho, United States.

Fifth Generation

16. **Johann Michael FOLLMER**-170 was born on 29 Sep 1744 in Tulpehocken Township, Berks, Pennsylvania, United States. He died on 14 Mar 1817. He was buried in 1817 in Milton, Northumberland, Pennsylvania, United States of America. Johann married (MRIN:86) Anna Juliana KESSLER-171.

17. **Anna Juliana KESSLER**-171 was born on 16 May 1745 in Weierbach, Idar-Oberstein, Birkenfeld, Rheinland-Pfalz, Germany. She died on 17 Jan 1820 in Reading, Berks, Pennsylvania, United States. She was buried after 17 Jan 1820 in Follmer Lutheran Church Cemetery, Milton, Northumberland, Pennsylvania, United States.

18. **Captain Johann Adam ZERFASS**-173 was born on 25 Jan 1742 in Whitehall Township, Northampton, Pennsylvania, United States. He was christened on 2 Feb 1742 in Whitehall Township, Lehigh, Pennsylvania, United States. He died on 18 Aug 1806 in Whitehall Township, Lehigh, Pennsylvania, United States. He was buried after 18 Aug 1806 in Egypt Churchyard, Lehigh, Lackawanna, Pennsylvania, United States. Johann married (MRIN:88) Mary Elizabeth SHAFER-174

on 6 Mar 1768 in Whitehall Township, Lehigh, Pennsylvania, United States.

19. **Mary Elizabeth SHAFER**-174 was born on 11 Feb 1746 in Whitehall Township, Northampton, Pennsylvania, United States. She was christened on 13 Jul 1775 in Egypt, Lehigh, Pennsylvania, United States. She died on 16 Mar 1800 in Whitehall Township, Northampton, Pennsylvania, United States. She was buried in Egypt, Northampton, Pennsylvania, United States.

20. **James Hutchings PRICE**-175 was born in 1759 in Kent Island, Queen Anne's, Maryland, United States. He died in 1811 in Scott, Kentucky, United States. James married (MRIN:89) Letitia KEENE-176 in 1789 in Baltimore, Maryland, United States.

21. **Letitia KEENE**-176 was born on 11 Feb 1760 in Baltimore, Baltimore, Maryland, United States. She died on 14 Sep 1832 in Nashville, Davidson, Tennessee, United States.

22. **Rev. James RUCKER**-177 was born on 4 Sep 1758 in Amherst, Amherst, Virginia, United States. He died on 10 Sep 1819 in , Rutherford, Tennessee, United States. He was buried in Sep 1819 in Rutherford, Tennessee, United States. James married (MRIN:90) Nancy Ann READE-178 on 31 Jan 1788 in Lynchberg, Amherst, Virginia.

23. **Nancy Ann READE**-178 was born on 12 May 1765 in Bedford, Virginia, United States. She died on 3 Nov 1843 in Murfreesboro, Rutherford, Tennessee, United States. She was buried in Oct 1843 in Rutherford, Gibson, Tennessee, United States.

24. **Andrew KENDALL**-179 was born on 17 Apr 1766 in Athol, Worcester, Massachusetts, United States. He died on 3 May 1829 in Royalston, Worcester, Massachusetts, United States. He was buried after 3 May 1829 in Royalston, Worcester, Massachusetts, United States. Andrew married (MRIN:91) Hannah JENNINGS-180 on 23 Feb 1796 in Royalston, Worcester, Massachusetts, United States.

25. **Hannah JENNINGS**-180 was born on 1 Apr 1768 in Brookfield, Worcester, Massachusetts, United States. She died on 14 Jul 1811 in Brookfield, Worcester, Massachusetts, United States. She was buried in Brookfield Cemetery, Brookfield, Worcester, Massachusetts, United States.

26. **Joseph Bradford LYMAN**-181 was born on 1 Sep 1767 in Lebanon, New London, Connecticut. He died on 11 Dec 1847 in Lebanon, New London, Connecticut, United States. Joseph married (MRIN:92) Hannah LYMAN-182 about 1804 in Of Lockport, Niagara, New York.

27. **Hannah LYMAN**-182 was born about 1776 in Connecticut, United States. She died after 1850 in Michigan, usa.

28. **James H CLEMENTS**-183 was born in 1780 in Saratoga, Saratoga, New York, United States. He died on 27 Aug 1866 in Glens Falls, Warren, New York, United States. He was buried in Aug 1866 in Harrisena Church, Warren, New York, United States. James married (MRIN:93) Lucy OWEN-184 in 1796 in Fort Ann, Washington, New York, United States.

29. **Lucy OWEN**-184 was born on 26 Jan 1781 in Fort Ann, Warren, New York, United States. She died on 26 Jan 1851 in Harrisburg, Warren, New York, United States. She was buried in Harrisena Church, Warren, New York, United States.

30. **Justus WINCHEL Jr.**-185 was born on 7 Dec 1759 in Brunswick, Braunschweig, Hanover, Germany. He died in Feb 1838 in Rose, Wayne, New York, United States. Justus married (MRIN:94) Eva SAVAGE-186 on 9 Apr 1787 in Westfield, Hampden, Massachusetts, United States.

31. **Eva SAVAGE**-186 was born in Oct 1770 in Westfield, Hampden, Massachusetts, United States. She died in 1841 in Rose, Wayne, New York, United States. She was buried in 1841 in New York, United States.

Sixth Generation

32. **Johann Jacob VOLLMAR**-346 was born on 2 Apr 1721 in Roßwag, Vaihingen, Württemberg, Germany. He was christened on 26 Apr 1721 in Roßwag, Vaihingen, Württemberg, Germany. He died on 20 Sep 1758 in Tulpehocken, Berks, Pennsylvania. He was buried in Inventory Of, Property Taken 3. Johann married (MRIN:181) Justina Catharina KAERCHER-347 on 25 Jan 1742 in Tulpehocken, Berks, Pennsylvania.

33. **Justina Catharina KAERCHER**-347 was born about 1720 in Dobel, Neuenbürg, Württemberg, Germany. She died on 17 Jan 1820 in Tulpehocken Township, Berks, Pennsylvania, United States.

34. **Johann Georg KESSLER**-348 was born on 11 Oct 1711 in Georg, Weierbach, Birkenfeld, Rheinland, Germany. He was christened on 11 Oct 1711 in Mettlach, Merzig, Rhineland, Prussia, Germany. He died on 1 Jul 1760 in Georg, Weierbach, Birkenfeld, Rheinland, Germany. He was buried on 2 Jul 1760 in Georg, Weierbach, Birkenfeld, Rheinland, Germany. Johann married (MRIN:182) UNKNOWN-349 on 17 Apr 1735 in Evangelisch, Mettlach, Rheinland, Prussia.

35. **UNKNOWN**-349 was born in 1715 in Of Georg-Weierbach, Birkenfeld, Rheinland, Germany. She died on 21 Oct 1762 in Georg, Weierbach, Birkenfeld, Rheinland, Germany. She was buried on 24 Oct 1762 in Georg, Weierbach, Birkenfeld, Rheinland, Germany.

36. **Johan Nicholas ZERFASS**-350 was born in 1709 in Rheinland-Pfalz, Germany. He was christened in farmer. He died on 1 Oct 1784 in Cocalico, Lancaster, Pennsylvania, United States. Johan married (MRIN:183) Maria Elisabeth HELWIG-351.

37. **Maria Elisabeth HELWIG**-351 was born in 1705 in Germany. She was christened on 23 Jan 1708 in Meddersheim, Meisenheim, Rhineland, Prussia, Germany. She died about 1742 in Salisbury Township, Lancaster, Pennsylvania, United States. She was buried in 1745.

38. **Peter SHAFER**-353 was born in 1720 in Schuylkill, Pennsylvania, United States. He was christened in 1720 in Schuylkill Township, Schuylkill, Pennsylvania, United States. He died in 1825 in White Hill, Cumberland, Pennsylvania, United States. Peter married (MRIN:185) Catherine LORICH-354 about 1745 in Of, Schuykill, Pennsylvania.

39. **Catherine LORICH**-354 was born in 1724 in Panama. She died on 16 Aug 1818. She was buried on 16 Aug 1818 in Germantown, , Ohio.

40. **John PRICE**-358 was born about 1732 in Kent Island, Queen Anne's, Maryland, United States. He died. John married (MRIN:188) Mary HUTCHINGS-359 on 28 Nov 1787.

41. **Mary HUTCHINGS**-359 was born in 1740 in Kent Island, Queen Anne's, Maryland, United States. She died in Kent Island, Queen Anne's, Maryland, United States.

42. **John Henry KEENE**-360 was born on 27 Mar 1720 in Taylors Island, Dorchester, Maryland, United States. He died in 1785. John married (MRIN:189) Sarah Elizabeth Young-361 in 1747 in Baltimore, Baltimore, Maryland, United States.

43. **Sarah Elizabeth Young**-361 was born in 1724 in Baltimore, Baltimore, Maryland, United States. She died.

44. **Benjamin RUCKER**-362 was born about 1730 in Orange, Orange, Virginia, United States. He died on 1 Feb 1810 in Amherst, Amherst, Virginia, United States. He was buried in 1810 in Orange, Orange, Virginia, United States. Benjamin married (MRIN:190) Elizabeth UNKNOWN-363 in <1755> in , , Virginia.

45. **Elizabeth UNKNOWN**-363 was born about 1725 in Amherst, Virginia, United States. She died.

46. **William READE**-366 was born after 1729 in Chesterfield, Virginia, United States. He died on 24 Sep 1798 in Bedford, Virginia, United States. William married (MRIN:192) Johanna JONES-367

about 1751 in , , Virginia, British Colony.

47. **Johanna JONES**-367 was born in 1736 in Henrico, Virginia, United States. She died on 23 Mar 1797 in Bedford, Virginia, United States.

48. **Jesse KENDALL**-368 was born on 15 May 1727 in Woburn, Middlesex, Massachusetts, United States. He died on 14 Apr 1797 in Athol, Worcester, Massachusetts, United States. He was buried in Old Pleasant Street Cemetery, Athol, Worcester, Massachusetts, United States. Jesse married (MRIN:193) Elizabeth EVANS-369 in Mar 1749 in Woburn, Middlesex, Massachusetts, United States.

49. **Elizabeth EVANS**-369 was born on 6 Jan 1732 in Woburn, Middlesex, Massachusetts, United States. She died on 22 Jun 1813 in Athol, Worcester, Massachusetts, United States. She was buried in Jun 1813 in Old Pleasant Steet Cemetery, Athol, Worcester, Massachusetts, United States.

50. **Benjamin JENNINGS**-370 was born on 16 Jul 1730 in Springfield, Hampden, Massachusetts, United States. He died on 18 Dec 1796 in Brookfield, Worcester, Massachusetts, United States. Benjamin married (MRIN:194) Elizabeth GILBERT-371 on 1 Nov 1750 in Brookfield, Worcester, MA.

51. **Elizabeth GILBERT**-371 was born on 16 Jun 1732 in Brookfield, Worcester, Massachusetts, United States. She died on 16 Sep 1785 in Brookfield, Worcester, Ma.

52. **Richard LYMAN**-372 was born on 23 Mar 1721/1722 in Lebanon, New London, Connecticut, United States. He died. Richard married (MRIN:195) Anna BRADFORD-373 on 15 Jun 1758.

53. **Anna BRADFORD**-373 was born on 23 Jul 1732 in New London, New London, Connecticut, United States. She died in Lebanon, New London, Connecticut, United States. She was buried in Lebanon, New London, Connecticut, United States.

56. **Peter CLEMENTS**-374 was born on 12 Feb 1747 in Sleepy Hollow, Westchester, New York, United States. He was christened on 3 May 1747 in Tarrytown, Westchester, New York, United States. He died on 21 Dec 1834 in Fort Ann, Washington, New York, United States. He was buried in Taylor Cemetery, Stillwater, New York. Peter married (MRIN:196) Anna SEELEY-375 about 1775/1776 in Fort Ann, Washington, New York, X.

57. **Anna SEELEY**-375 was born about 1755 in Stillwater, Saratoga, New York. She was christened in 1769 in Stillwater, Saratoga, New York, United States. She died on 10 Mar 1813 in Stillwater, Saratoga, New York, United States. She was buried in Saratoga, New York, Taylor Cemetery.

58. **Ananias OWEN**-376 was born in 1756 in Fort Ann, Washington, New York, United States. He died. Ananias married (MRIN:197) Lucy SALES-377 in 1775 in , , Tennessee.

59. **Lucy SALES**-377 was born in 1758 in Fort Ann, Washington, New York, United States. She died.

60. **Justus WINCHELL**-378 was born about 1729 in Hesson Kassel, Braunschweig, , Germany. He died. Justus married (MRIN:198) Hannah TAYLER-379 about 1758 in Hannover, Kingdom of Prussia, Germany.

61. **Hannah TAYLER**-379 was born about 1729 in <Hesson Kassel, Braunschweig, , Germany>. She died.

62. **John SAVAGE**-380 was born in 1733 in Dorset, England. He was christened on 21 Nov 1733 in Studland, Dorset, England. He died in 1809 in New York, United States. John married (MRIN:199) Martha GIPSON-381.

63. **Martha GIPSON**-381 was born on 28 Sep 1736 in Middletown, Middlesex, Connecticut, United States. She died on 15 Mar 1813 in Middletown, Middlesex, Connecticut, United States.

Seventh Generation

64. **Hans Jacob VOLLMAR**-663 was born on 6 Mar 1697 in Kohlstetten, Engstingen, Reutlingen, Baden-Württemberg, Germany. He was christened on 6 Mar 1698 in Lutheran Church, Turbot Twp., Kohlstetten, Donau, Wuertiemberg. He died on 25 Jan 1762 in Tulpehocken, Berks, Pennsylvania. He was buried on 25 Jan 1762 in Tulpehocken Township, Berks, Pennsylvania, United States. Hans married (MRIN:358) Marie Agnes RAU-664 on 16 Aug 1718 in Rosswag, Neckar, Württemberg.

65. **Marie Agnes RAU**-664 was born on 16 Nov 1695 in Eberdingen, Vaihingen, Neckarkreis, Württemberg, Germany. She was christened on 19 Nov 1695 in Eberdingen, Vaihingen, Neckarkreis, Württemberg, Germany. She died on 6 Apr 1735 in Roßwag, Vaihingen, Neckarkreis, Württemberg, Germany.

66. **John Michael KARCHER**-666 was born before 22 Aug 1685 in Konstanz, Baden, Germany. He was christened on 22 Aug 1685 in Dobel, Neuenbürg, Schwarzwaldkreis, Württemberg, Germany. He died in 1787. John married (MRIN:360) Maria Catharina KNOELLER-667.

67. **Maria Catharina KNOELLER**-667 was born on 23 Mar 1697 in Neuenburg, Schwarzwaldkreis, Wuerttemberg, Germany. She was christened on 24 Dec 1687 in Dobel Neuenbuerg, Schwarzwaldkreis, Wuerttemberg, Germany. She died on 11 Feb 1802 in Hamburg, Berks, Pennsylvania, United States. She was buried in Longswamp, Berks, Pennsylvania, United States.

68. **Hanss Otto KESSLER**-668 was born on 17 Feb 1673 in Idar-Oberstein, Rhineland, Prussia, Germany. He was christened on 17 Feb 1673 in Oberstein, Birkenfeld, Oldenburg, Germany. He died on 19 Sep 1749 in Idar-Oberstein, Rhineland, Prussia, Germany. He was buried on 21 Sep 1749 in Oberstein, Birkenfeld, Oldenburg, Germany. Hanss married (MRIN:361) Elisabeth Maria PURPUR-669 on 19 Feb 1697 in Birkenfeld, Oldenburg, Rheinland, Germany.

69. **Elisabeth Maria PURPUR**-669 was born about 1676 in Germany. She died.

70. **Johann Frantz KLEIN**-670 was born in 1681 in Windesheim, Bad Kreuznach, Rheinland-Pfalz, Germany. He died on 26 Jan 1733 in Windesheim, Bad Kreuznach, Rheinland-Pfalz, Germany. Johann married (MRIN:362) Anna Maria SECKLER-671 on 17 Jan 1707 in Weiderscheim, Rhineland, Germany.

71. **Anna Maria SECKLER**-671 was born in 1680 in Gensingen, Bingen, Rheinhessen, Hessen, Germany. She was christened about 1680 in Gensingen, Bingen, Rheinhessen, Hessen, Germany. She died on 1 Sep 1735 in Rhineland, Prussia, Germany.

72. **Ulysses (Zerfass) SURFACE**-672 was born about 1685 in Germany. He died in 1740 in Germany. Ulysses married (MRIN:363) Mrs. Ulysses Zerfass-673 about 1708 in Palatine Area, Germany.

73. **Mrs. Ulysses Zerfass**-673 was born about 1689 in Germany. She died.

74. **Herman HELWIG**-674 was born about 1676 in Kirschroth, Meisenheim, Rhineland, Prussia, Germany. He died. Herman married (MRIN:364) Sabina Elisabeth VON KIRSCHROTH-675 about 1702 in Rheinland, Germany.

75. **Sabina Elisabeth VON KIRSCHROTH**-675 was born about 1680 in Kirschroth, Meisenheim, Rhineland, Prussia, Germany. She died before 1779.

76. **Hanss Adam SCHNEIDER**-678 was born about 1694 in Germany. He died on 3 Nov 1769 in Haiterbach, Calw, Baden-Württemberg, Germany. Hanss married (MRIN:366) Anna HUNTZINGER-679 on 19 Jul 1722 in Heselwangen, Heselwangen, Württemberg, Germany.

77. **Anna HUNTZINGER**-679 was born on 11 Feb 1698 in Heselwangen, Balingen, Schwarzwaldkreis, Württemberg, Germany. She died on 26 Nov 1721.

80. **William PRICE**-683 was born on 18 Sep 1699 in Chirbury, Shropshire, England. He was christened

on 26 Dec 1691 in Astley Abbots, Shropshire, England. He died on 17 Apr 1740 in Kent Island, Queen Anne's, Maryland, United States. William married (MRIN:370) Elizabeth COLLINS-684.

81. **Elizabeth COLLINS**-684 was born in 1704 in Kent Island, Queen Anne's, Maryland, United States. She died on 21 Jun 1750 in Kent Island, Queen Anne's, Maryland, United States.

82. **James HUTCHINGS Sr.**-685 was born about 1715 in Kent Island, Queen Anne's, Maryland, United States. He died in 1770 in Kent Island, Queen Anne's, Maryland, United States. James married (MRIN:371) Mary ELLIOTT-686 in 1725 in Of, Kent Island, Queen Anne, Md.

83. **Mary ELLIOTT**-686 was born about 1712 in Kent Island, Queen Anne's, Maryland, United States. She was christened in 1715 in Kent Island, Queen Anne's, Maryland, United States. She died on 13 Feb 1764.

84. **Richard KEENE**-687 was born in 1689 in Dorchester, Maryland, United States. He died in 1787 in Queen Anne's, Maryland, United States. Richard married (MRIN:372) Susan POLLARD-688 on 4 Nov 1714 in Dorcester Co., Maryland.

85. **Susan POLLARD**-688 was born about 1695 in Dorchester, Maryland, United States. She died in 1794 in Maryland, United States.

86. **Samuel YOUNG**-689 was born in 1692 in Suffolk, New York, United States. He died in Baltimore, Maryland, United States. Samuel married (MRIN:373) Mary HILL-690.

87. **Mary HILL**-690 was born about 1694 in Maryland, United States. She was christened in 1694 in Maryland, United States. She died.

88. **John RUCKER**-691 was born in 1699 in Essex, Colony of Virginia, British Colonial America. He died in Jan 1743 in Orange, Virginia, United States. He was buried in Madison, Virginia, United States. John married (MRIN:374) Susannah Lloyd PHILLIPS-692 in 1729 in Essex, Colony of Virginia, British Colonial America.

89. **Susannah Lloyd PHILLIPS**-692 was born in 1684 in Orange, Virginia, United States. She died on 28 Aug 1742 in Orange, Orange, Virginia, United States.

90. **James BENNETT**-693 was born in 1706 in Amherst, Virginia, United States. He died. James married (MRIN:375) Mrs. James BENNETT-694 in 1730 in Orange, Virginia.

91. **Mrs. James BENNETT**-694 was born about 1710 in Virginia, United States. She died.

92. **John READE**-697 was born about 1708 in Elizabeth City, Virginia, United States. He died in 1739 in Henrico, Virginia, United States.

94. **Thomas JONES**-701 was born on 8 Jul 1715 in Chesterfield, Chesterfield, Virginia, United States. He died in 1782 in Shepherdstown, Jefferson, Virginia, United States. Thomas married (MRIN:382) Sarah HANCOCK-702 in 1735/1736.

95. **Sarah HANCOCK**-702 was born in 1719 in Henrico, Mecklenburg, Virginia, United States. She died in 1769 in Granville, North Carolina, United States.

96. **Samuel KENDALL**-703 was born in 1529 in Norfolk, England. He died in Norfolk, England. Samuel married (MRIN:383) Elizabeth PEIRCE-704.

97. **Elizabeth PEIRCE**-704 was born in 1687. She died on 10 Jan 1742 in Woburn, Middlesex, Massachusetts, United States. She was buried in Jan 1742 in First Burial Ground, Woburn, Middlesex, Massachusetts, United States.

98. **Andrew EVANS**-706 was born on 26 Jan 1708 in Malden, Middlesex, Massachusetts, United States. He was christened in Malden, Middlesex, Massachusetts, United States. He died on 18 Dec 1778 in Woburn, Middlesex, Massachusetts, United States. He was buried in Woburn, Middlesex, Massachusetts, United States. Andrew married (MRIN:385) Mary RICHARDSON-707 on 4 Dec

1730 in Woburn, Middlesex, Massachusetts, United States.

99. **Mary RICHARDSON**-707 was born on 13 Mar 1710 in Woburn, Middlesex, Massachusetts, United States. She died on 31 Aug 1781 in Woburn, Middlesex, Massachusetts, United States. She was buried in Woburn, Middlesex, Massachusetts, United States.

101. **Zerviah COOLEY**-708 was born on 29 Feb 1708 in Springfield, Hampshire, Massachusetts, United States. She died on 23 Feb 1781 in Springfield, Hampden, Massachusetts, United States.

102. **Thomas GILBERT 1V**-709 was born on 1 Aug 1695 in Brookfield, Worcester, Massachusetts. He died on 13 Feb 1781 in Brookfield, Worcester, Massachusetts, United States. Thomas married (MRIN:387) Judith GOSS-710 on 1 Dec 1718 in Brookfield, MA..

103. **Judith GOSS**-710 was born on 10 Apr 1699 in Lancaster, Worcester, Massachusetts, United States. She was christened in 1699 in Connecticut, United States. She died. She was buried about 1775 in Massachusetts, United States.

104. **Richard LYMAN IV**-711 was born in Apr 1678 in Northampton, Hampshire, Massachusetts, United States. He died on 3 Jun 1746 in Lebanon, New London, Connecticut, United States. He was buried in Jun 1746 in Lebanon, New London, Connecticut, United States. Richard married (MRIN:388) Mary WOODWARD-712 on 7 Apr 1700 in Lebanon, New London, Connecticut, United States.

105. **Mary WOODWARD**-712 was born on 26 Feb 1678 in Northampton, Hampshire, Massachusetts, United States. She died on 6 Jun 1746 in Lebanon, New London, Connecticut, United States. She was buried on 6 Jun 1746 in Lebanon, New London, Connecticut, United States.

106. **Joseph BRADFORD**-713 was born on 9 Apr 1702 in Lebanon, New London, Connecticut, United States. He was christened in Norwich, New London, Connecticut, United States. He died on 5 Jan 1778 in Haddam, Middlesex, Connecticut. Joseph married (MRIN:389) Heniretta SWIFT-714 in Mar 1729/1730 in New London, CT.

107. **Heniretta SWIFT**-714 was born in 1701 in New London, New London, Connecticut, United States. She died on 9 Oct 1758 in Higganum, Haddam, Middlesex, Connecticut, United States.

112. **Johannes Peter CLEMENTS**-715 was born on 8 Nov 1702 in Flammersfeld, Altenkirchen, Rhineland, Prussia, Germany. He was christened on 11 Nov 1702 in Flammersfeld, Altenkirchen, Rhineland, Prussia, Germany. He died on 31 Oct 1780 in Beekman, Dutchess, New York, United States. He was buried in Nov 1780 in Flushing, Queens, New York, United States. Johannes married (MRIN:390) Maritie Mary MEY-716 on 25 Jun 1727 in Tarrytown, Westchester, New York.

113. **Maritie Mary MEY**-716 was born in 1706 in , , Netherlands. She was christened in 1706 in Netherlands. She died in Nov 1780 in Flushing, Queens, New York, United States.

114. **James SEELEY**-717 was born about 1735 in Bedford, Westchester, New York, Usa. He died on 10 Feb 1819 in Stillwater, Saratoga, New York, United States. He was buried in Stillwater, Saratoga, New York, United States. James married (MRIN:391) Elizabeth BROWN-718 about 1750 in Stillwater, Saratoga, NY.

115. **Elizabeth BROWN**-718 was born in 1736 in Bedford, Westchester, New York, United States. She died on 25 Jan 1828 in Stillwater, Saratoga, New York, United States. She was buried in Stillwater, Saratoga, New York, United States.

120. **Johann Adam WENTZEL**-719 died. Johann married (MRIN:392) Anna Margaretha NICKEL-720 on 4 May 1742 in Evangelisch, Seeheim, Starkenburg, Hesse-Darmstadt.

121. **Anna Margaretha NICKEL**-720 was born on 24 Sep 1713 in Seeheim, Bensheim, Starkenburg, Hessen, Germany. She was christened in 1713 in Seeheim, Bensheim, Starkenburg, Hessen, Germany. She died on 24 Sep 1751 in Seeheim, Bensheim, Starkenburg, Hessen, Germany.

124. **Dea. William SAVAGE**-721 was born on 18 Sep 1699 in Middletown, Middlesex, Connecticut, United States. He died on 16 Apr 1774 in Middletown, Middlesex, Connecticut, United States. He was buried in 1774 in Cromwell, Middlesex, Connecticut, United States. William married (MRIN:393) Sarah SAVAGE-722 on 2 Jun 1726 in Connecticut, United States.

125. **Sarah SAVAGE**-722 was born on 2 Sep 1700 in Middletown, Middlesex, Connecticut, United States. She was christened on 8 Sep 1700 in First Church, Middletown, Middlesex, Connecticut, United States. She died on 10 Aug 1782 in Cromwell, Middlesex, Connecticut, United States. She was buried in 1782 in Cromwell Church, Cromwell, Middlesex, Connecticut, United States.

126. **John GIPSON**-725 was born on 28 Sep 1708 in Middleton, Middlesex, Connecticut. He died on 24 Jul 1757 in Middletown, Middlesex, Connecticut, United States. John married (MRIN:395) Marcy SAGE-726 on 27 Dec 1733 in Middletown, Middlesex, CT.

127. **Marcy SAGE**-726 was born on 20 Jan 1711 in Middletown, Middlesex, Connecticut, United States. She died on 24 Mar 1761 in Middletown, Middlesex, Connecticut, United States.

Eighth Generation

128. **Hans Joerg VOLLMER**-4743 was born about 1665 in Freudenstein, Maulbronn, Neckarkreis, Württemberg, Germany. He was christened in 1665 in Neckarkreis, Wuerttemberg, Germany. He died on 22 Apr 1745 in Roßwag, Vaihingen, Neckarkreis, Württemberg, Germany. Hans married (MRIN:3966) Anna BECK-4744 on 9 Jun 1696 in Kohlstetten, Donaukreis, Württemberg, Germany.

129. **Anna BECK**-4744 was born on 11 Mar 1671 in Kohlstetten, Münsingen, Donaukreis, Württemberg, Germany. She was christened on 11 Mar 1671 in Kohlstetten, Münsingen, Donaukreis, Württemberg, Germany. She died on 1 Jan 1710 in Roßwag, Vaihingen, Neckarkreis, Württemberg, Germany. She was buried in Roßwag, Vaihingen, Neckarkreis, Württemberg, Germany.

130. **Michael RAU**-4793 was born on 9 Apr 1665 in Eberdingen, Vaihingen, Neckarkreis, Württemberg, Germany. He was christened on 9 Apr 1665 in Wuerttemberg, Germany. He died on 10 Mar 1696 in Eberdingen, Vaihingen, Neckarkreis, Württemberg, Germany. Michael married (MRIN:3992) Anna Margaretha LUDWIG-4794 in 1683 in Eberdingen, Ludwigsburg, Baden-Württemberg, Germany.

131. **Anna Margaretha LUDWIG**-4794 was born about 1666 in Eberdingen, Vaihingen, Neckarkreis, Württemberg, Germany. She died about 1730.

132. **Moritz KARCHER Jr**-4851 was born on 21 Aug 1655 in Dobel, Neuenburg, W, Germany. He was christened in No Date. He died on 8 Sep 1727 in Rotensol, Neuenbürg, Schwarzwaldkreis, Württemberg, Germany. Moritz married (MRIN:4025) Margaret SIEB-4852.

133. **Margaret SIEB**-4852 was born about 1653 in Germany. She was christened on 25 Nov 1653 in Neuenburg, Schwarzwaldkreis, Wuerttemberg, Germany. She died on 31 May 1690 in Dobel, Neuenberg, Wuerttberg, Germany.

134. **Hanns Ludwig KNOELLER**-4861 was born on 2 Jan 1657 in Neusatz, Neuenbürg, Schwarzwaldkreis, Württemberg, Germany. He was christened on 22 Jan 1657 in Neuenburg, Schwarzwaldkreis, Wuerttemberg, Germany. He died on 2 May 1719 in Neusatz, Neuenbürg, Schwarzwaldkreis, Württemberg, Germany. Hanns married (MRIN:4030) Anna Maria-4862 about 1687 in of Neusatz, Neuenburg, Wuerttemberg.

135. **Anna Maria**-4862 was born about 1661 in Dobel, Neuenbuerg, Wurettemberg, Germany. She died in 1741.

137. **Anna Catharina HIRTZ**-4875 was born in Georg, Weierbach, Birkenfeld, Rheinland, Germany. She died. She was buried on 26 Apr 1674 in Oberstein, Birkenfeld, Oldenburg, Germany.

138. **Peter PURPUR**-4878 was born about 1652 in Oberstein, Birkenfeld, Oldenburg, Germany. He died. Peter married (MRIN:4041) Mrs. Peter PURPUR-4879 about 1676 in Of Oberstein, Birkenfeld, Oldenburg, Germany.

139. **Mrs. Peter PURPUR**-4879 was born about 1656 in Oberstein, Birkenfeld, Oldenburg, Germany. She died.

140. **Joseph KLEIN**-4880 was born in 1621 in Rhineland, Prussia, Germany. He was christened in 1629 in Windesheim, Bad Kreuznach, Rhineland, Prussia, Germany. He died on 24 May 1708 in Windesheim, Bad Kreuznach, Rhineland, Prussia, Germany. He was buried on 26 May 1708 in Windesheim, Bad Kreuznach, Rhineland, Prussia, Germany. Joseph married (MRIN:4042) Johanna FRANTZ-4881 about 1672 in Weiderscheim, Rhineland, Germany.

141. **Johanna FRANTZ**-4881 was born in 1633 in Windesheim, Bad Kreuznach, Rheinland-Pfalz, Germany. She died.

142. **Christoph SECKLER**-4914 was born about 1650 in Gensingen, Bingen, Rheinhessen, Hessen, Germany. He died. Christoph married (MRIN:4061) Mrs Christoph SECKLER-4915 about 1680 in Ginsingen, Rheinhessen, Hessen, Prussia.

143. **Mrs Christoph SECKLER**-4915 was born about 1655 in Preussen, Germany. She died.

144. **Von ZERFAS**-4936 was born about 1660 in Germany. He died. Von married (MRIN:4073) Jody BARTHOLEMEW-4937 about 1684 in Palatine Area, Germany.

145. **Jody BARTHOLEMEW**-4937 was born about 1664 in Germany. She died.

152. **Martin SCHULER**-4938 was born on 17 Sep 1658 in Wuerttemberg, Germany. He died on 25 Jan 1719. Martin married (MRIN:4074) Elisabetha HOFFMANN-4939 on 3 May 1681 in Haiterbach, Nagold, Württemberg.

153. **Elisabetha HOFFMANN**-4939 was born on 31 Jul 1656 in Haiterbach, Nagold, Schwarzwaldkreis, Württemberg, Germany. She died on 19 Jun 1736.

154. **Christian SCHULER**-4986 died on 9 Apr 1726 in Heselwangen, Balingen, Schwarzwaldkreis, Württemberg, Germany. Christian married (MRIN:4106) Catharina JETTER(IN)-4987 on 4 Jun 1695 in Heselwangen, Wuerttemberg, Germany.

155. **Catharina JETTER(IN)**-4987 died on 10 May 1704 in Heselwangen, Balingen, Schwarzwaldkreis, Württemberg, Germany.

Ninth Generation

256. **Hans Jerg VOLLMAR**-4745 was born in 1640 in Freudenstein, Neckar, Baden-Wuertemberg, Germany. He died before 9 Jun 1696 in Freudenstein, Neckar, Wuerttemberg, Germany.

258. **Hans BECK**-4746 was born on 31 Aug 1650 in Kohlstetten, Münsingen, Donaukreis, Württemberg, Germany. He was christened on 31 Aug 1650 in Kohlstetten, Münsingen, Donaukreis, Württemberg, Germany. He died on 17 Jan 1729 in Donaukreis, Wuerttemberg, Germany. He was buried on 17 Jan 1729. Hans married (MRIN:3968) Anna Maria TROESTER-4747 on 30 Oct 1669 in Kohlstetten, Donaukreis, Württemberg, Germany.

259. **Anna Maria TROESTER**-4747 was born in 1648 in Kohlstetten, Kohlstetten, Münsingen, Donaukreis, Württemberg, Germany. She died on 27 Oct 1678 in Kohlstetten, Kohlstetten, Münsingen, Donaukreis, Württemberg, Germany.

260. **Johannes RAU**-4795 was born on 13 Apr 1610 in Altburg, Calw, Schwarzwaldkreis, Württemberg,

Germany. He was christened on 13 Apr 1610 in Altburg, Calw, Schwarzwaldkreis, Württemberg, Germany. He died in Solingen, Rheinland, Preussen, Germany. Johannes married (MRIN:3993) Anna Maria TREIBER-4796 on 21 Jan 1662 in Eberdingen, Neckar, Wuerttemberg, Germany.

261. **Anna Maria TREIBER**-4796 was born on 24 Feb 1634 in Bad Wildbad im Schwarzwald, Neuenbürg, Schwarzwaldkreis, Württemberg, Germany. She died on 4 Sep 1693 in Eberdingen, Vaihingen, Neckarkreis, Württemberg, Germany.

264. **Moritz KARCHER**-4853 was born in 1600 in of Dobel, Neuenburg, W, Germany. He died on 18 Feb 1673 in Neckarkreis, Wuerttemberg, Germany. He was buried on 18 Feb 1673 in Neuenburg, Schwarzwaldkreis, Wuerttemberg, Germany. Moritz married (MRIN:4026) Anna Catharina KARCHER-4854.

265. **Anna Catharina KARCHER**-4854 was born in 1604 in Germany. She died in 1648 in Germany.

266. **Valentin SIEB**-4855 was born about 1630 in Württemberg, Rotenberg, Cannstatt, Württemberg, Germany. He was christened about 1630 in Reichental, Gernsbach, Rastatt, Baden, Baden, Germany. He died after 1694 in Bernbach, Wurttemberg, Germany. He was buried in Neuenburg, Schwarzwaldkreis, Wuerttemberg, Germany. Valentin married (MRIN:4027) Christina ZU ROTENSOL NEUENBUERG-4856 in 1659 in Baden-Württemberg, Germany.

267. **Christina ZU ROTENSOL NEUENBUERG**-4856 was born about 1636 in Dobel, Neuembuerg, Wuerttemberg, Germany. She was christened about 1645 in Of Bernbach, Wuerttemberg, Germany. She died on 5 Dec 1698 in Wuerttemberg, Germany. She was buried in Neuenburg, Schwarzwaldkreis, Wuerttemberg, Germany.

268. **Mathias KNOELLER**-4864 was born in Jan 1622 in Dobel, Calw, Baden-Württemberg, Germany. He was christened in Jan 1622 in Neuenburg, Schwarzwaldkreis, Wuerttemberg, Germany. He died on 31 May 1687. Mathias married (MRIN:4032) Martha RAU-4865 on 14 May 1650 in Dobel Neuenbuerg, Schwarzwaldkreis, Wuerttemberg.

269. **Martha RAU**-4865 was born on 20 Nov 1620 in Dobel, Calw, Baden-Württemberg, Germany. She was christened on 20 Nov 1626 in Neckarkreis, Wuerttemberg, Germany. She died on 24 Nov 1687. She was buried on 17 Nov 1695 in Dobel, Neuenburg, W, Germany.

274. **Debelt HIRTZ**-4876 was born about 1620 in Germany. He died in 1672. Debelt married (MRIN:4040) Mrs. Debelt HIRTZ-4877 in 1644 in Oberstein, Birkenfeld, Oldenburg, Rhineland, Germany.

275. **Mrs. Debelt HIRTZ**-4877 was born about 1624 in Germany. She died.

280. **Hans KLEIN**-4882 was born in 1595 in Bischmisheim, Saarbrücken, Rhineland, Prussia, Germany. He died before 9 Nov 1655 in Bischmisheim, Saarbrücken, Rhineland, Prussia, Germany. Hans married (MRIN:4043) Catharina SCHERER-4883 in 1620 in , , Prussia, (Germany).

281. **Catharina SCHERER**-4883 was born in 1595 in Bischmisheim, Saarbrücken, Rhineland, Prussia, Germany. She died on 24 Apr 1686 in Bischmisheim, Saarbrücken, Rhineland, Prussia, Germany.

282. **Eberhard FRANTZ**-4884 was born about 1610 in Kleinich, Bernkastel, Rhineland, Prussia, Germany. He died on 8 Mar 1690 in Kleinich, Bernkastel-Wittlich, Rheinland-Pfalz, Germany. He was buried on 8 Mar 1690 in Kleinich, Bernkastel-Wittlich, Rheinland-Pfalz, Germany. Eberhard married (MRIN:4044) Marie BAUR-4885 on 12 Aug 1632 in Evangelisch, Kleinich, Rheinland, Prussia.

283. **Marie BAUR**-4885 was born on 7 Oct 1603 in Hochscheid, Bernkastel, Rhineland, Prussia, Germany. She was christened on 7 Oct 1603 in Kleinich, Bernkastel, Rhineland, Prussia, Germany. She died on 10 May 1635 in Hochscheid, Bernkastel-Wittlich, Rheinland-Pfalz, Germany. She was buried on 10 May 1635 in Hochscheid, Bernkastel-Wittlich, Rheinland-Pfalz, Germany.

284. **Hans Ewald SECKLER**-4916 was born in 24 März 1616 in Manubach, Rheinland-Pfalz, Germany.

He was christened on 24 Mar 1616 in Manubach, Sankt Goar, Rhineland, Prussia, Germany. He died on 8 Nov 1676 in Manubach, Mainz-Bingen, Rheinland-Pfalz, Germany. Hans married (MRIN:4062) Catharine DIETZ-4917 on 31 Jan 1642 in Manubach, Mainz-Bingen, Rheinland-Pfalz, Germany.

285. **Catharine DIETZ**-4917 was born on 20 Feb 1625 in Steeg, Bacharach, Sankt Goar, Rhineland, Prussia, Germany. She was christened on 20 Feb 1625 in Steeg bei Bacharach, Rheinland, Preussen, Germany. She died on 11 Aug 1674 in Manubach, Palatinate, Bavaria, Germany.

304. **Hans Balthasar SCHULER**-4940 was born about 1620 in Kirchheim Unter Teck, Donaukreis, Wuerttemberg, Germany. He died on 3 Apr 1688 in Haiterbach, Calw, Baden-Württemberg, Germany. Hans married (MRIN:4075) Catarina EISELIN-4941 on 29 Jun 1647 in Haiterbach, Schwarzwaldkreis, Wuerttemberg.

305. **Catarina EISELIN**-4941 was born on 16 Feb 1618 in Deckenpfronn, Calw, Schwarzwaldkreis, Württemberg, Germany. She died on 15 Jan 1690 in Haiterbach, Calw, Baden-Württemberg, Germany.

306. **Andreas HOFFMANN**-4942 was born about 1630 in Oberiflingen, Schopfloch, Freudenstadt, Baden-Württemberg, Germany. He died. Andreas married (MRIN:4076) Agathe-4943 in <1655> in Haiterbach, Schwarzwald, Wuettemberg, Deutschland.

307. **Agathe**-4943 was born about 1640 in Oberiflingen, Schopfloch, Freudenstadt, Baden-Württemberg, Germany. She died. She was buried on 10 Jan 1679 in Oberiflingen, Freudenstadt, Schwarzwaldkreis, Württemberg, Germany.

Tenth Generation

512. **Martin VOLLMAR**-4748 was born on 13 Jul 1606 in Mötzingen, Herrenberg, Schwarzwaldkreis, Württemberg, Germany. He was christened on 9 Nov 1621 in Ehingen, Rottenburg am Neckar, Rottenburg, Schwarzwaldkreis, Württemberg, Germany. He died on 26 Sep 1635 in Öschelbronn, Waiblingen, Neckarkreis, Württemberg, Germany. Martin married (MRIN:3969) Margaretha BREINING-4749.

513. **Margaretha BREINING**-4749 was born in 1597 in Bondorf, Saulgau, Donaukreis, Württemberg, Germany. She died.

516. **Jerg BECK**-4750 was born in 1628 in Kohlstetten, Münsingen, Donaukreis, Württemberg, Germany. He died on 26 May 1675 in Kohlstetten, Münsingen, Donaukreis, Württemberg, Germany. Jerg married (MRIN:3970) Rosina BECK-4751 in 1646 in of Kohlstetten, Donau, Wuerttemberg.

517. **Rosina BECK**-4751 was born in Dec 1628 in Kohlstetten, Engstingen, Reutlingen, Baden-Württemberg, Germany. She died on 26 May 1675 in Donaukreis, Wuerttemberg, Germany.

518. **Ludvig TROESTER**-4752 was born about 1612 in Kohlstetten, Münsingen, Donaukreis, Württemberg, Germany. He died on 9 May 1675 in Kohlstetten, Kohlstetten, Münsingen, Württemberg, Germany. Ludvig married (MRIN:3971) Barbara TROESTER-4753 about 1647 in Kohlstetten, Donaukreis, Württemberg, Germany.

519. **Barbara TROESTER**-4753 was born about 1616 in Kohlstetten, Kohlstetten, Münsingen, Württemberg, Germany. She died on 15 Apr 1674 in Kohlstetten, Kohlstetten, Münsingen, Württemberg, Germany.

520. **Hans RAU**-4798 was born on 24 Dec 1577 in Altburg, Calw, Schwarzwaldkreis, Württemberg, Germany. He was christened on 6 Mar 1577 in Speßhardt, Calw, Calw, Schwarzwaldkreis, Württemberg, Germany. He died before 1687. Hans married (MRIN:3995) Helene Magdalena SEITZ-4799 on 28 Feb 1606/1607.

521. **Helene Magdalena SEITZ**-4799 was born on 3 Aug 1580 in Haugestett, Schwarzwald, Baden-Wuerttemberg, Germany. She was christened on 13 Aug 1580 in Schwarzwaldkreis, Württemberg, Germany. She died before 1690.

522. **Hans Jacob TREIBER**-4800 was born on 16 Sep 1613 in Wildbach, Schwarzw, Wuerttemberg, Germany. He died on 21 Sep 1682. He was buried on 21 Sep 1682 in Wildbad, Neuenbürg, Schwarzwaldkreis, Württemberg, Germany. Hans married (MRIN:3996) Dorethea LANG-4801 on 24 Jan 1631 in Wildbad, Neuenbürg, Schwarzwaldkreis, Württemberg, Germany.

523. **Dorethea LANG**-4801 was born in 1607 in Wildbad, Neuenbürg, Schwarzwaldkreis, Wuerttemberg, Germany. She died in UNKNOWN.

532. **Jacob SIEB**-4857 was born about 1602 in Wuerttemberg, Germany. He died in Oct 1649 in Württemberg, Germany. Jacob married (MRIN:4028) Anna Else Margritta ROHNS-4858 in 1622 in Wuerttemberg, Germany.

533. **Anna Else Margritta ROHNS**-4858 was born about 1603 in Wuerttemberg, Germany. She died.

537. **M**-4866 was born in 1594 in Dobel Neuenbuerg, Schwarzwaldkreis, Wuerttemberg, Germany. She died.

538. **Elias RAU**-4869 was born on 23 Apr 1592 in Dobel, Neuenbürg, Schwarzwaldkreis, Württemberg, Germany. He was christened on 23 Apr 1592 in Neuenburg, Schwarzwaldkreis, Wuerttemberg, Germany. He died on 21 Feb 1668 in Dobel, Neuenbürg, Schwarzwaldkreis, Württemberg, Germany. Elias married (MRIN:4036) Rosina STAHL-4870 on 2 Mar 1614/1615 in Dobel, Germany.

539. **Rosina STAHL**-4870 was born about 1598 in Dobel, Neuenbuerg, Wurettemberg, Germany. She died before 1660.

560. **Nickel KLEIN**-4886 was born in 1575 in Bischmisheim, Saarbrücken, Rhineland, Prussia, Germany. He died in 1621 in Bischmisheim, Saarbrücken, Rhineland, Prussia, Germany. Nickel married (MRIN:4045) Gertraud BECKER-4887 in 1593 in Bischmisheim, Saarbruchen, Germany.

561. **Gertraud BECKER**-4887 was born in 1576 in Germany. She died in 1621 in Bischmisheim, Saarbrücken, Rhineland, Prussia, Germany.

562. **Engeland SCHERER**-4888 was born about 1570 in Bischmisheim, Saarbrücken, Rhineland, Prussia, Germany. He died before 1622. Engeland married (MRIN:4046) Engel KLEIN-4889 about 1605 in of, Bischmisheim, Saar, Germany.

563. **Engel KLEIN**-4889 was born about 1570 in Bischmisheim, Saarbrücken, Rhineland, Prussia, Germany. She died before 11 Jun 1624.

564. **Eberhard FRANTZ**-4890 was born about 1590 in Irmenach, Bernkastel-Wittlich, Rheinland-Pfalz, Germany. He died on 30 Jan 1614 in Kleinich, Bernkastel-Wittlich, Rheinland-Pfalz, Germany. Eberhard married (MRIN:4047) Elisabetha HERBERTS-4891 about 1609 in Kleinich, , Rheinland-Pfalz, Germany.

565. **Elisabetha HERBERTS**-4891 was born about 1590 in Irmenach, Bernkastel-Wittlich, Rheinland-Pfalz, Germany. She died on 6 Nov 1632 in Kleinich, Bernkastel-Wittlich, Rheinland-Pfalz, Germany. She was buried on 6 Nov 1632 in Kleinich, Bernkastel-Wittlich, Rheinland-Pfalz, Germany.

566. **Hans BAUR**-4892 died. Hans married (MRIN:4048) Geze-4893.

567. **Geze**-4893 died.

568. **Johannes, Hans der Jüngste SECKLER**-4918 was born about 1589 in Manubach, Sankt Goar, Rhineland, Prussia, Germany. He died on 7 May 1669 in Manubach, Sankt Goar, Rhineland, Prussia, Germany. Johannes, married (MRIN:4063) Sophia KOCH-4919 on 19 Nov 1610 in Evangelisch, Manubach, Rheinland, Prussia.

569. **Sophia KOCH**-4919 was born on 26 Mar 1592 in Manubach, Mainz-Bingen, Rheinland-Pfalz, Germany. She was christened on 26 Mar 1592 in Manubach, Sankt Goar, Rhineland, Prussia, Germany. She died on 23 Oct 1620 in Manubach, Rheinland-Pfalz, Germany.

570. **Nikolaus DIETZ**-4920 was born about 1595 in Rheindiebach, Oberdiebach, Sankt Goar, Rhineland, Prussia, Germany. He died on 31 Jan 1642 in Steeg, Bacharach, Bacharach, Sankt Goar, Rhineland, Prussia, Germany. Nikolaus married (MRIN:4064) Maria Elisabeth HOLZ-4921 in 12 Juli 1619 in Steeg, Bacharach, Sankt Goar, Rheinland, Preußen, Deutschland.

571. **Maria Elisabeth HOLZ**-4921 was born about 1599 in Steeg, Bacharach, Sankt Goar, Rhineland, Prussia, Germany. She died.

608. **Andreas SCHULER**-4944 was born on 6 Jan 1594 in Kirchheim Unter Teck, Donaukreis, Wuerttemberg, Germany. He died on 23 Mar 1662 in Haiterbach, Calw, Karlsruhe, Baden-Württemberg, Germany. He was buried on 23 Mar 1662 in Haiterbach, Calw, Baden-Württemberg, Germany. Andreas married (MRIN:4077) Sara WEIßGERBER-4945 on 21 Apr 1617 in Calw, Schwarzwald, Württemberg.

609. **Sara WEIßGERBER**-4945 was born in 1595 in Calw, Schwarzwaldkreis, Württemberg, Germany. She died in 1645 in Haiterbach, Calw, Karlsruhe, Baden-Württemberg, Germany.

610. **Hans EISELIN**-4946 was born on 6 Mar 1591 in Sulz, Nagold, Schwarzwaldkreis, Württemberg, Germany. He died. Hans married (MRIN:4078) Ursula WALTZ-4947 on 19 Apr 1616 in Deckenpfronn, Calw, Schwarzwaldkreis, Württemberg, Germany.

611. **Ursula WALTZ**-4947 was born on 27 Oct 1595 in Merklingen, Leonberg, Neckarkreis, Württemberg, Germany. She died.

Eleventh Generation

1024. **Conrad VOLMAR**-4754 was born about 1581 in Mötzingen, Mötzingen, Herrenberg, Schwarzwaldkreis, Württemberg, Germany. He died in Sep 1614 in of Mötzingen, Schwarzwaldkreis, Württemberg, Germany. Conrad married (MRIN:3972) Marga VOLMAR-4755 about 1606 in Motzingen, Germany.

1025. **Marga VOLMAR**-4755 was born about 1586 in Mötzingen, Herrenberg, Schwarzwaldkreis, Württemberg, Germany. She died in Sep 1614 in Mötzingen, Herrenberg, Schwarzwaldkreis, Württemberg, Germany.

1026. **Hans " Deissen Hans" BREUNING**-4758 was born in 1558 in Böblingen, Neckarkreis, Württemberg, Germany. He died in 1622 in Württemberg, Germany. Hans married (MRIN:3974) Anna BERTSCH-4759 on 13 Feb 1581 in Böblingen, Neckarkreis, Württemberg, Germany.

1027. **Anna BERTSCH**-4759 was born on 30 Mar 1560 in Iselshausen, Nagold, Schwarzwaldkreis, Württemberg, Germany. She was christened on 10 Apr 1560 in Iselshausen, Nagold, Württemberg, Germany. She died in 1622 in Bondorf, Herrenberg, Württemberg, Germany.

1032. **Jacob BECK**-4760 died. Jacob married (MRIN:3975) Maria Apollonia HAEHN-4761 in 1627 in Kohlstetten, Donau, Wuerttemberg, Germany.

1033. **Maria Apollonia HAEHN**-4761 was born in 1608. She died on 12 May 1688.

1036. **TROESTER**-4764 was born about 1585 in Germany. He died. TROESTER married (MRIN:3977) Mrs. Troester-4765 about 1610 in Germany.

1037. **Mrs. Troester**-4765 was born in 1592 in Donaukreis, Wuerttemberg, Germany. She died.

1040. **Conrad RAU Jr.**-4802 was born in 1541 in Speßhardt, Calw, Calw, Schwarzwaldkreis, Württemberg, Germany. He was christened in 1542 in Speßhardt, Calw, Calw, Schwarzwaldkreis, Württemberg, Germany. He died before 1607. Conrad married (MRIN:3997) Agnes HIRNLEN-4803 in 5 MAR 15755 Mar 1575/1576 in Altburg, Schwartzwald, Württemberg, Germany.

1041. **Agnes HIRNLEN**-4803 was born in 1555 in Naislach, Würzbach, Calw, Schwarzwaldkreis, Württemberg, Germany. She was christened in 1555 in Schwarzwaldkreis, Wuerttemberg, Germany. She died.

1042. **Hans Sebastian Georg Bernherd SEITZ**-4804 was born on 18 Jan 1549 in Liebelsberg, Neubulach, Calw, Baden-Württemberg, Germany. He was christened in Rhodt, Palatinate, Bavaria, Germany. He died in 1610 in Rhodt, Rhodt unter Rietburg, Südliche Weinstraße, Rheinland-Pfalz, Germany. He was buried in Rheinland-Pfalz Lande, Germany. Hans married (MRIN:3998) Anna SCHURER-4805.

1043. **Anna SCHURER**-4805 was born about 1550 in Rohrau, Herrenberg, Schwarzwaldkreis, Württemberg, Germany. She died.

1044. **Johannes TREIBER**-4807 was born on 22 Jan 1583 in Nagold, Schwarzwaldkreis, Württemberg, Germany. He died. Johannes married (MRIN:4000) Catharina HOEFFEL OR HEFEL-4808 in 1605 in Wildbad, Schwarzw, Württemberg, Germany.

1045. **Catharina HOEFFEL OR HEFEL**-4808 was born on 31 Dec 1582 in Ehningen, Böblingen, Neckarkreis, Württemberg, Germany. She was christened on 31 Dec 1582 in Ehningen, Böblingen, Neckarkreis, Württemberg, Germany. She died.

1046. **Stephen Oswald LANG**-4809 was born on 5 Aug 1568 in Wildbad, Neuenbürg, Schwarzwaldkreis, Württemberg, Germany. He died. Stephen married (MRIN:4001) Barbara-4810 about 1591 in Wildbad, Neuenbürg, Schwarzwaldkreis, Wuerttemberg, Germany.

1047. **Barbara**-4810 was born in 1570 in Wildbad, Neuenbürg, Schwarzwaldkreis, Württemberg, Germany. She died.

1064. **Caspar SIEB**-4859 was born in 1591 in Reichental, Gernsbach, Rastatt, Baden, Baden, Germany. He died. Caspar married (MRIN:4029) Barbara-4860 in 1693 in Reichenthal, East Prussia, Germany.

1065. **Barbara**-4860 was born in aproximadamente 1580 in Reichental, Gernsbach, Rastatt, Baden, Germany. She died.

1076. **Johannes RAU**-4871 was born about 1560 in Neusatz, Calw, Germany. He died on 20 Apr 1613 in Neusatz, Neuenbürg, Schwarzwaldkreis, Württemberg, Germany. Johannes married (MRIN:4037) Martha-4872.

1077. **Martha**-4872 was born in 1564 in Neusatz, Neuenbürg, Schwarzwaldkreis, Württemberg, Germany. She died.

1078. **Johann STAHL**-4873 was born in 1564 in Dobel Neuenbuerg, Schwarzwaldkreis, Wuerttemberg, Germany. He died. Johann married (MRIN:4038) Mrs. Johann STAHL-4874 in 1595 in Of, Dobel Neuenbuerg, Srz, Wrt.

1079. **Mrs. Johann STAHL**-4874 was born in 1568 in Dobel Neuenbuerg, Schwarzwaldkreis, Wuerttemberg, Germany. She died.

1120. **Johannes Hans KLEIN**-4894 was born in 1550 in Bischmisheim, Saarbrücken, Rhineland, Prussia, Germany. He died in Bischmisheim, Saarbrücken, Rhineland, Prussia, Germany. Johannes married (MRIN:4049) Margaretha KLEINEN-4895 in 1570 in Bischmisheim, Saarbruchen, Germany.

1121. **Margaretha KLEINEN**-4895 was born in 1550 in Bischmisheim, Saarbrücken, Rhineland, Prussia, Germany. She died in Bischmisheim, Saarbrücken, Rhineland, Prussia, Germany.

1122. **Nickel BECKER**-4896 was born about 1549 in Bischmisheim, Saarbrücken, Rhineland, Prussia,

Germany. He died about 1625 in Bischmisheim, Saarbrücken, Rhineland, Prussia, Germany.

1124. **Hans SCHERER**-4897 was born about 1535 in Bischmisheim, Saarbrücken, Rhineland, Prussia, Germany. He died before 1587. Hans married (MRIN:4051) Meyet-4898 about 1569 in of, Bischmisheim, Saar, Germany.

1125. **Meyet**-4898 was born about 1539 in Bischmisheim, Saarbrücken, Rhineland, Prussia, Germany. She died.

1126. **Meyets Hans KLEIN**-4899 was born about 1534 in Bischmisheim, Saarbrücken, Rhineland, Prussia, Germany. He died in 1622/1626. Meyets married (MRIN:4052) Gertrud-4900 before 25 Jan 1591 in of, Bischmisheim, Saar, Germany.

1127. **Gertrud**-4900 was born about 1540 in Bischmisheim, Saarbrücken, Rhineland, Prussia, Germany. She died before 6 May 1616.

1128. **Hans FRANTZ**-4901 was born about 1560 in Irmenach, Bernkastel-Wittlich, Rheinland-Pfalz, Germany. He died on 7 Nov 1597 in Kleinich, Bernkastel-Wittlich, Rheinland-Pfalz, Germany. He was buried on 7 Nov 1597 in Kleinich, Bernkastel-Wittlich, Rheinland-Pfalz, Germany. Hans married (MRIN:4053) Eva TRONER-4902 about 1585 in Kleinich, , Rheinland-Pfalz, Germany.

1129. **Eva TRONER**-4902 was born about 1565 in Kleinich, Bernkastel-Wittlich, Rheinland-Pfalz, Germany. She died on 19 Apr 1621 in Kleinich, Bernkastel-Wittlich, Rheinland-Pfalz, Germany. She was buried on 19 Apr 1621 in Kleinich, Bernkastel-Wittlich, Rheinland-Pfalz, Germany.

1130. **Hamman HERBERTS**-4903 was born about 1550 in Irmenach, Bernkastel-Wittlich, Rheinland-Pfalz, Germany. He died after 1590 in Irmenach, Bernkastel-Wittlich, Rheinland-Pfalz, Germany. Hamman married (MRIN:4054) HERBERTS-4904.

1131. **HERBERTS**-4904 was born about 1550 in Germany. She died.

1136. **Hans (dit Roosen Hans) SECKLER**-4922 was born about 1564 in Manubach, Sankt Goar, Rhineland, Prussia, Germany. He died on 19 Jun 1634 in Manubach, Sankt Goar, Rhineland, Prussia, Germany. Hans married (MRIN:4065) Elizabeth ROOS-4923 on 22 Jan 1588 in Manubach, Sankt Goar, Rheinland, Preußen, Deutschland.

1137. **Elizabeth ROOS**-4923 was born about 1565 in Manubach, Sankt Goar, Rhineland, Prussia, Germany. She died on 24 Jun 1602 in Manubach, Sankt Goar, Rhineland, Prussia, Germany.

1138. **Heinrich KOCH**-4924 was born in Oberdiebach, Mainz-Bingen, Rheinland-Pfalz, Germany. He died on 23 Jan 1604 in Manubach, Mainz-Bingen, Rheinland-Pfalz, Germany. Heinrich married (MRIN:4066) Katharina-4925 on 19 Jan 1579 in Manubach, Rhineland, Germany.

1139. **Katharina**-4925 was born about 1556 in Oberdiebach, Mainz-Bingen, Rheinland-Pfalz, Germany. She died on 21 Oct 1608 in Oberdiebach, Mainz-Bingen, Rheinland-Pfalz, Germany.

1140. **Johannis DEUTZ**-4926 was born in gegen 1570. He died.

1142. **Johannes HOLZ**-4927 was born about 1575 in Steeg, Bacharach, Sankt Goar, Rhineland, Prussia, Germany. He died.

1216. **Johann SCHULER**-4948 was born in 1554 in Göppingen, Göppingen, Baden-Württemberg, Germany. He died in 1616 in Kirchheim unter Teck, Esslingen, Stuttgart, Baden-Württemberg, Germany. Johann married (MRIN:4079) Monica OSIANDER-4949 on 9 Apr 1578 in Stuttgart Collegiate Church, Stuttgart, Württemberg.

1217. **Monica OSIANDER**-4949 was born in 1559 in Blaubeuren, Alb-Donau-Kreis, Baden-Württemberg, Germany. She died on 23 Jul 1611.

1218. **Leonhard WEISSGERBER**-4950 was born about 1568 in Calw, Baden-Württemberg, Germany. He died. Leonhard married (MRIN:4080) Mrs. Leonhard WEISSGERBER-4951 about 1595 in

Calw, Baden-Wuerttemberg, Germany.

1219. **Mrs. Leonhard WEISSGERBER**-4951 was born about 1577 in Calw, Baden-Württemberg, Germany. She died.

1220. **Hans EISELIN**-4952 was born about 1562 in Sulz, Nagold, Schwarzwaldkreis, Württemberg, Germany. He died. Hans married (MRIN:4081) Margaretha-4953 about 1587 in Sulz, Nagold, Schwarzwaldkreis, Württemberg, Germany.

1221. **Margaretha**-4953 was born about 1566 in Sulz, Nagold, Schwarzwaldkreis, Württemberg, Germany. She died.

1222. **Jacob WALTZ**-4954 was born about 1566 in Haslach, Herrenberg, Schwarzwaldkreis, Württemberg, Germany. He died. Jacob married (MRIN:4082) Barbara HILTPURG-4955 on 23 Aug 1591 in Merklingen, Leonberg, Neckarkreis, Württemberg, Germany.

1223. **Barbara HILTPURG**-4955 was born about 1570 in Merklingen, Leonberg, Neckarkreis, Württemberg, Germany. She died.

Twelfth Generation

2048. **Martin VOLMAR**-4766 was born about 1553 in Öschelbronn, Herrenberg, Schwarzwaldkreis, Württemberg, Germany. He died in Mötzingen, Herrenberg, Schwarzwaldkreis, Württemberg, Germany. Martin married (MRIN:3978) Maria HARER-4767 on 27 Oct 1578 in Mötzingen, Schwarzwaldkreis, Württemberg, Germany.

2049. **Maria HARER**-4767 was born about 1557 in Mötzingen, Herrenberg, Schwarzwaldkreis, Württemberg, Germany. She died in Mötzingen, Herrenberg, Schwarzwaldkreis, Württemberg, Germany.

2052. **Matthaeus BREINING**-4768 was born in 1520 in Bondorf, Böblingen, Baden-Württemberg, Germany. He died in 1573 in Bondorf, Böblingen, Baden-Württemberg, Germany. Matthaeus married (MRIN:3979) Barbara-4769 in 1548 in Bondorf, Böblingen, Baden-Württemberg, Germany.

2053. **Barbara**-4769 died.

2054. **Jacob BERTSCH**-4770 was born in 1528 in Nebringen, Herrenberg, Schwarzwaldkreis, Württemberg, Germany. He died in 1598 in Nebringen, Herrenberg, Schwarzwaldkreis, Württemberg, Germany. Jacob married (MRIN:3980) Barbara SANWALD-4771 in 1552 in Iselshausen, Nagold, Württemberg, Germany.

2055. **Barbara SANWALD**-4771 was born in 1530 in Ottendorf, Gaildorf, Jagstkreis, Württemberg, Germany. She died in 1578 in Jagstkreis, Württemberg, Germany.

2080. **Lucas MÜLLER I**-4811 was born in 1490 in Altburg, Calw, Schwarzwaldkreis, Württemberg, Germany. He was christened in 1516 in Speßhardt, Calw, Calw, Schwarzwaldkreis, Württemberg, Germany. He died on 1 Dec 1560 in Augsburg, Augsburg, Schwaben, Bavaria, Germany. He was buried on 10 Jul 1689 in Eberdingen, Vaihingen, Neckarkreis, Württemberg, Germany. Lucas married (MRIN:4002) Margaretha-4812.

2081. **Margaretha**-4812 was born in Altburg, Schwarzw, Wuerttemberg, Germany. She was christened in 1620 in Spesshardt, Schwarzwald, Wuerttemberg, Germany. She died.

2082. **Hans HIRNLEN**-4814 was born in 1530 in Naislach, Oberreichenbach, Calw, Schwarzwaldkreis, Württemberg, Germany. He died. Hans married (MRIN:4004) Anna-4815 in 1553 in Naislach, Calw, Calw, Schwarzwaldkreis, Württemberg, Germany.

2083. **Anna**-4815 was born in 1533 in Schwarzwaldkreis, Württemberg, Germany. She was christened in 1533 in Schwarzwaldkreis, Wuerttemberg, Germany. She died before 1643.

2084. **Hans Sebastian Jacob SEITZ**-4816 was born about 1510 in Germany. He died in 1610 in Rheinland-Pfalz, GermanyUnknown. Hans married (MRIN:4005) Anna WOLFF-4806.

2085. **Anna WOLFF**-4806 was born about 1550 in Liebelsberg, Schwarzwald, Wuerttemberg, Germany. She died on 3 Apr 1620 in Rhodt, Rhodt unter Rietburg, Südliche Weinstraße, Rheinland-Pfalz, Germany. She was buried in 1620.

2086. **Gabriel SCHURER**-4817 was born about 1525 in Rohrau, Herrenberg, Schwarzwaldkreis, Württemberg, Germany. He died. Gabriel married (MRIN:4006) Katharina-4818 about 1549 in Rohrau, Herrenberg, Schwarzwaldkreis, Württemberg, Germany.

2087. **Katharina**-4818 was born about 1528 in Rohrau, Herrenberg, Schwarzwaldkreis, Württemberg, Germany. She died.

2088. **Hans Michael TREIBER**-4821 was born on 8 Sep 1560 in Nagold, Schwarzwaldkreis, Württemberg, Germany. He died. Hans married (MRIN:4008) Margaretha GASSENMUELLER-4822 on 5 Jul 1581 in Wildbad, Neuenbürg, Schwarzwaldkreis, Württemberg, Germany.

2089. **Margaretha GASSENMUELLER**-4822 was born on 12 Feb 1560 in Wildbad, Neuenbürg, Schwarzwaldkreis, Württemberg, Germany. She died.

2090. **Hans HOEFFEL**-4823 was born in 1555 in Naislach, Oberreichenbach, Calw, Schwarzwaldkreis, Württemberg, Germany. He died in 1617 in Württemberg, Germany. Hans married (MRIN:4009) Barbara KEPPELER-4824 in 1581 in Naislach, Oberreichenbach, Calw, Schwarzwaldkreis, Württemberg, Germany.

2091. **Barbara KEPPELER**-4824 was born on 7 Jun 1555 in Bitz, Balingen, Württemberg, Germany. She was christened on 7 Jun 1555 in Bitz, Balingen, Württemberg, Germany. She died in 1603 in Württemberg, Germany.

2092. **Peter LANG**-4826 was born about 1540 in Wildbad, Neuenbürg, Schwarzwaldkreis, Württemberg, Germany. He died. Peter married (MRIN:4011) Margaretha KUCH-4827 on 3 Sep 1565 in Wildbad, Schwarzwald, Wuertt., Germany.

2093. **Margaretha KUCH**-4827 was born about 1544 in Wildbad, Neuenbürg, Schwarzwaldkreis, Württemberg, Germany. She was christened on 11 Jul 1570 in Wildbad, Neuenbürg, Schwarzwaldkreis, Württemberg, Germany. She died.

2240. **Clesgin BALLIERER- BOHRER**-4906 was born in 1510 in Bischmisheim, Saarbrücken, Rhineland, Prussia, Germany. He died in 1583 in Engelfangen, Saarbrücken, Saarland, Germany. Clesgin married (MRIN:4057) Mrs. BALLIERER- BOHRER-4907 about 1534 in of, Bischmisheim, Saar, Germany.

2241. **Mrs. BALLIERER- BOHRER**-4907 was born in 1510 in Bischmisheim, Saarbrücken, Rhineland, Prussia, Germany. She died.

2244. **Jacob BECKER**-4908 was born in 1553 in Bischmisheim, Saarbrücken, Saar District, Germany. He died on 27 Feb 1622 in Bischmisheim, Saarbrücken, Saarland, Germany. Jacob married (MRIN:4058) Catharina BECKER-4909.

2245. **Catharina BECKER**-4909 was born in 1550 in Germany. She died on 27 Feb 1624 in Germany.

2272. **Jacob SECKLER**-4928 was born in 1528 in Manubach, Rheinland, Germany. He died in 19 março 1608 in Manubach, Rheinland, Germany. Jacob married (MRIN:4069) Elisabetha-4929 in gegen 1562 in Manubach, Rheinland-Pfalz, Alemanha.

2273. **Elisabetha**-4929 was born in gegen 1541 in Manubach, Mainz-Bingen, Rheinland-Pfalz, Deutschland. She died.

2274. **Hans ROOS**-4930 was born in gegen 1538 in Manubach, Sankt Goar, Rheinland, Preußen, Deutschland. He died on 27 Jan 1595 in Manubach, Sankt Goar, Rheinland, Preußen, Deutschland. Hans married (MRIN:4070) Catharina-4931 in gegen 1560 in Manubach, Sankt Goar, Rheinland, Preußen, Deutschland.

2275. **Catharina**-4931 was born in gegen 1540. She died on 6 Aug 1601 in Manubach, Sankt Goar, Rheinland, Preußen, Deutschland.

2276. **Hans KOCH**-4932 was born in aproximadamente 1525 in Oberdiebach, Mainz-Bingen, Rheinland-Pfalz, Alemanha. He died in Alemanha. Hans married (MRIN:4071) Mrs Hans KOCH-4933 about 1553 in Manubach, Rheinland, Prussia.

2277. **Mrs Hans KOCH**-4933 was born about 1533 in Manubach, Rheinland, Prussia. She died.

2432. **Peter SCHULER**-4956 was born about 1520 in Goppingen, Donaukreis, Wuerttemberg, Germany. He died. Peter married (MRIN:4083) Mrs. Peter SCHULER-4957 about 1550 in Goeppingen, Baden-Wuerttemberg, Germany.

2433. **Mrs. Peter SCHULER**-4957 was born about 1530 in Göppingen, Baden-Württemberg, Germany. She died.

2434. **Lucas OSIANDER**-4958 was born on 16 Dec 1534 in Nürnberg, Nürnberg, Middle Franconia, Bavaria, Germany. He died on 17 Sep 1604 in Stuttgart, Stuttgart, Baden-Württemberg, Germany. He was buried on 19 Sep 1604 in Stuttgart, Stuttgart, Baden-Württemberg, Germany. Lucas married (MRIN:4084) Margarete ENTRINGER-4959 in 1555 in Tubingen, Baden-Wuerttemberg, Germany.

2435. **Margarete ENTRINGER**-4959 was born in Jun 1524 in Tübingen, Tubingen, Baden-Württemberg, Germany. She died on 16 Jan 1566 in Stuttgart, Baden-Württemberg, Germany.

2440. **ICLIN**-4960 was born about 1510 in Schwarzwaldkreis, Württemberg, Germany. He died.

2444. **Caspar WALTZ**-4961 was born about 1540 in Haslach, Herrenberg, Schwarzwaldkreis, Württemberg, Germany. He died. Caspar married (MRIN:4086) Mrs Ursula WALTZ-4962 about 1565 in Haslach, Herrenberg, Schwarzwaldkreis, Württemberg, Germany.

2445. **Mrs Ursula WALTZ**-4962 was born about 1544 in Haslach, Herrenberg, Schwarzwaldkreis, Württemberg, Germany. She died.

2446. **Jacob HILTPURG**-4963 was born about 1529 in Merklingen, Leonberg, Neckarkreis, Württemberg, Germany. He died on 26 Dec 1580 in Merklingen, Leonberg, Neckarkreis, Württemberg, Germany. Jacob married (MRIN:4087) Mrs. Jacob HILTPURG-4964 about 1554 in Merklingen, Leonberg, Neckarkreis, Württemberg, Germany.

2447. **Mrs. Jacob HILTPURG**-4964 was born about 1533 in Merklingen, Leonberg, Neckarkreis, Württemberg, Germany. She died.

Thirteenth Generation

4098. **Johannes HARER**-4774 was born about 1531 in Mötzingen, Herrenberg, Schwarzwaldkreis, Württemberg, Germany. He died. Johannes married (MRIN:3982) Wife of Johannes HARER-4775 about 1556 in Moetzingen, Schwarzwald, Wuerttemberg, Germany.

4099. **Wife of Johannes HARER**-4775 was born about 1535 in Mötzingen, Herrenberg, Schwarzwaldkreis, Württemberg, Germany. She died.

4108. **Martin BERTSCH**-4776 was born in 1508 in Schwarzwaldkreis, Württemberg, Germany. He died in 1560 in Württemberg, Germany. Martin married (MRIN:3983) Maria LUPPLER-4777 on 23 Oct

1528 in Geislingen, Balingen, Schwarzwaldkreis, Württemberg, Germany.

4109. **Maria LUPPLER**-4777 was born in 1507 in Württemberg, Germany. She died in 1558 in Württemberg, Germany.

4110. **Seufridt SANWALD**-4778 was born in 1498 in Ottendorf, Gaildorf, Jagstkreis, Württemberg, Germany. He died in 1553 in Württemberg, Germany. Seufridt married (MRIN:3984) Barbara NEIFFER-4779 in 1519 in Württemberg, Germany.

4111. **Barbara NEIFFER**-4779 was born in 1500 in Donaukreis, Württemberg, Germany. She died in 1549 in Württemberg, Germany.

4160. **Georg MÜLLER I**-4828 was born in 1455 in Augsburg, Augsburg, Schwaben, Bavaria, Germany. He died in 1530 in Augsburg, Augsburg, Schwaben, Bavaria, Germany. Georg married (MRIN:4012) Ursula SPAN-4829 in Augsburg, Augsburg, Schwaben, Bayern, Germany.

4161. **Ursula SPAN**-4829 was born in 1465 in Augsburg, Augsburg, Schwaben, Bavaria, Germany. She died in Germany.

4162. **Leonhard KERCHER**-4830 was born in 1593 in Eberdingen, Baden-Württemberg, Deutschland. He died on 8 Aug 1647 in Eberdingen, Baden-Württemberg, Deutschland.

4170. **Veltin WOLFF**-4819 was born about 1524 in Rhodt, Palatinate, Bavaria, Germany. He died. Veltin married (MRIN:4007) Helen SEITA-4820 in 1549 in Germany.

4171. **Helen SEITA**-4820 was born in 1525 in Rhodt, Rhodt unter Rietburg, Südliche Weinstraße, Rheinland-Pfalz, Germany. She died in Unknown in Germany.

4176. **Cyriakus TREIBER**-4831 was born in 1534 in Nagold, Schwarzwaldkreis, Wuerttemberg, Germany. He died before 1592. Cyriakus married (MRIN:4014) Maria-4832.

4177. **Maria**-4832 died.

4178. **Blasius Stephan GASSENMUELLER**-4833 was born in 1534 in Wildbad, Neuenbürg, Schwarzwaldkreis, Württemberg, Germany. He died about 1600 in Germany. Blasius married (MRIN:4015) Anna-4834 about 1558 in Germany.

4179. **Anna**-4834 was born about 1538 in Wildbad, Neuenbürg, Schwarzwaldkreis, Württemberg, Germany. She died about 1600 in Germany.

4180. **Balthas HOEFFEL**-4835 was born in 1530 in Ehningen, Böblingen, Neckarkreis, Württemberg, Germany. He died in 1579 in Württemberg, Germany. Balthas married (MRIN:4016) Maria Salome FEYERABEND-4836 in 1555 in Ehningen, Böblingen, Neckarkreis, Württemberg, Germany.

4181. **Maria Salome FEYERABEND**-4836 was born in 1537 in Schwäbisch Hall, Hall, Jagstkreis, Württemberg, Germany. She died in 1579 in Württemberg, Germany.

4182. **Gallus KEPPELER**-4837 was born in 1525 in Württemberg, Germany. He was christened on 10 Sep 1525 in Bitz, Balingen, Schwarzwaldkreis, Württemberg, Germany. He died in 1577 in Württemberg, Germany. Gallus married (MRIN:4017) Magdalena KAUFMAN-4838 on 10 Mar 1545 in Ebingen, Balingen, Schwarzwaldkreis, Württemberg, Germany.

4183. **Magdalena KAUFMAN**-4838 was born in 1527 in Württemberg, Germany. She died in 1580 in Württemberg, Germany.

4184. **LANG**-4839 was born about 1510 in Germany. He died. LANG married (MRIN:4018) Mrs. Lang-4840 about 1535 in Germany.

4185. **Mrs. Lang**-4840 was born about 1515 in Germany. She died.

4186. **KUCH**-4841 was born about 1515 in Germany. He died. KUCH married (MRIN:4019) Mrs. Kuch-4842 about 1540 in Germany.

4187. **Mrs. Kuch**-4842 was born about 1520 in Germany. She died.

4480. **Clesgin Bohrer KLEIN**-4910 was born in 1485 in Bischmisheim, Saarbrücken, Saar District, Germany. He died in Bischmisheim, Saarbrücken, Saarland, Germany. Clesgin married (MRIN:4059) Sybille Bohrer KLEIN-4911.

4481. **Sybille Bohrer KLEIN**-4911 was born in 1486 in Germany. She died in Germany.

4488. **Jacob BECKER**-4912 was born in 1530 in Bischmisheim, Saarbrücken, Saar District, Germany. He died on 13 Feb 1616 in Schwerte, Unna, Nordrhein-Westfalen, Germany. Jacob married (MRIN:4060) Harriet BAKER-4913.

4489. **Harriet BAKER**-4913 was born in 1530 in Bischmisheim, Saarbrücken, Saar District, Germany. She died on 27 Feb 1622 in Bischmisheim, Saarbrücken, Saarland, Germany.

4544. **Hans SECKLER**-4934 was born in gegen 1503 in Manubach, Sankt Goar, Rheinland, Preußen, Deutschland. He died in Manubach, Sankt Goar, Rheinland, Preußen, Deutschland. Hans married (MRIN:4072) Mrs. SECKLER-4935 in vor 1528.

4545. **Mrs. SECKLER**-4935 was born in gegen 1507. She died in Manubach, Sankt Goar, Rheinland, Preußen, Deutschland.

4868. **Andreas OSIANDER**-4965 was born on 19 Dec 1498 in Gunzenhausen, Middle Franconia, Bavaria, Germany. He died on 17 Oct 1552 in Koenigsberg, Prussia. He was buried on 19 Oct 1552 in Königsberg, Königsberg, East Prussia, Prussia, Germany. Andreas married (MRIN:4088) Katharina PREU-4966 on 2 Nov 1525 in Nuernberg Stadt, Mittelfranken, Bavaria.

4869. **Katharina PREU**-4966 was born in 1502 in Weißenburg, Middle Franconia, Bavaria, Germany. She died on 14 Jul 1537 in Nuremberg, Bavern, Germany.

4870. **Johann ENTRINGER**-4967 was born about 1503 in Tubingen, Schwarzwaldkreis, Wuerttemberg, Germany. He died. Johann married (MRIN:4089) Anna PALM-4968.

4871. **Anna PALM**-4968 was born about 1500 in Rottenburg Am Neckar, Baden-Wuerttemberg, Germany. She died.

Fourteenth Generation

8222. **Johannes NEUFFER**-4782 was born in 1458 in Münsingen, Donaukreis, Württemberg, Germany. He died in 1522 in Württemberg, Germany. Johannes married (MRIN:3986) STROELIN-4783 in 1479 in Münsingen, Donaukreis, Württemberg, Germany.

8223. **STROELIN**-4783 was born in 1457 in Münsingen, Donaukreis, Württemberg, Germany. She died in 1519 in Württemberg, Germany.

8320. **Peter MULLER**-4843 was born in 1416 in Germany. He died.

8352. **TREIBER**-4844 was born about 1505 in Germany. He died.

8360. **HEFEL**-4845 was born about 1501 in Germany. He died. HEFEL married (MRIN:4022) Mrs. Hefel-4846 about 1525 in Germany.

8361. **Mrs. Hefel**-4846 was born about 1501 in Germany. She died.

8362. **Lienhard FEYERABEND**-4847 was born about 1501 in Württemberg, Germany. He died. Lienhard married (MRIN:4023) Katharina GEYER-4848.

8363. **Katharina GEYER**-4848 was born about 1501 in Württemberg, Germany. She died.

8364. **Greogor KEPPELER**-4849 was born in 1500 in Württemberg, Germany. He died in 1557 in Württemberg, Germany. Greogor married (MRIN:4024) Justin Anna Maria BUMILLER-4850 on 8 May 1520 in Jungingen, Hechingen, Hohenzollern, Prussia, Germany.

8365. **Justin Anna Maria BUMILLER**-4850 was born in 1502 in Württemberg, Germany. She died in 1555 in Württemberg, Germany.

9736. **Andreas OSIANDER**-4971 was born in 1444 in Gunzenhausen, Mittelfranken, Bayern Lande, Germany. He died in 1526 in Nürnberg, Nürnberg, Middle Franconia, Bavaria, Germany. Andreas married (MRIN:4092) Anna HERZOG-4972 before 1498 in Nuernberg, Bayern, Germany.

9737. **Anna HERZOG**-4972 was born about 1470 in Gunzenhausen, Mittelfranken, Bayern Lande, Germany. She died in 1540 in Nürnberg, Nürnberg, Middle Franconia, Bavaria, Germany.

9738. **Heinrich PREU**-4973 was born in 1464 in Weissenburg, Mittelfranken, Bayern Lande, Germany. He died before 1525. Heinrich married (MRIN:4093) Dorothea WOLFF-4974 about 1500 in Nuernberg Stadt, Mittelfranken, Bayern.

9739. **Dorothea WOLFF**-4974 was born before 1469 in Weissenburg, Mittelfranken, Bayern Lande, Germany. She died in 1533.

9740. **Johann ENTRINGER Snr**-4970 was born in 1502 in Tubingen, Schwarzwaldkreis, Wuerttemberg, Germany. He died in Apr 1546 in Tübingen, Schwarzwaldkreis, Württemberg, Germany.

9742. **Wilhelm PALM**-4975 was born in 1470. He died after 1505. Wilhelm married (MRIN:4095) Barbara PALM-4976 in 1500.

9743. **Barbara PALM**-4976 was born in 1480. She died after 1505.

Fifteenth Generation

16444. **Johannes NEIFER**-4786 was born before 1420 in Munsingen, Donaukreis, Wuerttemberg, Germany. He died after 1470 in Munsingen, Donaukreis, Wuerttemberg, Germany. Johannes married (MRIN:3988) Mrs. Hans NEUFFER-4787.

16445. **Mrs. Hans NEUFFER**-4787 was born about 1442 in Herrenberg, Schwarzwaldkreis, Wuerttemberg, Germany. She died.

19472. **Konrad OSIANDER**-4984 was born in 1410 in Anhausen, Ederheim, Donau-Ries, Schwaben, Bavaria, Germany. He died. He was buried in Auhausen, Bayern, Germany. Konrad married (MRIN:4105) Mrs OSIANDER-4985 in um 1440 in Anhausen, Bayern, Deutschland.

19473. **Mrs OSIANDER**-4985 was born in um 1420 in Anhausen, Mittelfranken, Bayern, Deutschland. She died.

19480. **Hensin ENTRINGER**-4982 was born in 1470 in Tubingen, Schwarzwaldkreis, Wuerttemberg, Germany. He died after 1544. Hensin married (MRIN:4104) N ENTRINGER-4983 in 1500 in Tübingen, Neckar, Württemberg.

19481. **N ENTRINGER**-4983 was born in 1475 in Tubingen, Schwarzwaldkreis, Wuerttemberg, Germany. She died after 1503.

Sixteenth Generation

32888. **Auberlin NIFER**-4790 was born in 1380. He died in 1454. Auberlin married (MRIN:3990) Mrs. Auberlin NIFER-4791 about 1410 in , Wuerttemberg, Germany.

32889. **Mrs. Auberlin NIFER**-4791 was born before 1400 in Wuerttemberg, Germany. She died.

Index

Name	ID	Page
HARER, Maria (b.1557)	2049	17
HARER, Wife of Johannes (b.1535)	4099	19
HEFEL, (b.1501)	8360	21
HELWIG, Herman (b.1676)	74	6
HELWIG, Maria Elisabeth (b.1705) .	37	4
HERBERTS, (b.1550)	1131	16
HERBERTS, Elisabetha (b.1590)	565	13
HERBERTS, Hamman (b.1550) .	1130	16
HERZOG, Anna (b.1470)	9737	22
HILL, Mary (b.1694)	87	7
HILTPURG, Barbara (b.1570) . .	1223	17
HILTPURG, Jacob (b.1529)	2446	19
HILTPURG, Jacob (b.1533)	2447	19
HIRNLEN, Agnes (b.1555)	1041	15
HIRNLEN, Hans (b.1530)	2082	17
HIRTZ, Anna Catharina	137	9
HIRTZ, Debelt (b.1620)	274	11
HIRTZ, Debelt (b.1624)	275	11
HOEFFEL OR HEFEL, C (b.1582)	1045	15
HOEFFEL, Balthas (b.1530) . . .	4180	20
HOEFFEL, Hans (b.1555)	2090	18
HOFFMANN, Andreas (b.1630) .	306	12
HOFFMANN, Elisabetha (b.1656) .	153	10
HOLZ, Johannes (b.1575)	1142	16
HOLZ, Maria Elisabeth (b.1599) . .	571	14
HUNTZINGER, Anna (b.1698)	77	6
HUTCHINGS, James Sr. (b.1715) . .	82	7
HUTCHINGS, Mary (b.1740)	41	4
ICLIN, (b.1510)	2440	19
JENNINGS, Benjamin (b.1730) . . .	50	5
JENNINGS, Hannah (b.1768)	25	3
JETTER(IN), Catharina (d.1704) .	155	10
JONES, Johanna (b.1736)	47	5
JONES, Thomas (b.1715)	94	7
KAERCHER, Justina C (b.1720) . . .	33	4
KARCHER, Anna Catharina (b.1604)	265	11
KARCHER, John Michael (b.1685) .	66	6
KARCHER, Moritz Jr (b.1655) . .	132	9
KARCHER, Moritz (b.1600)	264	11
KAUFMAN, Magdalena (b.1527)	4183	20
KEENE, John Henry (b.1720)	42	4
KEENE, Letitia (b.1760)	21	3
KEENE, Richard (b.1689)	84	7
KENDALL, Andrew (b.1766)	24	3
KENDALL, Jesse (b.1727)	48	5
KENDALL, Levi (b.1798)	12	2
KENDALL, Levi Newell (b.1822) . .	6	1
KENDALL, Roxey Jane (b.1859) . . .	3	1
KENDALL, Samuel (b.1529)	96	7
KEPPELER, Barbara (b.1555) . .	2091	18
KEPPELER, Gallus (b.1525) . . .	4182	20

Name	ID	Page
KEPPELER, Greogor (b.1500) . .	8364	22
KERCHER, Leonhard (b.1593) . .	4162	20
KESSLER, Anna Juliana (b.1745) . .	17	2
KESSLER, Hanss Otto (b.1673) . . .	68	6
KESSLER, Johann Georg (b.1711) . .	34	4
KLEIN, Clesgin Bohrer (b.1485) .	4480	21
KLEIN, Engel (b.1570)	563	13
KLEIN, Hans (b.1595)	280	11
KLEIN, Johann Frantz (b.1681)	70	6
KLEIN, Johannes Hans (b.1550) .	1120	15
KLEIN, Joseph (b.1621)	140	10
KLEIN, Meyets Hans (b.1534) . .	1126	16
KLEIN, Nickel (b.1575)	560	13
KLEIN, Sybille Bohrer (b.1486) .	4481	21
KLEINEN, Margaretha (b.1550) .	1121	15
KNOELLER, Hanns Ludwig (b.1657)	134	9
KNOELLER, Maria C (b.1697)	67	6
KNOELLER, Mathias (b.1622) . . .	268	11
KOCH, Hans (b.1525)	2276	19
KOCH, Hans (b.1533)	2277	19
KOCH, Heinrich (d.1604)	1138	16
KOCH, Sophia (b.1592)	569	14
KUCH, (b.1515)	4186	20
KUCH, Margaretha (b.1544) . . .	2093	18
LANG, (b.1510)	4184	20
LANG, Dorethea (b.1607)	523	13
LANG, Peter (b.1540)	2092	18
LANG, Stephen Oswald (b.1568) .	1046	15
LORICH, Catherine (b.1724)	39	4
LUDWIG, Anna Margaretha (b.1666)	131	9
LUPPLER, Maria (b.1507)	4109	20
LYMAN, Hannah (b.1776)	27	3
LYMAN, Joseph Bradford (b.1767) .	26	3
LYMAN, Lorena (Laura) (b.1804) . .	13	2
LYMAN, Richard (b.1721)	52	5
LYMAN, Richard IV (b.1678) . . .	104	8
MEY, Maritie Mary (b.1706)	113	8
MULLER, Peter (b.1416)	8320	21
MÜLLER, Georg I (b.1455)	4160	20
MÜLLER, Lucas I (b.1490)	2080	17
NEIFER, Johannes (b.1420) . . .	16444	22
NEIFFER, Barbara (b.1500)	4111	20
NEUFFER, Hans (b.1442)	16445	22
NEUFFER, Johannes (b.1458) . .	8222	21
NICKEL, Anna Margaretha (b.1713)	121	8
NIFER, Auberlin (b.1380)	32888	23
NIFER, Mrs. Auberlin (b.1400) .	32889	23
OSIANDER, (b.1420)	19473	22
OSIANDER, Andreas (b.1498) . .	4868	21
OSIANDER, Andreas (b.1444) . .	9736	22
OSIANDER, Konrad (b.1410) .	19472	22

Name	ID	Page	Name	ID	Page
VOLLMAR, Hans Jacob (b.1697) . .	64	6			
VOLLMAR, Hans Jerg (b.1640) . .	256	10			
VOLLMAR, Johann Jacob (b.1721) .	32	4			
VOLLMAR, Martin (b.1606)	512	12			
VOLLMER, Hans Joerg (b.1665) . .	128	9			
VOLMAR, Conrad (b.1581)	1024	14			
VOLMAR, Marga (b.1586)	1025	14			
VOLMAR, Martin (b.1553)	2048	17			
VON KIRSCHROTH, S E (b.1680) .	75	6			
WALTZ, Caspar (b.1540)	2444	19			
WALTZ, Jacob (b.1566)	1222	17			
WALTZ, Ursula (b.1595)	611	14			
WALTZ, Ursula (b.1544)	2445	19			
WEISSGERBER, L (b.1568) . . .	1218	16			
WEISSGERBER, L (b.1577) . . .	1219	17			
WEIßGERBER, Sara (b.1595) . . .	609	14			
WENTZEL, Johann Adam	120	8			
WINCHEL, Justus Jr. (b.1759)	30	3			
WINCHELL, Ada (b.1801)	15	2			
WINCHELL, Justus (b.1729)	60	5			
WOLFF, Anna (b.1550)	2085	18			
WOLFF, Dorothea (b.1469)	9739	22			
WOLFF, Veltin (b.1524)	4170	20			
WOODWARD, Mary (b.1678) . . .	105	8			
YOUNG, Samuel (b.1692)	86	7			
ZERFAS, Von (b.1660)	144	10			
ZERFASS, Johan Nicholas (b.1709) .	36	4			
ZERFASS, Johann Adam (b.1742) . .	18	2			
ZERFASS, Susannah (b.1783)	9	2			
ZU ROTENSOL NEUENB (b.1636)	267	11			

Ancestors of Edgar Osden FULLMER-10

```
                                    ┌─ Martin VOLMAR-4766 (b. Abt 1553-, , , Württemberg, Ger  d. , , , Württemberg, Germa)
                          ┌─ Conrad VOLMAR-4754 (b. Abt 1581-, , , Schwarzwaldkreis,  d. Sep 1614-o, S, W, Germany)
                          │          ┌─ Johannes HARER-4774 (b. Abt 1531-M, H, , Württemberg, Germany  d. Deceased)
                          └─ Maria HARER-4767 (b. Abt 1557-, , , Württemberg, German  d. , , , Württemberg, Germ)
                                     └─ Wife of Johannes HARER-4775 (b. Abt 1535-, , , Württemberg, Germ  d. Deceased)
               ┌─ Martin VOLLMAR-4748 (b. 13 Jul 1606-, , , Württemberg, Ger  d. 26 Sep 1635-, , , Württemberg, )
               │          └─ Marga VOLMAR-4755 (b. Abt 1586-, , , Württemberg, Ger  d. Sep 1614-, , , Württemberg, Ge)
   ┌─ Hans Jerg VOLLMAR-4745 (b. 1640-F, Neckar, B, Germany  d. Bef 9 Jun 1696-F, Neckar, W, Germany)
   │           │          ┌─ Matthaeus BREINING-4768 (b. 1520-B, B, Germany  d. 1573-B, B, B, Germany)
   │           │  ┌─ Hans " Deissen Hans" BREUNING-4758 (b. 1558-Böblingen, N, W, Germany  d. 1622-)
   │           │  │       └─ Barbara -4769 (d. Deceased)
   │           └─ Margaretha BREINING-4749 (b. 1597-, , , Württemberg, Germ  d. Deceased)
   │                      │          ┌─ Martin BERTSCH-4776 (b. 1508-S, W, Germany  d. 1560-Württemberg, Germany)
   │                      │  ┌─ Jacob BERTSCH-4770 (b. 1528-, , , Württemberg, Ger  d. 1598-, , , Württemberg, Germ)
   │                      │  │       └─ Maria LUPPLER-4777 (b. 1507-Württemberg, Germany  d. 1558-W, Germany)
   │                      └─ Anna BERTSCH-4759 (b. 30 Mar 1560-, , , Württemberg, Ger  d. 1622-B, H, W, Germany)
   │                                 │          ┌─ Seufridt SANWALD-4778 (b. 1498-O, G, J, Württemberg, Germany  d. 1553-)
   │                                 └─ Barbara SANWALD-4771 (b. 1530-, , , Württemberg, Ger  d. 1578-J, W, Germany)
   │                                            │          ┌─ Auberlin NIFER-4790 (b. 1380  d. 1454)
   │                                            │  ┌─ Johannes NEIFER-4786 (b. Bef 1420-M, D, W, Germany  d. Aft 1470-)
   │                                            │  │       └─ Mrs. Auberlin NIFER-4791 (b. Bef 1400-, Germany  d. Deceased)
   │                                            │  ┌─ Johannes NEUFFER-4782 (b. 1458-Münsingen, D, W, Germany  d. 1522-)
   │                                            │  │       └─ Mrs. Hans NEUFFER-4787 (b. Abt 1442-H, S, , Germany  d. Deceased)
   │                                            └─ Barbara NEIFFER-4779 (b. 1500-D, W, Germany  d. 1549-Württemberg, Germany)
   │                                                       └─ STROELIN-4783 (b. 1457-M, D, W, Germany  d. 1519-W, Germany)
   │  ┌─ Hans Joerg VOLLMER-4743 (b. Abt 1665-, , , Württemberg, Germany  d. 22 Apr 1745-, , , Württemberg, Germ)
   ┌─ Hans Jacob VOLLMAR-663 (b. 6 Mar 1697-, , , Baden-Württemberg, Germ  d. 25 Jan 1762-T, Berks, Pennsylvania)
   │  │          ┌─ Jacob BECK-4760 (d. Deceased)
   │  │  ┌─ Jerg BECK-4750 (b. 1628-K, M, , Württemberg, Germany  d. 26 May 1675-, , , Württemberg, Germ)
   │  │  │       └─ Maria Apollonia HAEHN-4761 (b. 1608  d. 12 May 1688)
   │  │  ┌─ Hans BECK-4746 (b. 31 Aug 1650-K, , , Württemberg, Germany  d. 17 Jan 1729-D, W, Germany)
   │  │  │       └─ Rosina BECK-4751 (b. Dec 1628-, , , Baden-Württemberg  d. 26 May 1675-D, W, Germany)
   │  └─ Anna BECK-4744 (b. 11 Mar 1671-K, M, D, Württemberg, Germany  d. 1 Jan 1710-, , , Württemberg, Germany)
   │             │          ┌─ TROESTER-4764 (b. Abt 1585-Germany  d. Deceased)
   │             │  ┌─ Ludvig TROESTER-4752 (b. Abt 1612-, , , Württemberg, Ger  d. 9 May 1675-, , , Württemberg, Ge)
   │             │  │       └─ Mrs. Troester -4765 (b. 1592-Donaukreis, W, Germany  d. Deceased)
   │             └─ Anna Maria TROESTER-4747 (b. 1648-, , , Donaukreis, Württe  d. 27 Oct 1678-, , , Donaukreis, Württem)
   │                        └─ Barbara TROESTER-4753 (b. Abt 1616-, , , Württemberg, Ger  d. 15 Apr 1674-, , , Württemberg, G)
┌─ Johann Jacob VOLLMAR-346 (b. 2 Apr 1721-Roßwag, Vaihingen, W, Germany  d. 20 Sep 1758-T, Berks, Pennsylvania)
│  │                        ┌─ Peter MULLER-4843 (b. 1416-Germany  d. Deceased)
│  │                ┌─ Georg MÜLLER I-4828 (b. 1455-A, , , Bavaria, Germany  d. 1530-, , , Bavaria, Ge)
│  │          ┌─ Lucas MÜLLER I-4811 (b. 1490-Altburg, C, S, Württemberg, Germany  d. 1 Dec 1560-)
│  │          │             └─ Ursula SPAN-4829 (b. 1465-A, A, S, Bavaria, Germany  d. Germany)
│  │          ┌─ Conrad RAU Jr.-4802 (b. 1541-, , , Schwarzwaldkreis, W  d. Bef 1607)
```

┌─ Leonhard KERCHER-4830 (b. 1593-Eberdingen, B, Deutschland d. 8 Aug 1647-)

└─ Margaretha -4812 (r. 1620-S, S, W, Germany d. Deceased)

Hans RAU-4798 (b. 24 Dec 1577-A, , , Württemberg, Germany d. Bef 1687)

┌─ Hans HIRNLEN-4814 (b. 1530-, , , Schwarzwaldkreis, d. Deceased)

Agnes HIRNLEN-4803 (b. 1555-, , , Schwarzwaldkreis, d. Deceased)

└─ Anna -4815 (b. 1533-S, Württemberg, Germany d. Bef 1643)

Johannes RAU-4795 (b. 13 Apr 1610-Altburg, C, S, Württemberg, Germany d. Solingen, R, P, Germany)

┌─ Hans Sebastian Jacob SEITZ-4816 (b. Abt 1510-Germany d. 1610-, GermanyUnknown)

┌─ Hans Sebastian Georg Bernherd SEITZ-4804 (b. 18 Jan 1549-, , , Baden-Württember d. 1610-)

┌─ Veltin WOLFF-4819 (b. Abt 1524-Rhodt, Palatinate, B, Germany d. Deceased)

└─ Anna WOLFF-4806 (b. Abt 1550-Liebelsberg, S, W, Germany d. 3 Apr 1620-)

└─ Helen SEITA-4820 (b. 1525-, , , Rheinland-Pfalz, G d. Unknown-Germany)

Helene Magdalena SEITZ-4799 (b. 3 Aug 1580-Haugestett, Schwarzwald, B, Germany d. Bef 1690)

┌─ Gabriel SCHURER-4817 (b. Abt 1525-R, H, S, Württemberg, Germany d. Deceased)

Anna SCHURER-4805 (b. Abt 1550-, , , Württemberg, Ger d. Deceased)

└─ Katharina -4818 (b. Abt 1528-, , , Württemberg, Ger d. Deceased)

Michael RAU-4793 (b. 9 Apr 1665-E, V, N, Württemberg, Germany d. 10 Mar 1696-, , , Württemberg, German)

┌─ TREIBER-4844 (b. Abt 1505-Germany d. Deceased)

┌─ Cyriakus TREIBER-4831 (b. 1534-Nagold, S, W, Germany d. Bef 1592)

┌─ Hans Michael TREIBER-4821 (b. 8 Sep 1560-Nagold, S, W, Germany d. Deceased)

└─ Maria -4832 (d. Deceased)

Johannes TREIBER-4807 (b. 22 Jan 1583-Nagold, S, Württemberg, Germany d. Deceased)

┌─ Blasius Stephan GASSENMUELLER-4833 (b. 1534-, , , Württember d. Abt 1600-)

└─ Margaretha GASSENMUELLER-4822 (b. 12 Feb 1560-, , , Württemberg, d. Deceased)

└─ Anna -4834 (b. Abt 1538-, , , Württemberg, Ger d. Abt 1600-Germany)

Hans Jacob TREIBER-4800 (b. 16 Sep 1613-Wildbach, Schwarzw, W, Germany d. 21 Sep 1682)

┌─ HEFEL-4845 (b. Abt 1501-Germany d. Deceased)

┌─ Balthas HOEFFEL-4835 (b. 1530-E, B, N, Württemberg, Germany d. 1579-)

└─ Mrs. Hefel -4846 (b. Abt 1501-Germany d. Deceased)

┌─ Hans HOEFFEL-4823 (b. 1555-, , , Schwarzwaldkreis, d. 1617-Württemberg, Germany)

┌─ Lienhard FEYERABEND-4847 (b. Abt 1501-W, Germany d. Deceased)

└─ Maria Salome FEYERABEND-4836 (b. 1537-, , , Württemberg, Germany d. 1579-)

└─ Katharina GEYER-4848 (b. Abt 1501-Württemberg, Germany d. Deceased)

Catharina HOEFFEL OR HEFEL-4808 (b. 31 Dec 1582-, , , Württemberg, Germ d. Deceased)

┌─ Greogor KEPPELER-4849 (b. 1500-Württemberg, Germany d. 1557-)

┌─ Gallus KEPPELER-4837 (b. 1525-Württemberg, Germany d. 1577-W, Germany)

└─ Justin Anna Maria BUMILLER-4850 (b. 1502-W, Germany d. 1555-)

Barbara KEPPELER-4824 (b. 7 Jun 1555-Bitz, Balingen, W, Germany d. 1603-)

└─ Magdalena KAUFMAN-4838 (b. 1527-Württemberg, Germany d. 1580-)

Anna Maria TREIBER-4796 (b. 24 Feb 1634-, , , Württemberg, Ger d. 4 Sep 1693-, , , Württemberg, Ger)

┌─ LANG-4839 (b. Abt 1510-Germany d. Deceased)

┌─ Peter LANG-4826 (b. Abt 1540-, , , Württemberg, Ger d. Deceased)

└─ Mrs. Lang -4840 (b. Abt 1515-Germany d. Deceased)

┌─ Stephen Oswald LANG-4809 (b. 5 Aug 1568-W, N, S, Württemberg, Germany d. Deceased)

┌─ KUCH-4841 (b. Abt 1515-Germany d. Deceased)

└─ Margaretha KUCH-4827 (b. Abt 1544-W, N, S, Württemberg, Germany d. Deceased)

    └─ Mrs. Kuch -4842 (b. Abt 1520-Germany d. Deceased)

└─ Dorethea LANG-4801 (b. 1607-, , , Wuerttemberg, German d. UNKNOWN)

    └─ Barbara -4810 (b. 1570-W, N, S, Württemberg, Germany d. Deceased)

└─ Marie Agnes RAU-664 (b. 16 Nov 1695-E, V, N, Württemberg, Germany d. 6 Apr 1735-, , , Württemberg, Germany)

    └─ Anna Margaretha LUDWIG-4794 (b. Abt 1666-, , , Württemberg, German d. Abt 1730)

─ Johann Michael FOLLMER-170 (b. 29 Sep 1744-TT, Berks, P, United States d. 14 Mar 1817)

┌─ Moritz KARCHER-4853 (b. 1600-of Dobel, N, W, Germany d. 18 Feb 1673-Neckarkreis, W, Germany)

┌─ Moritz KARCHER Jr-4851 (b. 21 Aug 1655-Dobel, N, W, Germany d. 8 Sep 1727-, , , Württemberg, Germany)

└─ Anna Catharina KARCHER-4854 (b. 1604-Germany d. 1648-Germany)

┌─ John Michael KARCHER-666 (b. Bef 22 Aug 1685-Konstanz, Baden, Germany d. 1787)

┌─ Caspar SIEB-4859 (b. 1591-, , , Baden, Baden, Germany d. Deceased)

┌─ Jacob SIEB-4857 (b. Abt 1602-Wuerttemberg, Germany d. Oct 1649-Württemberg, Germany)

└─ Barbara -4860 (b. aproximadamente 1580-Reichental, G, R, Baden, Germany d. Deceased)

┌─ Valentin SIEB-4855 (b. Abt 1630-W, R, C, Württemberg, Germany d. Aft 1694-Bernbach, W, Germany)

└─ Anna Else Margritta ROHNS-4858 (b. Abt 1603-Wuerttemberg, Germany d. Deceased)

└─ Margaret SIEB-4852 (b. Abt 1653-Germany d. 31 May 1690-Dobel, Neuenberg, Wuertteberg, Germany)

    └─ Christina ZU ROTENSOL NEUENBUERG-4856 (b. Abt 1636-Dobel, N, W, Germany d. 5 Dec 1698-)

└─ Justina Catharina KAERCHER-347 (b. Abt 1720-Dobel, Neuenbürg, W, Germany d. 17 Jan 1820-TT, B, P, United States)

┌─ Mathias KNOELLER-4864 (b. Jan 1622-Dobel, C, B, Germany d. 31 May 1687)

└─ M -4866 (b. 1594-Dobel Neuenbuerg, S, W, Germany d. Deceased)

┌─ Hanns Ludwig KNOELLER-4861 (b. 2 Jan 1657-, , , Württemberg, Ger d. 2 May 1719-, , , Württemberg, Ger)

┌─ Johannes RAU-4871 (b. Abt 1560-Neusatz, C, Germany d. 20 Apr 1613-, , , Württemberg, Ge)

┌─ Elias RAU-4869 (b. 23 Apr 1592-, , , Württemberg, Germa d. 21 Feb 1668-, , , Württemberg, Germ)

└─ Martha -4872 (b. 1564-N, N, S, Württemberg, Germany d. Deceased)

└─ Martha RAU-4865 (b. 20 Nov 1620-Dobel, Calw, B, Germany d. 24 Nov 1687)

┌─ Johann STAHL-4873 (b. 1564-DN, S, W, Germany d. Deceased)

└─ Rosina STAHL-4870 (b. Abt 1598-Dobel, N, W, Germany d. Bef 1660)

    └─ Mrs. Johann STAHL-4874 (b. 1568-DN, S, W, Germany d. Deceased)

└─ Maria Catharina KNOELLER-667 (b. 23 Mar 1697-N, S, W, Germany d. 11 Feb 1802-Hamburg, B, P, United States)

    └─ Anna Maria -4862 (b. Abt 1661-Dobel, Neuenbuerg, Wurettemberg, Germany d. 1741)

─ Peter FULLMER-83 (b. 25 Feb 1774-Reading, Berks, Pennsylvania, British America d. 6 Jan 1857-Salt Lake City, S, U, United States)

┌─ Hanss Otto KESSLER-668 (b. 17 Feb 1673-Idar-Oberstein, R, P, Germany d. 19 Sep 1749-I, Rhineland, P, Germany)

┌─ Debelt HIRTZ-4876 (b. Abt 1620-Germany d. 1672)

└─ Anna Catharina HIRTZ-4875 (b. Georg, W, B, Rheinland, Germany d. Deceased)

    └─ Mrs. Debelt HIRTZ-4877 (b. Abt 1624-Germany d. Deceased)

┌─ Johann Georg KESSLER-348 (b. 11 Oct 1711-Georg, W, B, Rheinland, Germany d. 1 Jul 1760-G, , , Rheinland, Germany)

┌─ Peter PURPUR-4878 (b. Abt 1652-Oberstein, Birkenfeld, O, Germany d. Deceased)

└─ Elisabeth Maria PURPUR-669 (b. Abt 1676-Germany d. Deceased)

    └─ Mrs. Peter PURPUR-4879 (b. Abt 1656-Oberstein, B, O, Germany d. Deceased)

└─ Anna Juliana KESSLER-171 (b. 16 May 1745-W, I, B, Rheinland-Pfalz, Germany d. 17 Jan 1820-Reading, B, P, United States)

┌─ Clesgin Bohrer KLEIN-4910 (b. 1485-B, S, SD, Germany d. B, S, S, Germany)

┌─ Clesgin BALLIERER- BOHRER-4906 (b. 1510-B, S, R, Prussia, Germany d. 1583-)

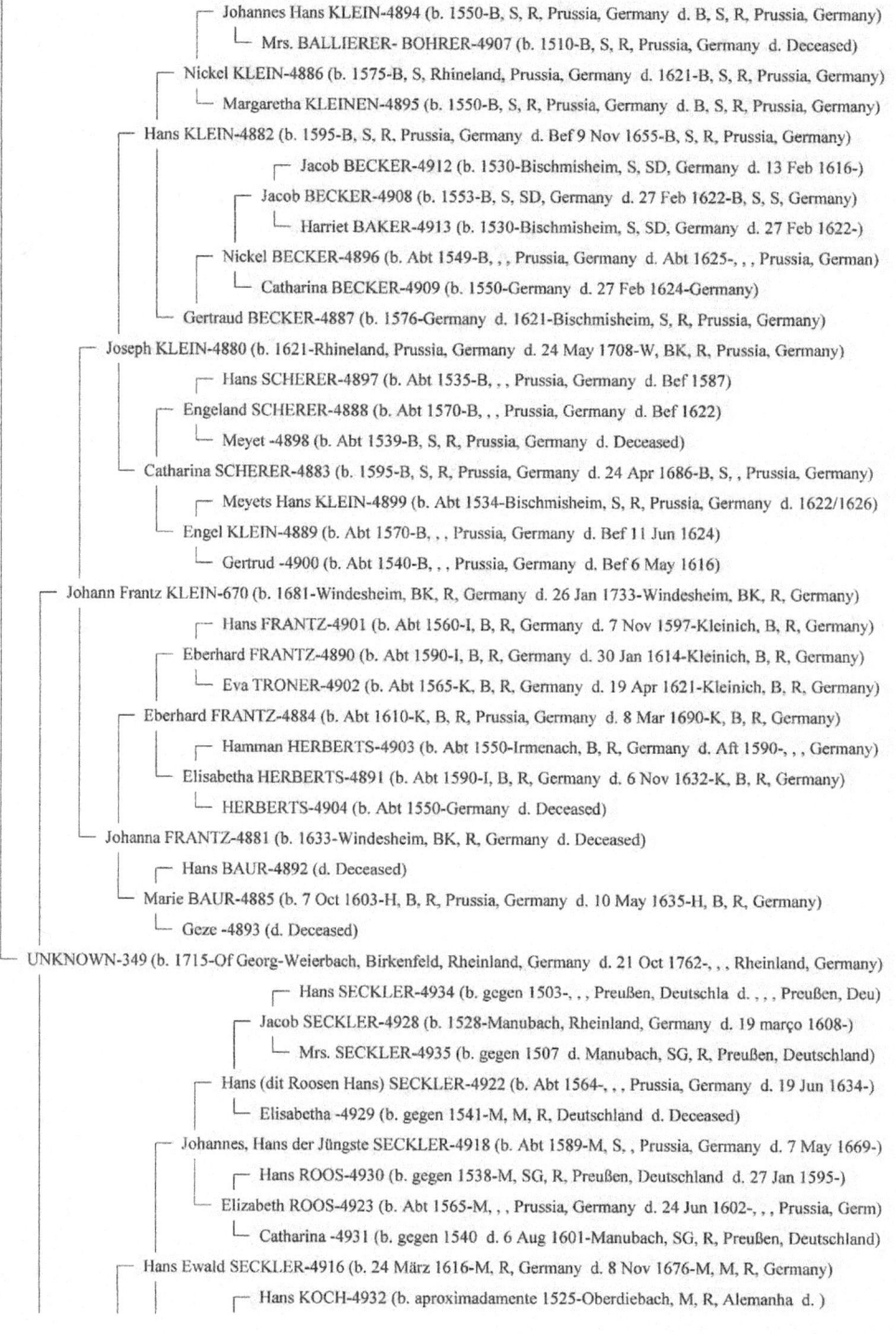

```
                                            └─ Sybille Bohrer KLEIN-4911 (b. 1486-Germany  d. Germany)

                                 ┌─ Johannes Hans KLEIN-4894 (b. 1550-B, S, R, Prussia, Germany  d. B, S, R, Prussia, Germany)
                                 │  └─ Mrs. BALLIERER- BOHRER-4907 (b. 1510-B, S, R, Prussia, Germany  d. Deceased)
                      ┌─ Nickel KLEIN-4886 (b. 1575-B, S, Rhineland, Prussia, Germany  d. 1621-B, S, R, Prussia, Germany)
                      │          └─ Margaretha KLEINEN-4895 (b. 1550-B, S, R, Prussia, Germany  d. B, S, R, Prussia, Germany)
           ┌─ Hans KLEIN-4882 (b. 1595-B, S, R, Prussia, Germany  d. Bef 9 Nov 1655-B, S, R, Prussia, Germany)
           │                             ┌─ Jacob BECKER-4912 (b. 1530-Bischmisheim, S, SD, Germany  d. 13 Feb 1616-)
           │                   ┌─ Jacob BECKER-4908 (b. 1553-B, S, SD, Germany  d. 27 Feb 1622-B, S, S, Germany)
           │                   │         └─ Harriet BAKER-4913 (b. 1530-Bischmisheim, S, SD, Germany  d. 27 Feb 1622-)
           │          ┌─ Nickel BECKER-4896 (b. Abt 1549-B, , , Prussia, Germany  d. Abt 1625-, , , Prussia, German)
           │          │        └─ Catharina BECKER-4909 (b. 1550-Germany  d. 27 Feb 1624-Germany)
           │          └─ Gertraud BECKER-4887 (b. 1576-Germany  d. 1621-Bischmisheim, S, R, Prussia, Germany)
  ┌─ Joseph KLEIN-4880 (b. 1621-Rhineland, Prussia, Germany  d. 24 May 1708-W, BK, R, Prussia, Germany)
  │                             ┌─ Hans SCHERER-4897 (b. Abt 1535-B, , , Prussia, Germany  d. Bef 1587)
  │                   ┌─ Engeland SCHERER-4888 (b. Abt 1570-B, , , Prussia, Germany  d. Bef 1622)
  │                   │         └─ Meyet -4898 (b. Abt 1539-B, S, R, Prussia, Germany  d. Deceased)
  │          └─ Catharina SCHERER-4883 (b. 1595-B, S, R, Prussia, Germany  d. 24 Apr 1686-B, S, , Prussia, Germany)
  │                             ┌─ Meyets Hans KLEIN-4899 (b. Abt 1534-Bischmisheim, S, R, Prussia, Germany  d. 1622/1626)
  │                   └─ Engel KLEIN-4889 (b. Abt 1570-B, , , Prussia, Germany  d. Bef 11 Jun 1624)
  │                             └─ Gertrud -4900 (b. Abt 1540-B, , , Prussia, Germany  d. Bef 6 May 1616)
┌─ Johann Frantz KLEIN-670 (b. 1681-Windesheim, BK, R, Germany  d. 26 Jan 1733-Windesheim, BK, R, Germany)
│                             ┌─ Hans FRANTZ-4901 (b. Abt 1560-I, B, R, Germany  d. 7 Nov 1597-Kleinich, B, R, Germany)
│                   ┌─ Eberhard FRANTZ-4890 (b. Abt 1590-I, B, R, Germany  d. 30 Jan 1614-Kleinich, B, R, Germany)
│                   │         └─ Eva TRONER-4902 (b. Abt 1565-K, B, R, Germany  d. 19 Apr 1621-Kleinich, B, R, Germany)
│          ┌─ Eberhard FRANTZ-4884 (b. Abt 1610-K, B, R, Prussia, Germany  d. 8 Mar 1690-K, B, R, Germany)
│          │                   ┌─ Hamman HERBERTS-4903 (b. Abt 1550-Irmenach, B, R, Germany  d. Aft 1590-, , , Germany)
│          │          └─ Elisabetha HERBERTS-4891 (b. Abt 1590-I, B, R, Germany  d. 6 Nov 1632-K, B, R, Germany)
│          │                   └─ HERBERTS-4904 (b. Abt 1550-Germany  d. Deceased)
│          └─ Johanna FRANTZ-4881 (b. 1633-Windesheim, BK, R, Germany  d. Deceased)
│                   ┌─ Hans BAUR-4892 (d. Deceased)
│          └─ Marie BAUR-4885 (b. 7 Oct 1603-H, B, R, Prussia, Germany  d. 10 May 1635-H, B, R, Germany)
│                   └─ Geze -4893 (d. Deceased)
└─ UNKNOWN-349 (b. 1715-Of Georg-Weierbach, Birkenfeld, Rheinland, Germany  d. 21 Oct 1762-, , , Rheinland, Germany)
                              ┌─ Hans SECKLER-4934 (b. gegen 1503-, , , Preußen, Deutschla d. , , , Preußen, Deu)
                    ┌─ Jacob SECKLER-4928 (b. 1528-Manubach, Rheinland, Germany  d. 19 março 1608-)
                    │         └─ Mrs. SECKLER-4935 (b. gegen 1507  d. Manubach, SG, R, Preußen, Deutschland)
           ┌─ Hans (dit Roosen Hans) SECKLER-4922 (b. Abt 1564-, , , Prussia, Germany  d. 19 Jun 1634-)
           │         └─ Elisabetha -4929 (b. gegen 1541-M, M, R, Deutschland  d. Deceased)
  ┌─ Johannes, Hans der Jüngste SECKLER-4918 (b. Abt 1589-M, S, , Prussia, Germany  d. 7 May 1669-)
  │                   ┌─ Hans ROOS-4930 (b. gegen 1538-M, SG, R, Preußen, Deutschland  d. 27 Jan 1595-)
  │          └─ Elizabeth ROOS-4923 (b. Abt 1565-M, , , Prussia, Germany  d. 24 Jun 1602-, , , Prussia, Germ)
  │                   └─ Catharina -4931 (b. gegen 1540  d. 6 Aug 1601-Manubach, SG, R, Preußen, Deutschland)
┌─ Hans Ewald SECKLER-4916 (b. 24 März 1616-M, R, Germany  d. 8 Nov 1676-M, M, R, Germany)
│                   ┌─ Hans KOCH-4932 (b. aproximadamente 1525-Oberdiebach, M, R, Alemanha  d. )
```

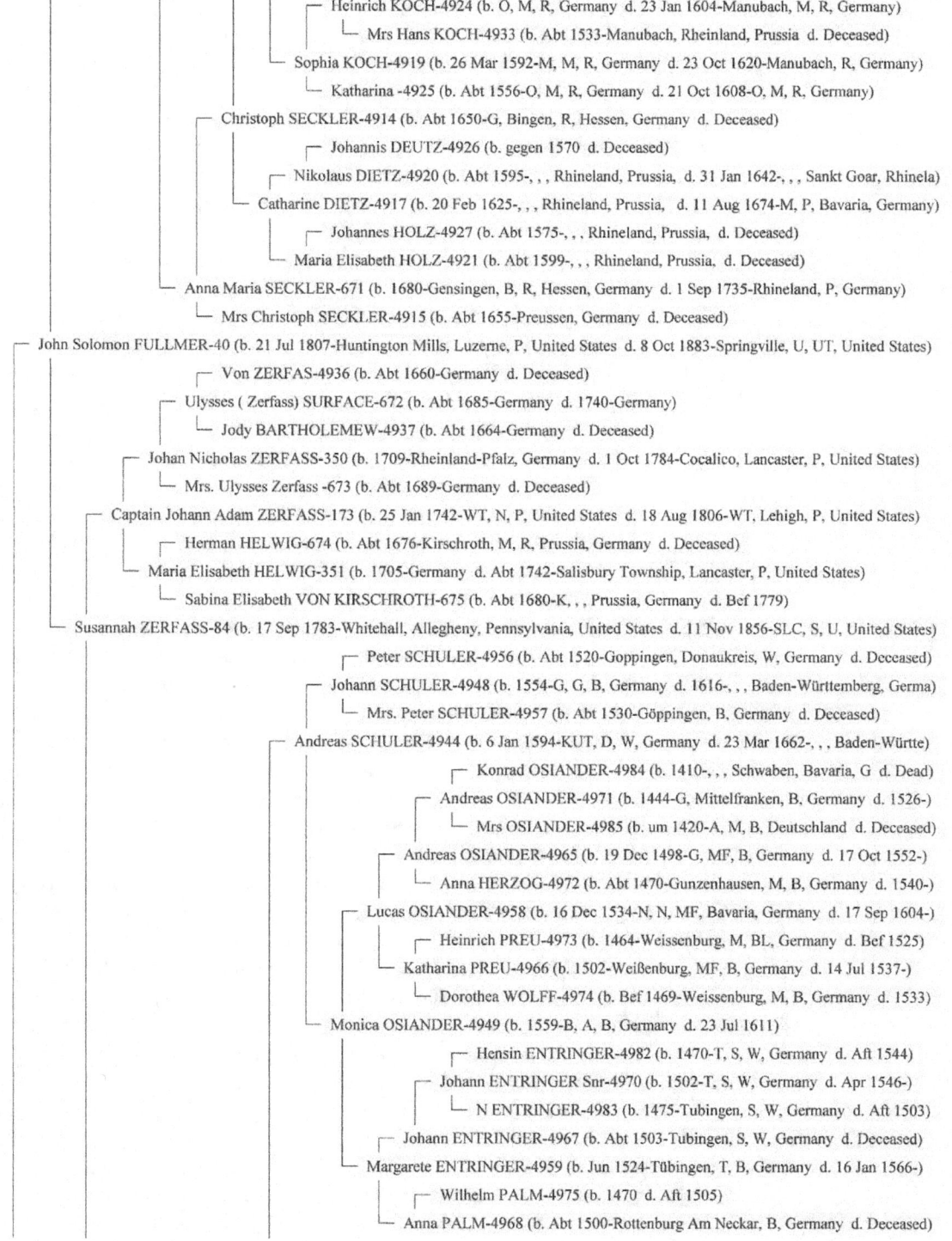

Heinrich KOCH-4924 (b. O, M, R, Germany d. 23 Jan 1604-Manubach, M, R, Germany)

Mrs Hans KOCH-4933 (b. Abt 1533-Manubach, Rheinland, Prussia d. Deceased)

Sophia KOCH-4919 (b. 26 Mar 1592-M, M, R, Germany d. 23 Oct 1620-Manubach, R, Germany)

Katharina -4925 (b. Abt 1556-O, M, R, Germany d. 21 Oct 1608-O, M, R, Germany)

Christoph SECKLER-4914 (b. Abt 1650-G, Bingen, R, Hessen, Germany d. Deceased)

Johannis DEUTZ-4926 (b. gegen 1570 d. Deceased)

Nikolaus DIETZ-4920 (b. Abt 1595-, , , Rhineland, Prussia, d. 31 Jan 1642-, , , Sankt Goar, Rhinela)

Catharine DIETZ-4917 (b. 20 Feb 1625-, , , Rhineland, Prussia, d. 11 Aug 1674-M, P, Bavaria, Germany)

Johannes HOLZ-4927 (b. Abt 1575-, , , Rhineland, Prussia, d. Deceased)

Maria Elisabeth HOLZ-4921 (b. Abt 1599-, , , Rhineland, Prussia, d. Deceased)

Anna Maria SECKLER-671 (b. 1680-Gensingen, B, R, Hessen, Germany d. 1 Sep 1735-Rhineland, P, Germany)

Mrs Christoph SECKLER-4915 (b. Abt 1655-Preussen, Germany d. Deceased)

John Solomon FULLMER-40 (b. 21 Jul 1807-Huntington Mills, Luzerne, P, United States d. 8 Oct 1883-Springville, U, UT, United States)

Von ZERFAS-4936 (b. Abt 1660-Germany d. Deceased)

Ulysses (Zerfass) SURFACE-672 (b. Abt 1685-Germany d. 1740-Germany)

Jody BARTHOLEMEW-4937 (b. Abt 1664-Germany d. Deceased)

Johan Nicholas ZERFASS-350 (b. 1709-Rheinland-Pfalz, Germany d. 1 Oct 1784-Cocalico, Lancaster, P, United States)

Mrs. Ulysses Zerfass -673 (b. Abt 1689-Germany d. Deceased)

Captain Johann Adam ZERFASS-173 (b. 25 Jan 1742-WT, N, P, United States d. 18 Aug 1806-WT, Lehigh, P, United States)

Herman HELWIG-674 (b. Abt 1676-Kirschroth, M, R, Prussia, Germany d. Deceased)

Maria Elisabeth HELWIG-351 (b. 1705-Germany d. Abt 1742-Salisbury Township, Lancaster, P, United States)

Sabina Elisabeth VON KIRSCHROTH-675 (b. Abt 1680-K, , , Prussia, Germany d. Bef 1779)

Susannah ZERFASS-84 (b. 17 Sep 1783-Whitehall, Allegheny, Pennsylvania, United States d. 11 Nov 1856-SLC, S, U, United States)

Peter SCHULER-4956 (b. Abt 1520-Goppingen, Donaukreis, W, Germany d. Deceased)

Johann SCHULER-4948 (b. 1554-G, G, B, Germany d. 1616-, , , Baden-Württemberg, Germa)

Mrs. Peter SCHULER-4957 (b. Abt 1530-Göppingen, B, Germany d. Deceased)

Andreas SCHULER-4944 (b. 6 Jan 1594-KUT, D, W, Germany d. 23 Mar 1662-, , , Baden-Württe)

Konrad OSIANDER-4984 (b. 1410-, , , Schwaben, Bavaria, G d. Dead)

Andreas OSIANDER-4971 (b. 1444-G, Mittelfranken, B, Germany d. 1526-)

Mrs OSIANDER-4985 (b. um 1420-A, M, B, Deutschland d. Deceased)

Andreas OSIANDER-4965 (b. 19 Dec 1498-G, MF, B, Germany d. 17 Oct 1552-)

Anna HERZOG-4972 (b. Abt 1470-Gunzenhausen, M, B, Germany d. 1540-)

Lucas OSIANDER-4958 (b. 16 Dec 1534-N, N, MF, Bavaria, Germany d. 17 Sep 1604-)

Heinrich PREU-4973 (b. 1464-Weissenburg, M, BL, Germany d. Bef 1525)

Katharina PREU-4966 (b. 1502-Weißenburg, MF, B, Germany d. 14 Jul 1537-)

Dorothea WOLFF-4974 (b. Bef 1469-Weissenburg, M, B, Germany d. 1533)

Monica OSIANDER-4949 (b. 1559-B, A, B, Germany d. 23 Jul 1611)

Hensin ENTRINGER-4982 (b. 1470-T, S, W, Germany d. Aft 1544)

Johann ENTRINGER Snr-4970 (b. 1502-T, S, W, Germany d. Apr 1546-)

N ENTRINGER-4983 (b. 1475-Tubingen, S, W, Germany d. Aft 1503)

Johann ENTRINGER-4967 (b. Abt 1503-Tubingen, S, W, Germany d. Deceased)

Margarete ENTRINGER-4959 (b. Jun 1524-Tübingen, T, B, Germany d. 16 Jan 1566-)

Wilhelm PALM-4975 (b. 1470 d. Aft 1505)

Anna PALM-4968 (b. Abt 1500-Rottenburg Am Neckar, B, Germany d. Deceased)

└─ Barbara PALM-4976 (b. 1480 d. Aft 1505)

┌─ Hans Balthasar SCHULER-4940 (b. Abt 1620-KUT, D, W, Germany d. 3 Apr 1688-H, C, B, Germany)

    ┌─ Leonhard WEISSGERBER-4950 (b. Abt 1568-Calw, B, Germany d. Deceased)

└─ Sara WEIßGERBER-4945 (b. 1595-Calw, S, W, Germany d. 1645-, , , Baden-Württemberg, Germa)

    └─ Mrs. Leonhard WEISSGERBER-4951 (b. Abt 1577-Calw, B, Germany d. Deceased)

┌─ Martin SCHULER-4938 (b. 17 Sep 1658-Wuerttemberg, Germany d. 25 Jan 1719)

    ┌─ ICLIN-4960 (b. Abt 1510-S, W, Germany d. Deceased)

    ┌─ Hans EISELIN-4952 (b. Abt 1562-, , , Württemberg, Ger d. Deceased)

┌─ Hans EISELIN-4946 (b. 6 Mar 1591-, , , Württemberg, German d. Deceased)

    └─ Margaretha -4953 (b. Abt 1566-, , , Württemberg, Germa d. Deceased)

└─ Catarina EISELIN-4941 (b. 16 Feb 1618-, , , Württemberg, Germ d. 15 Jan 1690-H, Calw, B, Germany)

    ┌─ Caspar WALTZ-4961 (b. Abt 1540-, , , Württemberg, Ger d. Deceased)

    ┌─ Jacob WALTZ-4954 (b. Abt 1566-, , , Württemberg, Ger d. Deceased)

    └─ Mrs Ursula WALTZ-4962 (b. Abt 1544-H, H, S, Württemberg, Germany d. Deceased)

└─ Ursula WALTZ-4947 (b. 27 Oct 1595-, , , Württemberg, Germ d. Deceased)

    ┌─ Jacob HILTPURG-4963 (b. Abt 1529-M, L, N, Württemberg, Germany d. 26 Dec 1580-)

└─ Barbara HILTPURG-4955 (b. Abt 1570-, , , Württemberg, Ger d. Deceased)

    └─ Mrs. Jacob HILTPURG-4964 (b. Abt 1533-M, L, , Württemberg, Germany d. Deceased)

┌─ Hanss Adam SCHNEIDER-678 (b. Abt 1694-Germany d. 3 Nov 1769-Haiterbach, Calw, B, Germany)

    ┌─ Andreas HOFFMANN-4942 (b. Abt 1630-, , , Baden-Württemberg, d. Deceased)

└─ Elisabetha HOFFMANN-4939 (b. 31 Jul 1656-, , , Württemberg, Germa d. 19 Jun 1736)

    └─ Agathe -4943 (b. Abt 1640-O, S, F, Baden-Württemberg, Germany d. Deceased)

┌─ Peter SHAFER-353 (b. 1720-Schuylkill, Pennsylvania, United States d. 1825-White Hill, Cumberland, P, United States)

    ┌─ Christian SCHULER-4986 (d. 9 Apr 1726-Heselwangen, Balingen, Schwarzwaldkreis, Württemberg, Germany)

└─ Anna HUNTZINGER-679 (b. 11 Feb 1698-H, B, S, Württemberg, Germany d. 26 Nov 1721)

    └─ Catharina JETTER(IN)-4987 (d. 10 May 1704-Heselwangen, Balingen, S, Württemberg, Germany)

└─ Mary Elizabeth SHAFER-174 (b. 11 Feb 1746-WT, Northampton, P, United States d. 16 Mar 1800-WT, N, P, United States)

└─ Catherine LORICH-354 (b. 1724-Panama d. 16 Aug 1818)

┌─ Samuel David FULLMER-20 (b. 4 Nov 1856-Salt Lake City, Salt Lake, Utah Territory, United States d. 29 Jul 1921-B, B, Idaho, United States)

    ┌─ William PRICE-683 (b. 18 Sep 1699-Chirbury, Shropshire, England d. 17 Apr 1740-KI, QAs, M, United States)

┌─ John PRICE-358 (b. Abt 1732-Kent Island, Queen Anne's, Maryland, United States d. Deceased)

    └─ Elizabeth COLLINS-684 (b. 1704-Kent Island, QAs, M, United States d. 21 Jun 1750-KI, QAs, M, United States)

┌─ James Hutchings PRICE-175 (b. 1759-Kent Island, Queen Anne's, Maryland, United States d. 1811-Scott, K, United States)

    ┌─ James HUTCHINGS Sr.-685 (b. Abt 1715-Kent Island, QAs, M, United States d. 1770-KI, QAs, M, United States)

└─ Mary HUTCHINGS-359 (b. 1740-Kent Island, Queen Anne's, Maryland, United States d. Kent Island, Q, M, United States)

    └─ Mary ELLIOTT-686 (b. Abt 1712-Kent Island, QAs, Maryland, United States d. 13 Feb 1764)

┌─ John PRICE-85 (b. 23 Dec 1790-Nashville, Davidson, Tennessee, United States d. 27 Dec 1848-Vicksburg, Warren, M, United States)

    ┌─ Richard KEENE-687 (b. 1689-Dorchester, Maryland, United States d. 1787-Queen Anne's, Maryland, United States)

┌─ John Henry KEENE-360 (b. 27 Mar 1720-Taylors Island, Dorchester, M, United States d. 1785)

    └─ Susan POLLARD-688 (b. Abt 1695-Dorchester, Maryland, United States d. 1794-Maryland, United States)

└─ Letitia KEENE-176 (b. 11 Feb 1760-Baltimore, Baltimore, Maryland, United States d. 14 Sep 1832-N, D, T, United States)

    ┌─ Samuel YOUNG-689 (b. 1692-Suffolk, New York, United States d. Baltimore, Maryland, United States)

└─ Sarah Elizabeth Young -361 (b. 1724-Baltimore, Baltimore, Maryland, United States d. Deceased)

    └─ Mary HILL-690 (b. Abt 1694-Maryland, United States d. Deceased)

└─ Mary Ann PRICE-41 (b. 16 Sep 1815-Nashville, Davidson, Tennessee, United States d. 28 Mar 1897-Marysvale, Piute, Utah, United States)

┌─ John RUCKER-691 (b. 1699-Essex, CoV, British Colonial America d. Jan 1743-Orange, Virginia, United States)

┌─ Benjamin RUCKER-362 (b. Abt 1730-Orange, Orange, Virginia, United States d. 1 Feb 1810-A, A, V, United States)

└─ Susannah Lloyd PHILLIPS-692 (b. 1684-Orange, Virginia, United States d. 28 Aug 1742-O, O, V, United States)

┌─ Rev. James RUCKER-177 (b. 4 Sep 1758-Amherst, Amherst, Virginia, United States d. 10 Sep 1819-, R, T, United States)

┌─ James BENNETT-693 (b. 1706-Amherst, Virginia, United States d. Deceased)

└─ Elizabeth UNKNOWN-363 (b. Abt 1725-Amherst, Virginia, United States d. Deceased)

└─ Mrs. James BENNETT-694 (b. Abt 1710-Virginia, United States d. Deceased)

└─ Johanna RUCKER-86 (b. 19 Apr 1786-Shockoe, Richmond City, Virginia, United States d. 6 Feb 1822-Nashville, D, T, United States)

┌─ John READE-697 (b. Abt 1708-Elizabeth City, Virginia, United States d. 1739-Henrico, Virginia, United States)

┌─ William READE-366 (b. Aft 1729-Chesterfield, Virginia, United States d. 24 Sep 1798-Bedford, Virginia, United States)

└─ Nancy Ann READE -178 (b. 12 May 1765-Bedford, Virginia, United States d. 3 Nov 1843-Murfreesboro, R, T, United States)

┌─ Thomas JONES-701 (b. 8 Jul 1715-Chesterfield, Chesterfield, V, United States d. 1782-S, J, Virginia, United States)

└─ Johanna JONES-367 (b. 1736-Henrico, Virginia, United States d. 23 Mar 1797-Bedford, Virginia, United States)

└─ Sarah HANCOCK-702 (b. 1719-Henrico, Mecklenburg, Virginia, United States d. 1769-Granville, N, United States)

Edgar Osden FULLMER-10 (b. 3 May 1884-Mapleton, Utah, Utah, United States d. 11 Apr 1959-Blackfoot, B, I, United States)

┌─ Samuel KENDALL-703 (b. 1529-Norfolk, England d. Norfolk, England)

┌─ Jesse KENDALL-368 (b. 15 May 1727-Woburn, Middlesex, M, United States d. 14 Apr 1797-Athol, W, M, United States)

└─ Elizabeth PEIRCE-704 (b. 1687 d. 10 Jan 1742-Woburn, Middlesex, Massachusetts, United States)

┌─ Andrew KENDALL-179 (b. 17 Apr 1766-Athol, Worcester, M, United States d. 3 May 1829-Royalston, W, M, United States)

┌─ Andrew EVANS-706 (b. 26 Jan 1708-Malden, Middlesex, M, United States d. 18 Dec 1778-W, M, M, United States)

└─ Elizabeth EVANS-369 (b. 6 Jan 1732-Woburn, Middlesex, M, United States d. 22 Jun 1813-Athol, W, M, United States)

└─ Mary RICHARDSON-707 (b. 13 Mar 1710-Woburn, M, M, United States d. 31 Aug 1781-W, M, M, United States)

┌─ Levi KENDALL-87 (b. 13 Jun 1798-Royalston, Worcester, Massachusetts, United States d. 19 Apr 1822-L, Niagara, N, United Staes)

┌─ Benjamin JENNINGS-370 (b. 16 Jul 1730-Springfield, H, M, United States d. 18 Dec 1796-B, W, M, United States)

└─ Zerviah COOLEY-708 (b. 29 Feb 1708-Springfield, H, M, United States d. 23 Feb 1781-S, H, M, United States)

└─ Hannah JENNINGS-180 (b. 1 Apr 1768-Brookfield, Worcester, M, United States d. 14 Jul 1811-B, Worcester, M, United States)

┌─ Thomas GILBERT 1V-709 (b. 1 Aug 1695-Brookfield, W, Massachusetts d. 13 Feb 1781-B, W, M, United States)

└─ Elizabeth GILBERT-371 (b. 16 Jun 1732-Brookfield, Worcester, M, United States d. 16 Sep 1785-Brookfield, W, Ma)

└─ Judith GOSS-710 (b. 10 Apr 1699-Lancaster, Worcester, M, United States d. Deceased)

┌─ Levi Newell KENDALL-42 (b. 19 Apr 1822-Lockport, Niagara, New York, United States d. 10 Mar 1903-Mapleton, Utah, U, United States)

┌─ Richard LYMAN IV-711 (b. Apr 1678-Northampton, H, M, United States d. 3 Jun 1746-L, NL, C, United States)

┌─ Richard LYMAN-372 (b. 23 Mar 1721/1722-Lebanon, New London, C, United States d. Deceased)

└─ Mary WOODWARD-712 (b. 26 Feb 1678-Northampton, H, M, United States d. 6 Jun 1746-L, NL, C, United States)

┌─ Joseph Bradford LYMAN-181 (b. 1 Sep 1767-Lebanon, New London, Connecticut d. 11 Dec 1847-L, NL, C, United States)

┌─ Joseph BRADFORD-713 (b. 9 Apr 1702-Lebanon, NL, C, United States d. 5 Jan 1778-Haddam, M, Connecticut)

└─ Anna BRADFORD-373 (b. 23 Jul 1732-New London, New London, Connecticut, United States d. L, NL, C, United States)

└─ Heniretta SWIFT-714 (b. 1701-New London, New London, C, United States d. 9 Oct 1758-, , , Connecticut, United)

└─ Lorena (Laura) LYMAN-88 (b. 27 Jul 1804-Canada d. 27 Dec 1860)

└─ Hannah LYMAN-182 (b. Abt 1776-Connecticut, United States d. Aft 1850-Michigan, usa)

└─ Roxey Jane KENDALL-21 (b. 21 Dec 1859-Springville, Utah, Utah, United States d. 18 Jun 1934-Rexburg, Madison, Idaho, United States)

┌─ Johannes Peter CLEMENTS-715 (b. 8 Nov 1702-F, A, R, Prussia, Germany d. 31 Oct 1780-B, D, NY, United States)

┌─ Peter CLEMENTS-374 (b. 12 Feb 1747-Sleepy Hollow, W, NY, United States d. 21 Dec 1834-FA, W, NY, United States)

└─ Maritie Mary MEY-716 (b. 1706-, , Netherlands d. Nov 1780-Flushing, Queens, New York, United States)

James H CLEMENTS-183 (b. 1780-Saratoga, Saratoga, New York, United States d. 27 Aug 1866-GF, Warren, N, United States)

James SEELEY-717 (b. Abt 1735-Bedford, Westchester, New York, Usa d. 10 Feb 1819-S, S, NY, United States)

Anna SEELEY-375 (b. Abt 1755-Stillwater, Saratoga, New York d. 10 Mar 1813-Stillwater, Saratoga, NY, United States)

Elizabeth BROWN-718 (b. 1736-Bedford, Westchester, NY, United States d. 25 Jan 1828-S, S, NY, United States)

Albert N CLEMENTS-89 (b. 19 Mar 1801-Fort Ann, Washington, New York, United States d. 2 Apr 1883-S, Utah, U, United States)

Ananias OWEN-376 (b. 1756-Fort Ann, Washington, New York, United States d. Deceased)

Lucy OWEN-184 (b. 26 Jan 1781-Fort Ann, Warren, New York, United States d. 26 Jan 1851-Harrisburg, W, NY, United States)

Lucy SALES-377 (b. 1758-Fort Ann, Washington, New York, United States d. Deceased)

Elizabeth CLEMENTS-43 (b. 17 May 1836-Liberty, Clay, Missouri, United States d. 1 Feb 1924-Oxford, Franklin, Idaho, United States)

Johann Adam WENTZEL-719 (d. Deceased)

Justus WINCHELL-378 (b. Abt 1729-Hesson Kassel, Braunschweig, , Germany d. Deceased)

Anna Margaretha NICKEL-720 (b. 24 Sep 1713-S, B, S, Hessen, Germany d. 24 Sep 1751-S, B, S, Hessen, Germany)

Justus WINCHEL Jr.-185 (b. 7 Dec 1759-Brunswick, Braunschweig, Hanover, Germany d. Feb 1838-Rose, W, N, United States)

Hannah TAYLER-379 (b. Abt 1729-<Hesson Kassel, Braunschweig, , Germany> d. Deceased)

Ada WINCHELL-90 (b. 24 Dec 1801-Hebron, Washington, New York, United States d. 4 Mar 1890-Oxford, F, Idaho, United States)

Dea. William SAVAGE-721 (b. 18 Sep 1699-M, M, C, United States d. 16 Apr 1774-M, Middlesex, C, United States)

John SAVAGE-380 (b. 1733-Dorset, England d. 1809-New York, United States)

Sarah SAVAGE-722 (b. 2 Sep 1700-Middletown, M, C, United States d. 10 Aug 1782-C, M, C, United States)

Eva SAVAGE-186 (b. Oct 1770-Westfield, Hampden, Massachusetts, United States d. 1841-Rose, Wayne, NY, United States)

John GIPSON-725 (b. 28 Sep 1708-Middleton, Middlesex, Connecticut d. 24 Jul 1757-M, M, C, United States)

Martha GIPSON-381 (b. 28 Sep 1736-Middletown, Middlesex, C, United States d. 15 Mar 1813-M, M, C, United States)

Marcy SAGE-726 (b. 20 Jan 1711-Middletown, Middlesex, C, United States d. 24 Mar 1761-M, M, C, United States)